The Joy of Not Working

The Joy of Not Working

A Book for the Retired, Unemployed, and Overworked

Ernie J. Zelinski

Ten Speed Press
Berkeley

All rights reserved. Published in the United States by Ten Speed Press, an imprint of the Crown Publishing Group, a division of Random House, Inc., New York.
www.crownpublishing.com
www.tenspeed.com

Ten Speed Press and the Ten Speed Press colophon are registered trademarks of Random House, Inc.

Also published in Japanese by Voice Incorporated, Tokyo, Japan; in Chinese traditional characters by Yuan-Liou Publishing Co., Taipei, Taiwan; in Chinese simplified characters by CITIC Publishing House, Beijing, China; in Korean by Mulpure, Seoul, South Korea; in Spanish by Gestión 2000, Barcelona, Spain; in French (for Europe) by Group Eyrolles, Paris, France; in French (for North America) by Stanké International, Montreal, Canada; in German by Deutscher Taschenbuch Verlag, Munich, Germany; in Polish by Wydawnictwo MUDRA, Krzeszowice, Poland; in Portuguese by Editorial Presença, Lisbon, Portugal; in Dutch by Mirananda, The Hague, The Netherlands; in Greek by Kedros, Athens, Greece; in Finnish by Kustannusosakeyhtiö Nemo, Helsinki, Finland; in Czech by Portal, Prague, Czech Republic; and in Italian by Editorial Armenia, Milan, Italy.

Illustration on p. 79 is reprinted with permission of Randy Glasbergen. All rights reserved.

Library of Congress Cataloging-in-Publication Data Zelinski, Ernie J. (Ernie John), 1949–
    The joy of not working: a book for the retired, employed, and overworked / Ernie J.
    Zelinski.—21st-Century ed.
      p. cm.
    1. Retirement. 2. Early retirement. 3. Unemployment. 4. Leisure. I. Title.
    HQ1062 .Z45 2003
    306.3'8—dc21   2003013338

ISBN-13: 978-1-58008-552-6 (pbk.)

Printed in USA

Cover design by Betsy Stromberg
Text design by Jeff Brandenberg
Production by Chloe Nelson

20 19

First Edition

Contents

Chapter 4: Working Less Just for the Health of It

Chapter 5: Unemployed: The True Test of Who You Really Are

Chapter 6: Somebody Is Boring Me; I Think It Is Me

Chapter 7: Lighting Your Own Fire Rather than Being Warmed by Someone Else's

Chapter 12: The End Has Just Begun

Preface

This book can make you a winner. *The Joy of Not Working* has now been published in sixteen languages and has sold over 200,000 copies worldwide. Although the last edition was still selling well, I have updated it to make it more appropriate for the twenty-first century. I want to thank Phil Wood, Kirsty Melville, and Meghan Keeffe at Ten Speed Press for making the new edition possible.

Not only has the content been updated, a new section has been added at the back: a collection of some of the more interesting letters that I have received from readers since the last edition was published in 1997. I believe that you will find these letters just as inspiring as the material that I have written, if not more so. Moreover, I have inserted a few letters throughout the book. I want to thank the individuals who wrote these letters; they have contributed immensely to this book.

Unlike most how-to books on winning, this book is not about winning at a job or making money. Nor is it a book about winning at competitive games. It is about winning when you aren't working, in a way that is not competitive, but still very rewarding.

You're a winner when you have a zest for life. You're a winner when you wake up every morning excited about the day. You're a winner when you enjoy what you're doing. And you're a winner when you pretty well know what you want to do with the rest of your life.

> My father taught me to work, but not to love it. I never did like to work, and I don't deny it. I'd rather read, tell stories, crack jokes, talk, laugh— anything but work.
> —Abraham Lincoln

Whether you are retired, unemployed, or working, you can use *The Joy of Not Working* as a practical and reliable guide to create a paradise away from the workplace. Because all of us need reminders from time to time about the obvious and the not-so-obvious, we can all use a handy guide on how to enjoy life more.

This book is the result of my education—an education that has nothing to do with the curricula in place at schools and universities. I acquired this education through my personal experiences, far removed from my formal education.

At the age of twenty-nine, I embarked on a new career. Having lost my job, I decided that I wanted be a creative loafer for a year or so. Although my new career was supposed to be temporary, I have yet to return to a regular job.

In my last traditional job, I allowed myself to be imprisoned by a system that wasn't designed for free spirits. For almost six years, I worked for a government-owned utility, where I was hired to work from nine to five. The nine-to-five job was more often an eight-to-six job with weekend work, mostly without extra compensation.

Having skipped vacations for over three years, I decided to spend ten weeks away from work one summer. Aside from the fact that I did not have approval from my superiors, this was a great idea. In short, I truly enjoyed those ten weeks. Despite my ingenuity in coming up with the idea, I was fired from my job as a professional engineer. The verdict was that I had violated company policy by taking the extended vacation.

> What's the use of being a genius if you can't use it as an excuse for being unemployed?
> —Gerald Barzan

Obviously, my superiors didn't like what I had done. Regardless of my high performance evaluations and my lengthy period without a vacation, the company terminated my employment shortly after I returned to work. I am not sure whether my termination was solely due to my violating company policy. Perhaps my superiors were envious of how much I enjoyed myself during my extended vacation. After all, many supervisors—particularly those employed in government—don't like dealing with subordinates who are not only creative workers, but also creative loafers.

Not surprisingly, for the first few weeks I was bitter about being fired. Having been a dedicated and productive worker, I had made many important contributions to this company. No doubt a great injustice was committed when they fired me, a valuable employee.

Mr. Zelinski, Harvard University, always thankful for all major contributions to society, today would like to grant you the honorary degree of Doctor of Leisure.

A big turning point for me occurred the day I realized my firing was a blessing in disguise. Not only did I admit I wasn't an indispensable employee, but I also lost interest in a regular nine-to-five job. I decided to spend as much time as possible away from the workplace, particularly in summers. A normal job was now out of the question. What's more, my career as a professional engineer was over.

For the next two years, I didn't work at all, nor did I attend any educational institution. My overriding purpose was to be happy without a job. All things considered, I succeeded.

What did I do during this period? Although at times I had very little money, I lived what I consider to be a truly prosperous life. I engaged in constructive and satisfying activities too numerous to mention. Above all, I made a celebration out of being unemployed. I grew as a person and went through a transformation of my values. In my view, during those two years I truly earned my Doctorate in Leisure. Alas, no university has as yet granted me this degree.

After two years of total leisure, I decided from then on, if at all possible, not to ever work in any month without an "r" in its name. After all, in North America, May, June, July, and August are most suited for leisure activities. Because I enjoy my freedom, I have successfully avoided a regular nine-to-five job for over two decades. For all intents and purposes, I have been in temporary retirement or semiretirement since I was in my late twenties.

> *Leisure is the most challenging responsibility a man can be offered.*
> —William Russell

Over the years, many people have asked me how I am able to utilize so much leisure time without getting bored. This made me realize that many individuals have problems attaining satisfaction in their spare time. It also occurred to me that very little had been written on how to manage and enjoy leisure time. That is when the idea for this book was conceived. My premise is that anyone can learn how to fill spare time with constructive and exciting activities. It follows that a book on how to enjoy leisure time can help many people.

Throughout this book, I share my thoughts about how to lead a leisurely life, often using my experiences away from the workplace as examples. To give a broad perspective on how to be happily unemployed or retired, however, I don't draw only from my own experiences.

CALVIN AND HOBBES © Watterson. Dist. by UNIVERSAL PRESS SYNDICATE. Reprinted with permission. All rights reserved.

The greater part of this book is the result of studying and listening to the stories, experiences, and aspirations of other people.

You will find that this book isn't highly academic in nature. I avoid great detail and academic jargon, because these simply don't appeal to most readers. The format includes text, exercises, cartoons, diagrams, and quotations to appeal to the many learning styles of different individuals. The many positive comments that I have received in hundreds of letters from readers have confirmed that this format works best in getting my message across in an interesting and entertaining way.

He enjoys true leisure who has time to improve his soul's estate.

—Henry David Thoreau

If you want to add to the variety, tone, and quality of your life, you should find this book a valuable asset, as have tens of thousands of people throughout the world. Based on the responses of readers, I trust *The Joy of Not Working* will entertain, challenge, influence, or motivate you in more ways than one.

"The Life of Riley," a popular expression for decades, denotes a good life. A person living the Life of Riley is satisfied and happy. This book is about how you can live the Life of Riley, whether you are retired, unemployed, or working. What it takes to live the Life of Riley may surprise you, however.

CHAPTER 1

You Too Can Live the Life of Riley

A Grand Time to Loaf

On the second day of his visit to a large city, a wealthy and somewhat eccentric traveler encountered six panhandlers whom he had seen soliciting money the previous day. The panhandlers were now all lying in the sun, obviously taking a break from the responsibilities of their chosen profession. The panhandlers looked up curiously as the traveler approached.

The traveler decided to have some fun. He offered $1,000 to the panhandler who could prove that he was the laziest. Hoping to claim the prize, five of the panhandlers jumped up to take part in the contest. Each one proceeded to demonstrate in varying ways—such as by sitting down while soliciting money from tourists—how much lazier he could be than his colleagues.

> I am a friend of the working-man, and I would rather be his friend, than be one.
>
> —Clarence Darrow

After an hour, having watched the five competitors with amusement, the traveler made his decision and awarded the $1,000. He concluded that the sixth panhandler, who had refrained from the competition, was definitely the laziest. The sixth panhandler had remained lying on the grass, reading a paper and enjoying the sun.

There is a moral to this story: not working, when you can enjoy yourself loafing, has its rewards.

This book is about the many pleasures that you can experience away from the workplace. If you are retired, you will learn how to manage and enjoy your unlimited leisure time. If you are temporarily unemployed, you will learn how to enjoy your leisure time and be happy without a job until you find one. And if you are employed, you will learn how to enjoy your limited spare time and create some more if you want more. You may even quit your job, never to work again.

In short, regardless of your situation, you can get more satisfaction and pleasure away from the workplace by reading this book. Welcome to the joy of not working.

Leisure: The Opposite of Work, but Not Quite

"How do you define leisure?" This is an interesting question, but one that is difficult to answer. It was posed to me by a participant in a leisure-planning seminar that I presented at a Canadian Association of Pre-Retirement Planners' conference.

Unable to give a definite answer, I decided to utilize one of my many principles of creativity—give the problem away. I asked the other seminar participants how they define leisure.

After a great deal of discussion, we arrived at a consensus. The definition that we created was: "Spare time over and above the time required to provide the necessities in life." Luckily for me, the definition was adequate for us to continue the seminar.

Nonetheless, this definition can lead to another interesting question: "How do you define necessities in life?" Eating may be a necessity, but casual dining for an hour or two at a bistro is a pleasure. Indeed, casual dining is one of my favorite leisure activities. Yet to some, eating is always a necessity, one that interferes with their other pursuits in life.

Later, I looked up the definition of leisure in several dictionaries. Dictionaries commonly define leisure in such terms as "time free from required work, in which one may rest, amuse oneself, and do the things one likes to do."

DICTIONARY

lei-sure (le'zher or lezh'er), n. 1. the opposite of work but not quite. 2. somewhat of a paradox. 3. what a person does living the Life of Riley.—adj. and adv. **lei'sure-ly**.

lem-on (lem'un) n. 1. a small tropical fruit with pale yellow skin and very acid juice; 2. the tree, related to the orange, which bears this fruit; 3. a pale yellow color.—adj.

lem-on-ade (lem'un-ād) n. a drink of sweetened water flavored with lemon juice.

So where does eating fit into the dictionary definition? Is eating work? Is eating leisure? Or is eating something altogether different?

I wasn't about to take the time to locate the people responsible for the dictionary definition of leisure to see if they could clarify this confusion. I suspected they couldn't.

I hate definitions.
—Benjamin Disraeli

After pondering this question for some time, I was still a little puzzled. How can I define leisure to prevent the potential for endless questioning in my seminars? I just want to present my ideas on how to enjoy leisure. I don't want to be a philosopher, determining whether eating is leisure or leisure is eating.

Eventually I decided that the purpose of my seminars (and this book) is not to establish a universal and perfect definition for leisure. Leisure will always mean different things to different people. Loosely defined, however, leisure is the time an individual spends away from work to do the things he or she wants to do.

Ultimately, it is up to you and me to define work and leisure for our personal needs. Moreover, it is up to you and me to find out what we, as unique human beings, want to do in our spare time. Of course, we also have to actually do what we would like to do.

Doing what we want to pursue in our leisure time is easier said than done. An interesting paradox arises: Leisure is about not working; in order to attain satisfaction from our leisure, however, we have to "work" at it. Weirdly enough, leisure is the opposite of work, but for it to be enjoyable, it requires a great deal of effort.

BIZARRO © Dan Piaro. Reprinted with permission of UNIVERSAL PRESS SYNDICATE. All rights reserved.

The Illusions of Leisure, Retirement, and Lotteries

By choice or by chance, all of us, sooner or later, will have to learn how to utilize and enjoy leisure time. No doubt what we do with our spare time will determine the quality of our lives.

Because it was once a rather rare commodity, leisure was considered a luxury for many centuries. Only recently has leisure become abundant enough that some people are able to enjoy it for decades, particularly when they retire.

Leisure in great measure is the ultimate goal of many people throughout the world. Everyone desires at least a certain amount. Some people, in fact, claim their goal is to have nothing but leisure on their hands. They want to live the Life of Riley. Even so, most aren't prepared for handling unlimited leisure time. Sustained leisure has become a burden to many, even those who are healthy and in a financial position to never work again.

> It is paradoxical but nonetheless true that the nearer man comes to his goal to make his life easy and abundant, the more he undermines the foundations of a meaningful existence.
>
> —Franz Alexander

Whether we find our jobs exciting and stimulating or boring and depressing, many of us are in for a big surprise when confronted with an increase in spare time. Most of us reserve the enjoyment of leisure for the future; often the future arrives too soon. When we retire or are laid off, we end up with much more spare time than we are accustomed to handling.

Various studies confirm that many people have difficulty in effectively utilizing their spare time. For example, one study by the U.S. Department of Commerce reported that only 58 percent of people were experiencing "a great deal" of satisfaction from how they spend their leisure time. This means that 42 percent of individuals could use substantial help in enhancing the quality of their leisure. Even some of the people who are getting a great deal of satisfaction may not be experiencing as much satisfaction as they would like. Many of these people probably could use some help as well.

FACULTY OF LEISURE STUDIES

Most of us will spend the greater part of our adult lives working. Taking into account getting ready for work, commuting to work, talking about our jobs, and worrying about getting laid off, we will have spent more time during our working lives thinking about work than thinking about all our other concerns in life.

Many of us also spend a great amount of time thinking about how great life will be when we don't have to work anymore. Indeed, many dream about how much better life will be with much more leisure time. When I worked as an engineer, I was amazed (and dejected) at how much time engineers and technicians in their twenties spent talking about the potential size of their pensions and all the activities they could pursue in retirement. Although I too was in my twenties, I had more interesting subjects to discuss with others. (If you are interested in what they were, buy me dinner, and we'll have a most interesting conversation.)

As a matter of course, society leads us to believe that retirement and happiness are one and the same. Retirement is supposed to be the great escape from the stresses inherent in most jobs, a time to experience a fulfilling life derived from many enjoyable and rewarding activities. Unfortunately, this is not the case for everyone who retires.

> He lacks much who has no aptitude for idleness.
> —Louise Beebe Wilder

Embarrassingly, I admit that until my thirties, I, not unlike most baby boomers, was influenced by society's programming as to what constitutes the good life. I believed that increased leisure was something everyone looked forward to and enjoyed when they took a long sabbatical or retired. Soon after, I realized that it is often dangerous to go along with beliefs that most people adopt—about the good life or otherwise. Indeed, the masses are frequently wrong. The problem is that the finer things in life often turn out far different from what society's influential factions lead us to believe they will be.

Winning a major lottery, for example, is supposed to immeasurably enhance our lives. Most of us have no doubt that becoming a millionaire will enable us to experience the Life of Riley that we have always dreamed about. The Life of Riley with no work and all play is supposed to be not only trouble-free, but also satisfying and happy. Not all evidence supports this notion, however.

For their book, *Suddenly Rich,* Jerry LeBlanc and Rena Dictor LeBlanc studied several wealthy people who had acquired sudden fortunes. The LeBlancs found most people with unlimited leisure time on their hands weren't very happy. After having been subject to a mandatory work routine for so long, these people had trouble dealing with days totally lacking in structure and purpose. "I really miss that truck driving job," admitted a New York resident who had won a major lottery and then retired. "The biggest loss of my life is not having someone to tell me what to do."

The act of retiring can actually be as much of a problem as not being able to retire. A study by Challenger, Gray & Christmas, Inc. found that

In this world there are only two tragedies. One is not getting what you want, and the other is getting it.
—Oscar Wilde

over 50 percent of people accepting early retirement packages were more than happy to return to work after three months of retirement. The Life of Riley wasn't all that enjoyable. Surprisingly, despite all its shortcomings, work wasn't so bad after all.

Taking It Easy Isn't All That Easy for Some People

Perhaps living the Life of Riley wasn't easy even for Riley. For people who have not learned how to handle leisure time effectively, the Life of Riley is a dilemma, filled with anxiety and uncertainty.

Chances are that you will experience the same difficulties if you don't develop the ability to enjoy many leisure activities. Indeed, if you haven't adopted a love for leisure by the time you retire, you will feel the Life of Riley is the biggest rip-off since the last time you were conned into buying the Brooklyn Bridge.

Following are some common problems that people have in their leisure time:

Guess I'll apply for work again. After having been retired for six months, I am really looking forward to returning to the misery of a job.

➤ Boredom
➤ No real satisfaction from leisure activities
➤ All dressed up and nowhere to go
➤ All dressed up, somewhere to go, but no one to go with
➤ Friction with spouse when time together increases
➤ Not enough things to do
➤ So much to do and no time to do it
➤ Hard time deciding what to do
➤ Bankroll of a peasant but tastes of a millionaire
➤ Bankroll of a millionaire but poverty consciousness of a peasant
➤ Feeling guilty about taking it easy and having fun
➤ Enjoying only those things that are illegal, immoral, or unhealthy

Luckily, leisure has two sides to it; the other side is much more positive. Unlimited spare time can, in fact, be an incredible blessing rather than a dull curse. To some, the leisurely life is even more satisfying than they expected. They become more active than ever before. Each day is a new adventure. To these individuals, nothing can be as enjoyable as a leisurely lifestyle. Indeed, they would do Riley proud if he were to show up and see them in action.

The time you enjoy wasting is not wasted time.

—Laurence J. Peter

When you are able to enjoy leisure time to the fullest, your life will be enhanced to immeasurable levels. Success at leisure will contribute to a life that many on this earth can only dream about. Whether you are retired, unemployed, or overworked, your ability to handle leisure time will result in:

- ➤ Personal growth
- ➤ Improved health
- ➤ Higher self-esteem
- ➤ Less stress and a more relaxed lifestyle
- ➤ Satisfaction from challenging activities
- ➤ Excitement and adventure
- ➤ A more balanced lifestyle
- ➤ Improved family life
- ➤ A sense of self-worth
- ➤ A higher quality of life overall

The difference between success and failure at anything in life is often slim. Handling unlimited spare time is no exception. Having covered the problems and benefits of increased leisure time, it's time for us to look at what factors are essential for solving the problems of leisure and reaping its benefits.

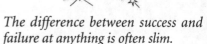

The difference between success and failure at anything is often slim.

The following exercise is just one of several you will encounter in this book. You will get a lot more out of the content if you attempt all the exercises. When a choice of answers is given in an exercise, you can add your own if none is suitable to you.

Exercise 1-1. The Essentials

Read through the following list of personal attributes and other factors and check any that you feel are essential for attaining success at managing and enjoying leisure time.

- ❏ Excellent health
- ❏ Living in an exciting city

- ❏ Having many friends from different walks of life
- ❏ A charming personality
- ❏ Owning a motor home
- ❏ A love for travel
- ❏ Athletic ability
- ❏ Good looks
- ❏ Excellent physical condition
- ❏ Abundant financial resources
- ❏ A beach cabin
- ❏ Living in a warm climate
- ❏ Having had good parents
- ❏ A great marriage or relationship
- ❏ Having many hobbies

Now that you've chosen those you think are essential, let's look at two people who had trouble handling the Life of Riley and one individual who was a master at it.

The Life of Riley Can Be Elusive

A few years ago, I discussed retirement with Delton, who was sixty-seven at the time, financially secure, and played tennis (often better than I did even though I was thirty years younger) at the club where I was a member. Although Delton had liked the company he worked at for many years, he didn't like its policy of mandatory retirement at sixty-five.

After he was forced to retire, Delton had no idea what he should do with his time. Indeed, he was lost. Two years after his retirement, Delton was happy that his company allowed him to return to work part-time. His time away from the job had not been well spent (except when he whipped me in a game of tennis). Delton even confided in me that he hadn't liked weekends when he was working full-time. Weird as it may seem, he always had difficulty deciding what to do on his days off.

Rich, another former member at the same tennis club, is another example of someone who had problems with his spare time. The difference between Delton and Rich was that Rich yearned to retire early. Like many people in my hometown, Rich fantasized about moving to the West Coast to live the Life of Riley. Rich had his wish come true when he was only forty-four. Having worked with a police force since he was nineteen, Rich was able to retire with a decent pension after working only twenty-five years.

After Rich moved west to enjoy the Life of Riley, he realized that he didn't have too much in common with Riley. Rich found handling unlimited spare time extremely difficult. He responded by opening a business. When he lost his shirt on that venture (not serious—you don't need a shirt in West Coast weather), he tried several other things, including going back to work for a short time. The last time I talked to him, Rich was still undecided on how he could best deal with retirement. This is somewhat unfortunate, considering that Rich was in an enviable position to which many people aspire.

People waste more time waiting for someone to take charge of their lives than they do in any other pursuit.
—Gloria Steinem

Unemployed Stockbroker Lives Life of Riley

A number of years ago, North American newspapers reported on the plight of stockbrokers, who were having a tough time after a severe market crash. Young executives, who had known a bull market and the expensive lifestyles it brought, were bewildered and astounded. Many, who were about to lose their $200,000-to-$500,000-a-year jobs, claimed that they couldn't take other jobs at $100,000 a year because their personal expenses were too high. (I'm sure these stories brought tears to many readers' eyes, as they did to mine.)

My friend Denny was a stockbroker before the crash. Denny hadn't been a top producer and had saved very little money. After the crash, Denny left the business altogether. He didn't immediately go looking for another job, however (not even a low-paying one at $100,000 a year). Although Denny had little money, he decided to take it easy for over a year so he could enjoy a different lifestyle.

During the time Denny was unemployed, he was content as anyone could be in this world. He was relaxed, he had a smile he couldn't lose, and he was a treat to be around because of his positive nature. I knew many working people who were making above-average incomes in their high-status jobs, but not one was as happy as Denny.

Hard work pays off in the future. Laziness pays off now.
—Graffiti

Denny has since returned to the workforce in another field of endeavor. The last time I saw Denny, he mentioned that he was enjoying his new career. Even so, he was yearning for the time when he again could leave the workforce for a year or two just to enjoy life. No doubt Denny, unlike Rich and Delton, will get at least as much satisfaction and enjoyment out of retirement as he did from any one of his careers.

Riley's Secret

Let's return to exercise 1-1 to clarify which factors are essential for living the Life of Riley. Why was my friend Denny so content to have nothing but free time on his hands, while Delton and Rich both found the free time that comes with retirement to be a burden?

If you chose any item that was on the list, you are a victim of your own incorrect thinking about what it takes to master leisure. Not one item that I listed is essential for successfully living the Life of Riley. Every item on the list may help, but none is essential.

Some people will argue vehemently that abundant financial resources are essential. Yet Delton and Rich were much better off financially than Denny was. If abundant financial resources are essential, Delton and Rich should have been happy to be unemployed and Denny unhappy, instead of the other way around. (In chapter 11, we will look at the role money plays in the enjoyment of a leisurely lifestyle.)

Some may also feel that excellent health is essential. No doubt excellent health is an important asset. Nonetheless, many retirees with health problems are still able to enjoy their leisure time and life in general.

Then what is essential? The Life of Riley is nothing more than a state of mind. Denny has the one essential ingredient—a healthy attitude—that Riley surely had to have in order to live the good life.

ED STEIN reprinted by permission of Newspaper Enterprise Association, Inc.

Provided that you have a healthy attitude, you can adjust to a life of total leisure without missing a stride. Dick Phillips of Portsmouth, Hampshire, England, couldn't agree with this more. He wrote to me after reading a previous edition of this book.

Dear Ernie,

My wife Sandy and I were on an Air Canada flight to Vancouver this summer to commence a "Life of Riley" retirement holiday in your lovely country when a fellow female passenger introduced me to your book *The Joy of Not Working*.

I later obtained a copy at Duthie's Bookstore and read it when I returned home. (Riley did not allow time for reading on holidays.) I am fifty-four years of age and have worked since I was fifteen years old: first as a fitter and turner apprentice, then as a seagoing-ships engineer before joining the County Police for a thirty-year career. Your book gives much sound advice, some I have been following for years. I have enjoyed developing interests outside work while still working. When I retired last November, I enjoyed the freedom to parcel up my time and develop interests which include hiking, cycling, old car restoration, model engineering, painting, and D. I. Y. projects. You are right—a positive attitude to life in retirement is essential.

In your book, you write about a fellow officer named Rich who, like me, retired in an enviable position but found life difficult. I hope he has now read your book, and he is developing that inner self that makes all things possible. Meanwhile, I am looking forward to next year, when I will join a team building a large, wooden sailing ship for disabled people, and later find time to revisit Canada.

Regards to Riley,

Dick Phillips

Note that Dick Phillips, like Denny, also has a healthy attitude about being unemployed—an important attribute for enjoying all aspects of life. Regardless of your age, sex, occupation, and income, you too can experience the many joys of not working, provided you adopt the right attitude. I can say this simply because I have been able to be as happy when unemployed as when I was in the workforce—if not happier. If I can do it, so can you.

> There exists above the "productive" man a yet higher species.
> —*Friedrich Nietzsche*

My firsthand experience with unemployment is extensive. I have spent over half of my adult years without a job. This has given me important insight into what it takes to be a success away from the workplace. I am not blessed with any special talents and abilities that you don't have. Other people who, like Denny, experience enjoyment in their spare time are also normal human beings with no exceptional intelligence, talent, or skills.

All things considered, living a leisurely lifestyle isn't dependent on having some huge advantage over others. We all have the ability to live the Life of Riley. The key is to acknowledge our own skills and talents and put them to good use.

Never adopt the excuse that you weren't born as talented or fortunate as others. The hand that you were dealt at birth isn't as important as what you do with it. You can always make up in creativity what you lack in talent or good fortune. Playing the game of leisure is like playing poker; playing three aces badly won't get you as far as playing a terrible hand well.

"Leisure consists in all those virtuous activities by which a man grows morally, intellectually, and spiritually," stated the Roman statesman and philosopher Marcus Tullius Cicero. "It is that which makes a life worth living." I suggest that you take Cicero's advice and run with it. It will be most valuable to you on your journey through life.

CHAPTER 2

What You See Is What You Get

Thinking for a Change

We can change the quality of our lives by changing the context in which we view our circumstances. Two people can be faced with the same situation, such as being fired from a job. While one may view it as a blessing, the other may view it as a curse. The degree to which we are able to change the context of a situation depends on how flexible our thinking is. What's more, it depends on our willingness to challenge our beliefs and values.

Most people think only once or twice a year. I have made myself an international reputation by thinking once or twice a week.
—George Bernard Shaw

Unfortunately, most of us don't take the time to question what we are thinking or why we think the way we do. Indeed, to affect a change in our thinking, we must start thinking for a change. By challenging our thinking, we welcome fresh perspectives and new values to replace outmoded ones. For example, challenging the way we think about work can help us develop a healthy attitude toward leisure.

Never challenging the way we think has at least two inherent dangers:

> ➤ We lock ourselves into one mode of thinking and don't see more workable solutions or alternatives.

> ➤ We adopt a set of values that are appropriate at the time. Time passes, and, of course, things change. Our original values are no longer appropriate, but we still hang on to them.

Old Dogs Can Learn New Tricks

Draw a black dot like the one above on a white board and ask a class of adult students what they see. Practically everyone will say they see a black dot, and only a black dot. Place a similar dot in front of a grade-school class and ask what they see. Children will give you fascinating answers, such as:

> ➤ Darkness outside a round window

> ➤ A black bear rolled up in a ball

> ➤ A black hubcap

> ➤ A horse's eye

> ➤ A black marble

> ➤ A dirty quarter

> ➤ A chocolate cookie

We all come into this world blessed with creativity and a great imagination. As children, we have the capacity and flexibility to see the world from many interesting perspectives and different points of view. Because we pay attention to everything around us, we see more and enjoy life more.

At some point in childhood, most of us start to lose these abilities. Society, educational institutions, and our parents tell us how we should think and act. Because we want to be accepted socially, we stop questioning. Moreover, we stop paying attention and lose our mental flexibility. When we see a black dot, we can't imagine that it could represent something else, such as the inside of a pipe.

Grown-ups never understand anything by themselves, and it is tiresome for children to be always and forever explaining things to them.
—From The Little Prince by Antoine de Saint-Exupéry

By the time we are adults, our thinking has become too structured for our own good. Our resistance to changing our beliefs and values fosters erroneous, incomplete, or outdated perceptions of the world. Structured thinking also suppresses most of the creativity we had as children. Unless we learn to think differently, our creativity remains dormant and our perceptions of the world suppress our enjoyment of life.

What's the matter, Mitch? Did you lose all of your creativity when you turned fifty-five? Use what I use to get out of these situations!

Creativity is a powerful tool for anyone who is willing to put forth the necessary effort to develop it—and use it. Researchers in the area of creativity indicate that the major difference between those who use their creativity and those who don't is that those who do simply think they are creative. Put another way, people who are regularly creative are aware of their natural ability and use it to their advantage.

Creativity and mental agility are crucial to being able to adapt to a rapidly changing world. We must continually challenge our values and perceptions to avoid inhabiting a delusional world. People who don't develop the habit of carefully examining their own premises and beliefs run the risk of seeing a world that has little relationship to reality. This destructive practice can have serious consequences, ranging from disappointment to depression and other mental illnesses.

Many people are uncomfortable with the notion that their own attitudes and beliefs are all that stop them from achieving true success and happiness. What frightens them most is having to give up their excuses for not winning at the game of life. People who resist change and the notion that their perceptions may be wrong need to start thinking differently to get their lives back on track to fulfillment.

> The dog too old to learn new tricks always has been.
>
> —Unknown wise person

Contrary to popular belief, old dogs *can* learn new tricks, but only if they want to learn them. The only thing that stops any one of us from learning new behaviors is ourselves. People who become structured in their thinking at an early age often use the age-old excuse that they are too old to change. Conversely, people who are open-minded and use their imaginations aren't hindered by age. To them, developing new values and behaviors is something that comes naturally, regardless of how old they get.

In the Land of the Blind, the One-Eyed Man Is King

Exercise 2-1. The Three Secrets to Fulfillment

A successful American entrepreneur acquired a lot of wealth but realized that he was unhappy. He decided to retire and take it easy. He soon realized, however, that he still wasn't happy.

Because his life was so empty, the entrepreneur decided to go in search of a Zen master who supposedly knew three important secrets for living life to the fullest. After twenty months of searching, the entrepreneur finally found the Zen master on top of an obscure high mountain.

The Zen master was happy to reveal his three secrets for a happy and satisfying life. The entrepreneur was surprised by what he was told.

What were the three secrets?

1. _____

2. _____

3. _____

You're telling me, "Life is a joke!" Is that all there is to enlightenment?

To enjoy the world more, we must perceive more. There is a saying: "In the land of the blind, the one-eyed man is king." Put another way, keeping your eyes wide open will allow you to see things in this world that others don't see.

Let's return to the exercise. According to the Zen master, the three secrets for a happy and satisfying life are:

1. Pay attention

2. Pay attention

3. Pay attention

Awareness is the first step in changing our lives for the better. When we have some pattern deeply buried within us, before we can change or eliminate it we must first become aware of it. The condition may be pointed out to us by others. Sometimes we see the condition in other people before we see it in ourselves. Perhaps, through synchronistic events, we attract a friend, a guru, a workshop, or a book into our lives that not only points out the condition to us, but also helps us awaken to new ways to dissolve the problem.

Only the most foolish of mice would hide in a cat's ear. But only the wisest of cats would think to look there.

—Scott Love

The following letter was sent to me by a professor in the Faculty of Education at the University of Victoria:

> Dear Mr. Zelinski,
>
> I very much enjoyed your book, *The Joy of Not Working*. I decided that I am boring myself; I plan to do something about it.
>
> Thank you,
>
> John

Out of several hundred letters that I have received about this book, John's letter is one of the most powerful, despite being the shortest. No doubt chapter 6 on boredom made an impact on John. First, he realized that he was bored in life. Moreover, he realized that there was only one person who could do something about his boredom—John! Assuming that he opened his eyes to all the exciting things that he could pursue in his leisure time, John likely had few problems in overcoming his boredom.

Whether your problem is how to enjoy yourself while unemployed or how to create a better work/life balance, you can find many solutions to your problem. Above all, you must be more attentive to all the opportunity around you. Anything important—which takes only five minutes to spot—will exceed the attention span of most people by at least four and a half minutes. Learn to pay attention for five minutes at a time and you will spot more opportunity than you know what to do with.

Are You Paying Attention?

All of us, to some degree, are not paying attention. We allow our perceptions to be affected by our judgments, so we don't see all there is to see.

The obscure we see eventually. The completely obvious, it seems, take longer.
—Edward R. Murrow

To see how well you pay attention, try the four following exercises. Your presence of mind will determine whether you see everything there is to see. Allow yourself a few minutes to do all the exercises.

Exercise 2-2. Looking at Perception

View the two figures and then proceed to the other exercises.

Figure 1

| A bird in the the hand | is worth two in the bush |

Figure 2

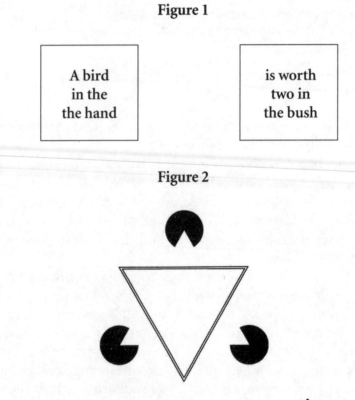

Exercise 2-3. Triangles Galore

The diagram on the right is a perspective builder. You simply have to count the number of triangles in the diagram.

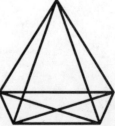

Exercise 2-4. Playing with Matches

The following equation is made from matchsticks. Each line in a character is one matchstick.

This equation is wrong. Move just one matchstick to make the equation correct.

Exercise 2-5. Cycle Designed by a Psycho?

Although my undergraduate degree is in electrical engineering, a while ago I decided to design something mechanical. This is a design for a new tandem bicycle that I created to help people enjoy leisure. (I know you are impressed.)

Analyze the merits of this design for a new tandem bicycle.

Perception Is Everything

If you noticed everything there was to see in figure 1 of exercise 2-2, you should have read the following in the two boxes:

A bird in **the the** hand is worth two in the bush.

If you missed the double *the*, you are not seeing all there is to see. You may be overlooking many solutions to solving your problems in life. Moreover, you may be overlooking a lot of opportunity in personal and business affairs.

In figure 2, you probably noticed two triangles. Upon closer examination, one triangle actually exists and the other doesn't. The imaginary triangle even appears whiter than the rest of the page. Just as you imagined a brighter triangle that doesn't even exist, you may be imagining many barriers or obstacles to solving your life's problems that aren't there. Even worse, you may be imagining *problems* that don't exist.

Like most people, you probably saw fewer than twenty-five triangles in the figure in exercise 2-3. There are, in fact, thirty-five different triangles in this figure. Likewise, in exercise 2-4, you may have generated a solution. If you did, that's great. If you stopped after only one solution, however, that's not so great. I have generated over thirty solutions to this exercise—you can, too, by taking the time to generate them yourself (or by paying a fortune to attend one of my seminars). The point is, if you stop after generating only one or two solutions to your problems at work or play, you are not seeing many more solutions, some of which could be more exciting and effective.

> Some men see things as they are and ask, "Why?" I see them as they have never been and ask, "Why not?"
> —George Bernard Shaw

What did you think of my bicycle design in exercise 2-5? Most people see only the negative when they look at this design. If your thoughts were all negative, you did not fully explore the design. Unless you saw some positive and some negative features, you did not give my unusual design due consideration. Your voice of judgment stepped in too soon, as it may when you are confronted with new ideas.

There are many positive features to the bicycle design: The rear wheel can be used as a spare in case the front tire goes flat. With the two back wheels, the bicycle will give a more comfortable ride. This bicycle will also have an advantage over conventional ones for carrying heavy loads. It will be more suitable for overweight people than a standard two-wheeler. Some people may want to buy it as a status symbol because it is a new and different design.

In life, perception is everything; what you see is what you get. You can be the judge of how well you paid attention in the exercises. If you didn't see all there was to see, you may want to start paying more attention to the world around you.

Only the Foolish and the Dead Don't Change

As a young lawyer, Abraham Lincoln had to plead two similar cases one day. He happened to get the same judge for both cases and both cases involved the same principle of law. In the case heard in the morning, Lincoln appeared for the defendant. He made an eloquent plea and easily won his case.

Ironically, in the case heard in the afternoon, Lincoln happened to be acting for the plaintiff. Lincoln was arguing this case with the same eagerness, only from the opposite point of view, when the judge, somewhat amused, asked Lincoln why he had changed his point of view since the morning. "Your Honor, I could have been wrong this morning," declared Lincoln, "but I know I'm right this afternoon."

The moral of this true story is: Don't get stuck in your beliefs. Only the foolish and the dead don't change. Rigid thinking limits your ability to see things in a different light. Today's world is changing at an unprecedented pace. To deal effectively with this rapid change, you must ensure that your opinions, beliefs, and values aren't carved in stone.

Our problems—particularly the whoppers—begin with our belief systems. For some strange reason, we find it easier to hang on to belief systems that don't work than to adopt new ones that do. For example, you may subscribe to the belief that hard work is the only way to success and happiness. Such being the case, you may want to look at hard work from a different point of view.

Giving up your present values and beliefs about hard work may open up new dimensions to your life. Opting out of the rat race and putting more leisure time into your days can lead to a far richer life. To be sure, you will need courage and trust in your creative ability to make such a dramatic change in your life—and to forgo security and a regular paycheck in the process.

To him, this bicycle represents leisure. To me, it represents work.

People who make dramatic changes in their lives, however, often find that their beliefs and values were holding them back from enjoying life to the fullest. Rita Ueda of Vancouver, B.C., decided to make a big change in her life. She took a sabbatical from work by quitting her job. In the letter she sent me, Rita had this to say about her decision:

Dear Mr. Zelinski;

I have just finished reading your book *The Joy of Not Working* (yes, I did all the exercises too). I had been teaching seven days a week, six to twelve hours a day without a holiday at a music school for the last twelve years. I originally took the job to earn my way through my commerce degree, but I continued to habitually work after my graduation five years ago.

The job was ruining my life—so I "retired" (after all, I'm still in my twenties) two months ago. Although I was happy with my decision, I was not prepared for my new lifestyle. My friends and colleagues severely criticized me, and I had to find new ways to spend my extra time.

Having read your book, I am convinced that I made the right decision. I am now even proud to be not working.

Yours truly,

Rita

I had the opportunity to talk to Rita about six months after she wrote to me. Her sabbatical had done her a lot of good. She told me that she was back at work, but working fewer hours, enjoying herself more, and being more productive. Changing her beliefs about the merits of working long and hard hours had clearly changed her life for the better. Above all, Rita realized that working less can contribute to a lot more happiness, satisfaction, and fulfillment.

> Faced with having to change our views or prove that there is no need to do so, most of us immediately get busy on the proof.
> —John Kenneth Galbraith

As Rita has shown, it's important to challenge all our beliefs—especially the ones we cherish most. As difficult and uncomfortable as it may be to accept, our most cherished beliefs are potentially the most dangerous. In fact, some hard-core beliefs end up being a disease, harming our physical, psychological, and spiritual well-being.

We all need a mental framework, points of view, and values to function as human beings. Nonetheless, we should regularly question these, especially when they become hard-core beliefs. Most people's beliefs—especially those related to what brings satisfaction and happiness in life—are often erroneous assumptions, myths, and pure fiction perpetuated by society and advertisers.

CHAPTER 3

The Morality of Work Is the Morality of Slaves

Thinking about Work

If you want to enhance the quality of your life, challenging your perceptions about work is a good place to start. Most people aren't able to correctly value work. Indeed, they overvalue work and undervalue leisure. This is the result of years of programming by religious organizations, educational institutions, corporations, society, and advertisers.

The seventeenth-century French writer François, Duc de La Rochefoucauld, declared, "The greatest gift is the power to estimate correctly the value of things." As you put some old notions about the value of work to sleep, you will come into your own as a person. Above all, when you accept that work is not all that society makes it out to be, you will be better prepared to live happily and prosperously.

> Work: The thing that interferes with golf.
> —Frank Dane

Exercise 3-1. Something to Think About

As mentioned in chapter 2, your ability to enjoy spare time will depend, in part, on how open-minded you are. To get a grip on your values and attitudes about work, answer the following questions:

Do you believe that hard work is the key to success in this world? Why?

Do you think that it is productive for North American society to have every able person between the ages of eighteen and sixty-five years old gainfully employed at least forty hours a week?

Are unemployed panhandlers a drain on society?

There are no right or wrong answers to the above questions. If you are a strong convert to the idea that working long and hard hours is the only way to personal success, however, you may not be as right as you think you are. This chapter is meant to challenge your beliefs and values about work and leisure so that you can direct your life in directions that it might not otherwise take.

The richest people in the world are those who have fun earning their living and at the same time have a healthy work-life balance. Personally, I believe in erring on the side of having a good time at the expense of my work. Because my career is so enjoyable, I have probably blurred the line between work and play as well as anyone can. Still, I wouldn't imagine working more than an average of four or five hours a day on my work-related projects.

You can argue that extracurricular play is not important if one enjoys one's work; work then becomes play. I disagree with this argument, simply because this world offers so much in the way of excitement, adventure, and learning. To confine yourself to a world of work is to miss out on many of life's other rewarding experiences. And for those who don't enjoy their work and see it primarily as a means to meet financial obligations, finding the right balance between work and play is even more crucial for contentment.

> The best test of the quality of a civilization is the quality of its leisure.
> —Irwin Edman

Contrary to what work-crazed individuals believe, you don't have to work hard for fifty or sixty hours a week so you may eventually enjoy yourself sometime in the future. One of the greatest dangers of adopting the workaholic lifestyle is the possibility of sacrificing your present-day happiness for twenty or thirty years, only to die of a heart attack or get hit by a bus just before you are able to retire and enjoy life.

Alas, the Protestant Work Ethic Ruined a Good Thing

The work ethic is not a traditional value. Work hasn't always been held in the high regard that it is today. Many of our ancestors, in fact, would have rejected the Protestant work ethic outright, considering what it signifies.

Indeed, some of the best-known ancient Greek philosophers thought that work was vulgar. Working, just for the sake of working, signified slavery and a lack of human dignity. Socrates felt that because manual laborers had no time for friendship or for serving the community, they made bad citizens and undesirable friends. The early Greeks and Romans relegated all activities done with the hands, done under orders, or done for wages to the lower-class citizens or to the slaves.

Other early Greek philosophers, such as Plato and Aristotle, cited total leisure as ultimate wealth; leisure was desirable as an end in itself so people could use it to think, learn, and develop themselves. Conversely, pursuing wealth, power, and status through work was considered a form of voluntary slavery that failed to enhance the human condition. Plato and Aristotle were critical of people who kept working after they had satisfied their basic needs. They concluded that these people were working and pursuing luxury and power in an attempt to cover up their fear of freedom.

Moreover, Plato and Aristotle did not associate leisure with idleness and slothfulness as many people do today. They placed leisure on a much higher level than work. Plato described leisure as "activity, not passiveness, a mind and body in action, not frozen contemplation." In other words, leisure time was an opportunity for human beings to exercise their minds, bodies, and spirituality in new, exciting, and satisfying ways that couldn't be experienced in the workplace.

Today, popular belief holds that it is natural for human beings to work long and hard hours. This is far from the truth. Although European peasants in the Middle Ages were poor and oppressed, they didn't work long hours. They celebrated holidays in honor of even the most obscure saints; consequently, over time they had more holidays and fewer workdays. At one point, the normal number of annual holidays was up to 115. Alas, the Protestant work ethic ruined a good thing.

> There is no more fatal blunderer than he who consumes the greater part of his life getting his living.
>
> —Henry David Thoreau

In the few remaining primitive societies today, people also work less than people in industrialized societies do. Men residing in the Sandwich Islands of Hawaii only work four hours a day. Similarly, aborigines in Australia work only as hard as they have to for their necessities. To the surprise of many in developed nations, people in these societies lead happy and fulfilling lives and have far fewer wants than those in the rest of the world.

Working long hours is a recent bad habit initiated by the factory system during the Industrial Revolution. Over time, the number of regular hours in a workweek did fall from sixty hours in 1890 to about forty hours in 1950. But since then, regular work hours haven't declined significantly. Indeed, the length of the workweek in some professions is on the rise.

> Let us be grateful to Adam: he cut us out of the blessing of idleness and won for us the curse of labor.
> —Mark Twain

With the reversal in the roles of work and leisure, work has become the sole organizing principle and means for expression. In the modern world, leisure has a much lower status than work. To many people, leisure represents idleness and a waste of time. Without work, many people experience a loss of self-esteem, and some even exhibit deterioration in their personalities. Indeed, when people lose their jobs, new faults often appear, such as drinking, gambling, and unfaithfulness.

Oddly, the majority today view work with such high regard that they boast about how many hours a day they work. Even if their jobs are routine and tiresome, and they gain nothing financially from working overtime, people can't resist bragging about how hard they have been working. They have become martyrs, giving up the opportunity for self-actualization in return for the privilege of being slaves, primarily benefiting the company rather than themselves.

Influenced by the work ethic, many people even exaggerate or lie about how much they actually work. Researchers recently discovered that people actually worked less than they, themselves, estimated. When the researchers compared the actual hours recorded in time diaries to the workers' estimates, they found a significant gap between the estimates and the actual time worked.

> Hard work never killed anybody, but why take a chance?
> —Charlie McCarthy
> (Edgar Bergen)

Not surprisingly, workaholics had the biggest difference; they said they worked seventy-five-hour weeks when, in fact, the diaries showed they worked only fifty to sixty hours a week.

As in ancient Greece, a meaningful and prosperous life today shouldn't be based only on hard work and the accumulation of material possessions; it also requires challenging and rewarding leisure activities, including some that develop the mind, body, and soul. Most people today can attain a more holistic approach to life—one that integrates the material with the nonmaterial—if they really want it. Unfortunately, few people do what is required to attain it.

No doubt the progressive philosophers in ancient Greece would be saddened to learn that many people in the modern world don't know how to constructively use their leisure time. Moreover, Socrates, Aristotle, and Plato would conclude that individuals

All keeping my nose to the grindstone for twenty-five years has given me is a sore nose.

who work long hours even though they are financially well-off either have serious kinks in their brains or masochistic tendencies. Needless to say, I would agree with them.

Workaholism Provides a Perverse Form of Gratification

Working at an unpleasant job when it is necessary for one's survival is rational. Working at an unpleasant job when one is financially well-off and doesn't have to work is irrational. Nevertheless, many well-off people toil away at unpleasant jobs because they believe it's more moral to be working than not working.

Most people fail to consider that a great deal of harm may result from adopting the belief that work is a virtue. Although work is necessary for our survival, it doesn't contribute as much to individual well-being as many think it does.

Just to set things straight, I am not saying that we should avoid work at all costs. You may have erroneously assumed I suffer from ergophobia (the fear of work). On the contrary, I get a great deal of satisfaction from most work I choose to do. Writing this book is one example.

Don't be too moral. You may cheat yourself out of life so.
—Henry David Thoreau

My point is that working for the sake of working can be detrimental to our well-being and enjoyment of life. This, of course, is by no means a new revelation. Bertrand Russell stated some time ago that North America's attitude toward work and leisure was outdated and contributed to the misery in society. In his essay "In Praise of Idleness," Russell stated, "The morality of work is the morality of slaves, and the modern world has no need of slavery."

I would like you to believe that Bertrand borrowed this line from me, but this would sound far-fetched considering he wrote this in 1932, over seventy years ago. Reading Russell's essay today is eye-opening because of its relevance in this day and age. Although our world has dramatically changed, it is interesting to see how little our values have changed in over seventy years. Old values and beliefs are hard to surrender.

> They intoxicate themselves with work so they won't see how they really are.
>
> —Aldous Huxley

With all the modern technology at our disposal, none of us need slave away to the extent that people did seventy years ago. After all, greater opportunity to seek a balanced and wholesome lifestyle exists now than ever before in the history of humankind. Today's prosperous times should be able to support millions of people seeking their true selves through creative pursuits and self-expression, while only working a few hours a day. Unfortunately, most people are too uncreative or too afraid of such freedom.

We would be hard pressed to find one person in twenty who is taking advantage of working only four hours a day, or taking a one-year sabbatical to relax and enjoy life. Paradoxically, more people actually seek their true selves in bad times than in good times—due to the high number of unemployed with free time on their hands to do something other than work.

The poet W. H. Auden stated: "In order that people may be happy in their work, these three things are needed: They must be fit for it: they must not do too much of it: and they must have a sense of success in it." The second of Auden's three ingredients is the one that most people in the modern world overlook and violate. In western societies, most people today put way too much time into their work lives and not enough into their personal lives.

When it comes to earning a living and having a good life, most people think that the most important thing is to work hard. These people are wrong. What they need, in fact, to learn is how not to work hard. Learned workaholism is difficult to give up because it provides a perverse form of gratification. Moreover, the Protestant work ethic has influenced us to believe there is some virtue in working hard regardless of how much harm it does.

A Nation Gone Mad with the Work Ethic

Can you imagine this? Everyone in the nation loves working more than anything else. The work ethic gets so out of hand that factory workers, even though they are entitled to only seven days' annual vacation, routinely refuse to take their entire vacations, preferring instead to stay at the plant and work.

The whole nation has gone mad. Businesspeople, like everyone else, still insist on working six days a week. Although they are entitled to twenty days vacation, they take no more vacation than factory workers. When businesspeople take vacations, they don't know how to relax. Instead, they behave like maniacs, rushing back and forth, exhausting themselves trying to get in as many leisure activities as possible. They are so brainwashed with the work ethic that they don't quite know what leisure is. Things get so bad that health in the nation starts to suffer. The government eventually steps in with programs to teach people how to have more leisure.

Imagine the Human Resources Department in Canada or the Department of Labor in the United States promoting more leisure. This would be severely criticized in either country. The situation described above is real, however. In fact, it happened in Japan in the early 1990s.

Faced with a crisis of overwork, the Japanese government made one of its objectives the improvement of the quality of life by increasing leisure. Through the Japanese Ministry of Labor, the government created a poster series promoting more time off

Just watching people work makes me tired. Thanks to the two of you for working harder than the Japanese, I am now terribly exhausted and have to go home early for my afternoon nap.

for workers. One such poster said, "Let's realize a five-day workweek society." The ministry also published a handbook under the title *Try Your Best: Salaryman's Guide to Relaxation.* It gave workers ideas on how to take time off.

Alas, around this time, Japan went into a ten-year economic slump, reducing the pursuit of more leisure to a low priority on the government's agenda. Today the work ethic is as strong as ever, particularly among workers age forty and over. Japan's work ethic has been so strong over the years that they even identified a new disease: *karoshi* is the Japanese term for sudden death from overwork. Reports indicate that up to 10 percent of male fatalities are attributed to *karoshi*.

In earlier editions of this book I indicated that I feel individuals who die from overwork—whether Japanese, American, or Canadian—have no one to blame but themselves. Anyone crazy enough to work that hard, when there are so many wonderful things to do in life, will get little sympathy from me. Furthermore, I don't know why Japan had to come up with another term for this disease. They already had one; the term *hara-kiri* would have done nicely.

Apparently *hara-kiri* was not good enough. By the late 1990s, the hardworking Japanese had actually coined a new word, *karojisatsu*, to signify suicide from overwork. Because of the economic slide throughout the decade, the number of such suicides swelled to an estimated 1,000 or more a year, according to lawyers specializing in work-related deaths. What these victims—whether businesspeople or factory workers—had in common was working ten to twelve hours a day with no days off for months at a time

> Death is nature's way of telling us to slow down.
> —Graffiti

Weird as it may seem, the victims of *karojisatsu* rarely blame their companies. Instead, many leave notes behind to apologize for not having done better. "I no longer have the strength to go on," wrote forty-six-year-old Tadashi Shimonaka, who committed suicide because of chronic overwork and a lack of sleep. "I am really sorry," added Shimonaka.

In 1997, the Japanese appeal courts for the first time upheld an earlier court decision that employers can be held liable for *karojisatsu*. Ichiro Oshima, a twenty-four-year-old worker at Tokyo's largest advertising agency, was the first suicide legally attributed to overwork. Oshima averaged thirty minutes to two hours of sleep a night and didn't get a day off for seventeen months. Dentsu, his employer, argued that Oshima had personal problems that contributed to his suicide, but the Tokyo High Court ruled otherwise and ordered Dentsu to pay $1.2 million to his family.

Unfortunately, the work ethic and obsession with having a job have not abated much since the Japanese government tried to promote more leisure in the early 1990s. By 2002, the official unemployment rate had reached 5 percent—not high by North American standards, but considered excessive in Japan. The stigma of joblessness has been deadly, indeed. Suicides in 2002 hit an all-time high, with more than 30,000 people taking their lives.

Homelessness, unheard of in Japan not that long ago, has also become a problem there, mainly because of the unemployed. Sadao Yamashita, thirty-eight, became one of Tokyo's homeless in 2002 after losing his job. There is a bright side to his plight, however. "Passersby give us dirty looks," Yamashita told a reporter, but he said that being unemployed and homeless had taught him to live without fear of not fitting into Japan's conformist society. "In Japan it's always been one rule after another," declared Yamashita. "But here I can be my own man."

In a country obsessed with work, where joblessness carries a particular stigma, it is little wonder that the first Japanese edition of *The Joy of Not Working*, published in 1995, didn't sell as well as expected. The editors of Kodansha, Japan's largest publisher, told me that they had high hopes for the book. Even so, the editors thought that it would be too radical to call the book *The Joy of Not Working*. The editors called it *Zelinski's Law* instead, to play on *Murphy's Law*, a best-seller in Japan.

Surprisingly, after Kodansha let the first Japanese edition go out of print due to disappointing sales, another Japanese publisher picked up rights for a new edition to be published in 2004.

Let's hope, for the sake of the Japanese, that the new edition will reach more readers and help save a few lives from *karoshi* or *karojisatsu*.

> It is better to have loafed and lost than never to have loafed at all.
>
> —James Thurber

Another Nation Tries to Catch Up to the Madness

Most politicians, economists, and corporate executives in western nations see the recent unleashing of capitalism as an incredibly good thing for mainland China. Yet as China enters the global economy head first, many of its people are finding out that hard work, and the money and consumerism that come with it, are dangerous, indeed. All three can be as addictive as many potent drugs and can lead to serious physical and mental health problems.

In their pursuit of happiness, many Chinese have become obsessed with getting the best jobs, having their children attend the

I always wanted to be a degenerate panhandler, but I couldn't quite make it. That's why I got myself an office job.

most prestigious universities, purchasing the fanciest gadgets, and living in the most exclusive apartments. Business executives are known to work long hours, often without a vacation, competing for career promotion and salaries. Ironically, some of the most successful Chinese are the most insecure and have the hardest time relaxing.

In 2003, Xiao Zeping, chief psychiatrist at the Shanghai Medical Health Center, told a *Globe and Mail* reporter, "They work without a rest or a holiday, and they feel so tired that they lose almost all interest in life. They're rich, but they don't pay attention to their health. In Shanghai, everyone focuses on their work and their salary. It determines whether you are successful or not. If someone loses his job, he feels that he is no good. It's very shameful."

Many Chinese are stressed out because of the rising number of factory layoffs and the corporate job turmoil that capitalism has brought with it. "People are floating from one job to another. Life is much quicker, and they don't have much spare time," states Dr. Xiao. "There used to be ten people sitting and chatting with you every weekend, and there was time to talk. Now you might meet your extended family only twice a year."

The stresses and anxieties of working life have become so intense that many wealthy Chinese can't sleep at night, despite the fact they are living what others consider the Chinese dream. The burdens of the capitalist life have contributed to social problems that were unheard of not that long ago. There has been a dramatic increase in alcoholism and drug addiction. Moreover, for the first time, Chinese are suffering from gambling, Internet addiction, and eating disorders such as anorexia.

"China is not a very relaxed society any more," declared Margarete Haass-Wiesegart, a psychiatrist from Germany who was instrumental in setting up China's first psychotherapy training program. "There's a lot of instability. Money is very important now. People have to pay for good schools and health care, and they have to work very hard."

Indeed, mainland China seems to be succeeding in catching up to the madness of the strong Japanese work ethic and all the problems it can create. The major causes of premature death and disability in China are psychological disorders and suicide. Studies estimate that more than sixty million Chinese suffer from mental disorders, with depression the most common. More than two million attempt suicide every year.

Interestingly, a recent newspaper article cited the dramatic increase in everyday stresses as the major reason for the significant increase in sales of self-help books in mainland China. In fact, in 2003, the Chinese rights for *The Joy of Not Working* were sold to a Beijing publisher. Only time will tell how well my philosophy is received.

To Be Highly Successful in North America Is to Fail Badly

There are two things phonier than a three-dollar bill: One is a tree filled with elephants; the other is a successful yuppie. During the 1980s and into the early 1990s, yuppies, with their pasted-on smiles and masks of false happiness, lived Halloween 365 days a year. They liked to portray themselves as highly successful individuals, but how successful were they really?

Yuppies, in their madness, made the work ethic trendy. Indeed, not only did they make the work ethic trendy, they also made being a workaholic trendy. With hard work were supposed to come incredible success and the good life. Being a yuppie meant it was easier and better to be recognized for what one owned than for who one was.

Clearly, the "good life" that yuppies first pursued in the 1980s and 1990s was far from as good as it could have been. Due to their wealth-warped mentality and addiction to overwork, yuppies suffered in great numbers from hypertension, alcohol abuse, and drug dependence. Despite their abundant salaries, yuppies found leisure time the hardest thing to buy.

All my possessions for a moment of time.

—Queen Elizabeth I

Unfortunately, things have gone from bad in the 1980s and 1990s to worse in the twenty-first century. Today most of these baby boomers are working longer and harder, sacrificing what could be the well-balanced life that constitutes the true "good life." Moreover, today corporations in North America try to impose the baby boomers' workaholic ethic—which made hard work and long hours the order of the day in the 1980s and 1990s—on everyone, regardless of how detrimental it can be to workers and society in general.

Paradoxically, to be highly successful in North America is to fail badly at living a balanced life. Generally speaking, the people with the best jobs tend to have the worst work/life balance. Workers at all salary levels are affected, however. A recent study concluded that tens

Harold, it's been ten years since we were in the MBA program at Stanford. What in the world are you doing driving cabs?

I used to be a successful yuppie, but I gave up my nervous twitches, pasted-on smile, and therapist, and it ruined my career.

of millions of workers in the United States are dissatisfied with the balance between their careers and personal lives. Indeed, half of employed people between age twenty-five and forty-four work so many hours that they don't have sufficient time to spend with their friends and family.

Millions of people are working long hours, taking few vacations, and tying their identities to the workplace. Instead of having their emotional needs satisfied by friends, family, and church, they are relying on their bosses and colleagues at work. Sadly, work has become the primary source of self-esteem, recognition, and approval.

Therapists today are seeing more and more patients who have lost their true selves in their work. Maynard Brusman, a San Francisco–based consulting psychologist, recently told *Fast Company* magazine, "The workplace has become their community center—where they work out, get a massage, go to parties. They come to me anxious, and they don't know why. They've become caught up in the culture. The question is, Is that healthy? From what I've seen, it isn't."

Clearly, not only is the loss of identity unhealthy, so are the physical and mental stresses that come from overwork. Too much work, like too much exercise, leaves us with nothing in reserve. Health researchers have verified that overwork eventually leads to ailments such as ulcers, back problems, insomnia, depression, and heart attacks. Any one of these can knock the wind out of our sails in no time. For good measure, we can add "an early death" to this list, regardless of whether we live in Japan, China, North America, Europe, or anywhere else in this world.

What the "G" in GNP Really Stands For

Economists, businesspeople, and politicians tell us that we will all be better off if our gross national product (GNP) increases substantially. Gross national product is the value of all services and products sold in a country during any given year. It is the measurement that supposedly tells us if we have been successful as a nation. Therefore, the goal of any country's economy is growth in GNP. A healthy dose of GNP is supposed to provide jobs for everyone able to work—whether they want to work or not—as well as happiness to the masses.

Having taught economics courses at private vocational schools and universities, I have always had a problem with GNP as a yardstick of prosperity. GNP is improved by increases in question-able activities such as consumption of cigarettes and the production of weapons. Moreover, a substantial increase in car accidents will favorably affect GNP because more funerals, hospital visits, car repairs, and new car purchases will result.

If all economists were laid end to end, they would not reach a conclusion.

—George Bernard Shaw

Given that the growth in GNP is such an important yardstick, it surprises me that the skipper of the *Exxon Valdez* didn't receive a Nobel Prize for economics. In fact, the gross national product of the United States increased by $1.7 billion due to the *Valdez* oil spill. Following that logic, the United States should have hundreds of major spills a year— they would do wonders for its GNP. Moreover, the unemployment rate would drop to zero because of all the people required to clean up the oil. (Perhaps I should be the one awarded a Nobel Prize for Economics for this great insight. A Nobel would go nicely with my honorary Doctorate in Leisure, if I ever receive one.)

If all economists were laid end to end, it would not be a bad idea.

—Unknown wise person

Contrary to popular belief, growth in a coun-try's GNP doesn't necessarily benefit its citizens or make them happier. Yet bubbleheaded politicians, economists, and businesspeople advocate growth just for the sake of growth. This is the philosophy of cancer cells. In my view, GNP should actually stand for the Grossness of the National Product because of the many question-able activities in the economy that increase GNP.

Why Panhandlers Contribute More to a Better World than SUV Owners

Michael Enright, host of CBC radio's *This Morning*, recently stated that city dwellers who purchase sport utility vehicles "must be (mentally) arrested or not highly evolved." Given that only a small fraction of SUV owners actually use their vehicles to go camping or skiing, or to reach other hard-to-get-to locations—whereas the majority drive them alone, to work and back, and at very low gas mileage—I have to agree with him.

SUVs are nothing more than status symbols that many people feel pressured into buying. These oversized, overpriced, overrated, and over-built supertoys are designed to make people feel superior to those who don't have SUVs, while substantially increasing the profits of the auto manufacturers. Just because people work long and hard hours to pay for their expensive SUVs doesn't mean that owning their SUV makes them happier. Granted, the sales of expensive SUVs increase the GNP. But to what end? Unfortunately for all of us, the gas-guzzling SUVs are more harmful to the environment than vehicles need to be.

> Millions long for immortality who don't know what to do on a rainy Sunday afternoon.
> —Susan Ertz

More than a hundred years ago, the British philosopher and economist John Stuart Mill predicted that the environment would eventually be totally destroyed if the world continued on its path of economic growth. His premise was that accumulation of wealth, as defined by western nations, is dependent upon defacing the environment. As some of us are now aware, the environment cannot withstand the increasing demands we place on it. Owning an SUV is just one example.

Although caring for the environment has become a more important concern to most of us lately, few of us are willing to admit that our wealth-warped values and excessive drive for success contribute to serious environmental pollution. The work ethic plays a major role. If people were to work less, consume less, and take it easy more, they would help create a greener world. No doubt panhandlers who take it easy, never work, and consume little make a much more important contribution to a greener and better world than the rest of us, particularly SUV owners.

Virtually all work involves altering matter at or near the earth's surface relative to other matter—that is, utilization of natural resources. It follows that work of any kind contributes to pollution—and that increases in GNP come at a substantial cost to our environment.

Sometimes I get an irresistible urge to work hard like you two guys, but I just lie down until the feeling goes away, and then I'm okay.

We don't need SUVs or increases in GNP to be happy. We can get by on half the resources we use and still maintain a high standard of living. This can be accomplished, in part, by changing our values, including getting rid of the work ethic. Eliminating frivolous work—such as production of SUVs—is a good place to start.

Less work and more leisure will not only help the environment, it will contribute to our personal well-being. Unfortunately, most economists and businesspeople see more leisure as a positive event only if we have money and use it to buy more leisure items and services. In other words, more leisure is good if it increases the GNP. Perhaps these economists and businesspeople should pay attention to John Kenneth Galbraith, the well-known economist, who doesn't always view more money as a good thing.

> The end of labor is to gain leisure.
> —Aristotle

"I am not quite sure what the advantage is in having a few more dollars to spend," stated Galbraith, "if the air is too dirty to breathe, the water too polluted to drink, the commuters are losing out in the struggle to get in and out of the city, the streets are filthy and the schools so bad that the young perhaps wisely stay away, and the hoodlums roll citizens for some of the dollars they saved in the tax cut."

Saving our planet will require more than recycling bottles and cans. Most important, our values must change. There is something ridiculous about having people produce unnecessary trinkets and various other products, just to keep them working, because they don't know what to do in their leisure time.

The Real Stuff of Life

To sum up: the values dear to North American society have their limitations and shortcomings. If you have blindly adopted these values, seeing things differently can improve the quality of your life. Holding onto strict beliefs that work is virtuous and play is frivolous will impair your ability to happily handle unemployment and retirement. These same values will also contribute to a poor work/life balance.

Sadly, in the last few decades we have lost our sense of moderation. Today most of us cherish Donald Trump values of habitually striving for more and bigger stuff, and of working longer and harder for it. Yet the profile of the eighteenth-century gentleman, who made a modest amount of money and then retired to more worthwhile pursuits, makes greater sense today than ever. Personal growth from leisure activities would contribute to greater satisfaction and well-being than material growth from working hard.

In the higher order of life, all kinds of stuff around us—cars, houses, stereos, jobs—are conveniences and nothing else. These aren't the source of happiness. The things we own, the places we live, and the jobs we have are secondary. Above all, success shouldn't be measured by how hard we work or what we own.

Our true essence is of a higher order. Ultimately, the most important thing is how well we are living today—what are we learning, how much are we laughing and playing, and how much love we are showing toward the world around us. This is the real stuff of life!

CHAPTER 4

Working Less Just for the Health of It

The Trap with No Cheese

Try an experiment in which you test a rat by consistently placing cheese in tunnel #3 of several tunnels; you are likely to find that the rat will eventually figure out the cheese is in tunnel #3. As should be the case, the rat will not waste its time looking in other tunnels once it knows tunnel #3 is where the cheese is. If you start putting the cheese in tunnel #6, however, the rat will keep going to tunnel #3 for only so long. Sooner or later, the rat will realize there is no cheese in tunnel #3; the rat will then start looking in other tunnels until it discovers that the cheese is in tunnel #6. Not surprisingly, the rat will again consistently show up in the tunnel with the cheese.

I don't want the cheese, I just want to get out of the trap.
—Spanish proverb

The difference between rats and human beings is that the majority of people will remain in a tunnel when it is obvious there is no cheese in it. Oddly enough, most human beings remain in tunnels from which they never venture; they wonder where the cheese is, but they never do find any. After all, it's pretty hard to find cheese when one remains in a tunnel that either has no cheese left in it or, in some cases, had no cheese in the first place.

"Cheese" here represents happiness, satisfaction, and fulfillment as they relate to the workplace and life in general. In early 2003, Towers Perrin Management Consultants polled a sample group of U.S. and Canadian employees: more than half reported negative feelings about their jobs, and one-third of those described their feelings as intensely negative. They cited boredom, overwork, concern about their futures, and a lack of support and recognition from their bosses as key reasons for their unhappiness, dissatisfaction, and lack of fulfillment in the workplace.

There is more to life than increasing its speed.
—Mohandas K. Gandhi

Other research concludes that up to 70 percent of white-collar workers are unhappy with their jobs. Ironically, although a majority of workers are dissatisfied with their jobs, many are spending more and more time working. Yet few try to change the circumstances that contribute to their unhappiness and dissatisfaction. Put another way, they don't look in other tunnels for the cheese.

For some strange reason, we often use the term "being in the rat race." It isn't an appropriate term, however, simply because it's demeaning to rats. Rats wouldn't stay in a tunnel without cheese. It would be more appropriate for rats to use the term "being in the human race," particularly if they were to do something so ridiculous as returning to the same tunnel over and over again without finding any cheese in it.

One of the symptoms of an approaching nervous breakdown is the belief that one's work is terribly important.
—Bertrand Russell

Unfortunately, jobs don't always provide all the types of cheese that we are looking for. Tunnel vision keeps us in the trap with no cheese. This means no happiness, satisfaction, and fulfillment in our work lives. You can skip the rest of this chapter if you are a rat or a happily retired human being. This chapter will be beneficial to you, however, if you are either employed or unemployed and planning to go back to work sometime in the future. This chapter is designed to help you overcome tunnel vision so that you can create a great work/life balance and prepare yourself for a happy retirement.

Do You Know Who You Are?

To help you get a proper perspective on whether you are in a tunnel with lots of cheese, try the following exercise:

Exercise 4-1. A Simple Question?

Take a few moments to answer this simple question:

> Who are you?

When doing this exercise, practically all working people will write down various combinations of what they do for a living, what nationality they are, what religion they follow, whether they are married, where they live, and how old they are. However, what they do for a living is the main focus—often, the only one. Sadly, few people associate interests away from their workplace with their identity. They think they are their jobs.

Yes, this job will definitely enhance my identity. If I get it, my BMW won't be repossessed.

Preposterous as it may seem, the work world constitutes a tragic case of many mistaken identities. Career identities keep people in bondage because their identities hide their true selves. People weren't born into this world as doctors, lawyers, teachers, or laborers. These are things that they decided to become to earn a living. Of course, some higher-status careers may have also been chosen for their prestige—to give individuals a "better" identity.

So, how much of your identity is tied to your job? There is nothing wrong with associating yourself with your job at times, but your job should comprise only a small part of your identity. This is true even if you love your work so much that you are totally blown away by it. After all, if your identity is mainly tied to your work, you are limiting yourself as a human being.

Luckily, you are a thousand times more than your work. You just haven't realized it because practically everyone else in society is going through life thinking that they are their work.

Exercise 4-1, continued

To get a better idea of your true identity, first ask yourself:

> What sort of person would you want to be if work were totally abolished in this world?

Write this down. Also record your five best traits, not including any work-associated traits—such as ambitious, well-organized, or hard worker.

The truth is that your essence is much more than your work and always has been. Being in touch with your deeper self will reveal that a career by itself doesn't make you a whole person; neither do possessions, status, power, or net worth. Your true self is based on more profound things, such as your creativity, kindness, passionate pursuits, generosity, love, joy, spontaneity, connection with others, sense of humor, and spirituality. A new, healthy identity based on these traits will put you in the tunnel containing lots of cheese.

Ignorance Runs Rampant in Today's Corporate World

Sadly, outmoded attitudes and values still cherished by many corporate executives in the twenty-first century help to perpetuate a work environment characterized by workaholism. Given the serious health and social problems that result from workaholism, a visitor from another planet whose inhabitants are more intelligent than those of Earth would have to conclude that ignorance at all levels—including the higher echelons in management—is pervasive in major corporations across North America.

Comfortable in this sea of ignorance, workaholics are not only tolerated, they're respected. Because workaholism is about greed and power, many business leaders love workaholics. In many departments where most workers can be classified as workaholics, it's even fashionable to put in sixty to eighty hours a week (or, at least, claim to do so). Moreover, no one complains about being overextended in one's work. After all, most workaholics feel heroic when they're overcommitted all of the time, because they have nothing else in life to feel heroic about.

Ignorance is never out of style. It was in fashion yesterday, it is the rage today, and it will set the pace tomorrow.

—*Frank Dane*

Workaholics are addicts, no different from other addicts, such as alcoholics and drug addicts. All addicts are neurotics with serious problems, in denial about their addiction. The same can be said about people in corporations and society who support workaholics. They are no better than addicts; at best, they are neurotics.

Why do society and corporations support addiction? Anne Wilson Schaef explains this in great detail in her 1988 book, *When Society*

Becomes an Addict. She states that addictive behavior is the norm in American society: society itself functions as an addict, as do a lot of organizations. In her later book, *The Addictive Organization,* Schaef and her coauthor, Diane Fassel, go into great detail about why most large organizations are affected by addictions and function like addictive individuals.

Promoting the importance of work and emphasizing the need to be in a hurry go hand in hand with promoting productivity. In reality, this only appears to promote productivity. Having company employees work longer, harder, and faster, while sacrificing their leisure time, doesn't necessarily mean more will be accomplished. The result can be quite the contrary. Less will be accomplished in the long run, because sooner or later productivity and efficiency will be impacted by the decreased effectiveness of workers suffering from stress and burnout. Employees who have no time to think will inevitably make careless mistakes, and in the long run this will make the organization less innovative and productive.

The detrimental consequences of the mad world of corporate life are far-reaching. In the frenzy of hard work and day-to-day survival, many employees have lost their personal dreams. Their overwork leads to deprived family lives, forgotten social lives, even separation or divorce. For those feeling burnout, there is no more purpose, meaning, or zest for living.

> He worked like hell in the country so he could live in the city, where he worked like hell so he could live in the country.
> —Don Marquis

Interestingly enough, many baby boomers are caught in the trap with no cheese, but they have contributed to it individually as much as corporations have. It all started in the 1970s. When the baby boomers first began hitting the workforce, they were well-educated, committed, and loyal. Because there were more baby boomers than jobs, many worked long, hard hours, believing this was the path to promotions and job security. Their sacrifices paid off: the monetary and career rewards kept coming for some time—but not forever.

Unfortunately, corporations took advantage of the boomers' willingness to give their heart and soul to the organization. From the 1990s into the twenty-first century, many employees were downsized out of jobs because the remaining employees were willing to work even longer and harder. This has led to twenty-first-century lifestyles that leave much to be desired.

Some good has come out of this mess. Most children of baby boomers, having seen what workaholism did to their parents, define work-life balance very differently. To them, having a work-life balance means having a life—one with eight hours or less of work a day and plenty of leisure time to pursue the truly important things in life.

Hard Work Is the Enemy of Creativity

Years ago, an efficiency expert was hired by Henry Ford to examine the performance of the Ford Motor Company. The expert presented a report that was highly favorable, except for one employee whom he regarded with great suspicion. The expert told Henry Ford, "That lazy man over in that office is wasting your money. Every time I go by, he's just there sitting with his feet on his desk."

By working faithfully eight hours a day you may eventually get to be a boss and work twelve hours a day.
—Robert Frost

Henry Ford replied, "That man once had an idea that saved us millions of dollars." Ford added: "At the time he had the idea, his feet were planted right where they are now—on that same desk."

The moral of this story is straightforward: You must relax and use your imagination if you want to come up with the blockbuster idea that is going to save your company millions of dollars or earn you a cool million or two. Creative loafing—or productive relaxation, if you will—is actually good for your cash flow. Just one good session of creative thinking could be worth an extra million dollars to you sometime in the future.

Sadly, many of us today desperately want something different in our lives, yet we can find neither the time nor the space to generate the ideas that would contribute to a better lifestyle in the future. We are too preoccupied with the drudgery of our everyday lives to sit back and do some relaxed creative thinking.

Inasmuch as we live in a work-oriented society, most of us feel that we must be continually busy to be successful. We are led to believe that fabulous wealth and fame await the person who works the hardest. Indeed, we fear that taking it easy will prevent us from capturing even a small measure of wealth. The irony is that taking it easy now and then would help us achieve wealth a lot sooner—in fact, overwork can be hazardous to our creative ability.

The work ethic is an insidious force in our society; it dictates that we must always be busy doing something constructive in order to be productive members of society. Many people think loafing is an evil activity that stifles ambition and interferes with productivity. To the contrary, loafing can be a sign of ambition. It makes some individuals much more productive—and wealthier in the long run.

Throughout history, many highly creative people have been productive because they were able to goof off and indulge in some serious constructive loafing. Mark Twain did most of his writing in bed. Samuel Johnson rarely rose before noon. Other lazy achievers who were considered notorious layabouts include Oscar Wilde, Bertrand Russell, Robert Louis Stevenson, and W. Somerset Maugham.

Like most people in western society, you have probably been programmed to be hard-working, straight and narrow, and analytical. You may thus have difficulty accepting the fact that you could benefit from intentionally being a slacker on a regular basis.

> I have never liked working. To me a job is an invasion of privacy.
> —Danny McGoorty

To be highly creative, experience prosperity consciousness, and work toward financial independence, you must be able to sit back, ponder the big picture, and take the long-term view. Certain conditions and attitudes tend, more than others, to support the generation of new and blockbuster money-making ideas. The best environment for generating a bigger cash flow over the long term, while also preparing for financial independence, is a relaxed one with few distractions.

Always reserve enough time in your day to loaf, relax, and think creative thoughts. This will have much more of a positive effect on your financial and personal well-being than two or three hours of extra work. Not only does loafing take your imagination to greater heights, it's good for your long-term health, because it reduces stress and helps prevent many diseases. Moreover, when you loaf, you are preparing for the time when you achieve enough wealth to take it easy. You are giving yourself a taste of the freedom and prosperity that are coming to you.

> America has become so tense and nervous it has been years since I've seen anyone sleep in church—and that is a sad situation.
> —Norman Vincent Peale

One of the most productive things you can do is take a week or two to vacation away from home and your workplace and generate ideas for putting your talents and knowledge to better use. The income-producing ideas will be a big step toward your continued prosperity and wealth building. Concentrate on opportunities for three or four hours a day; forget everything else related to your workplace. Don't worry about the income you lose while you are away. The ideas you generate will be worth a hundred times what you sacrifice being away from work.

Keep in mind that you don't have to be a millionaire to take a few days off here and there. I have done this all my adult life, even when I was over $30,000 in debt. Taking time off hasn't prevented me from getting out of debt and creating some wealth for myself. In fact, my creative loafing has helped me to better evaluate my ability and potential so that

I could find an occupation that suited my desired lifestyle. Consequently, today I don't have to succumb to the frenzied, stressed-out lives that most people in western nations lead.

An unexpected day off work provides an opportunity to reflect on life and let your mind wander in all directions. This can pay big dividends—psychological, physical, and financial. Your immediate payoff won't be in the numbers of hours worked and in how much money you have earned. Instead, the return on your investment will be in your interesting thoughts and great ideas that you can put to good use for earning more money in the future.

> Personally, I have nothing against work, particularly when performed quietly and unobtrusively by someone else.
>
> —Barbara Ehrenreich

Hard work is the enemy of creativity. The more hard work you indulge in, the less creative you become. Only when you have plenty of time to loaf and think wildly will you be creative and come up with the great ideas that make the world a better place—and that will earn you a comfortable living in the process. Indeed, just one great idea can change your life dramatically. Look for it. It's there somewhere!

To Be a Peak Performer, Work Less and Play More

Perhaps you are like millions of people in today's world whose need to make a living has gotten out of hand and become an obsession. You yearn for more excitement, more adventure, more satisfaction, more happiness, and an overall higher quality of life, but you never find the time for these things. If this is your situation, you are probably a workaholic or close to being one. If you admit that you have a small problem with overwork, the problem is likely much bigger than you would like to acknowledge.

The universe defies you to answer the following questions: What good is a high-paying career if it leaves you continually stressed out and miserable? What good is owning a large stately house if the only time you spend in it is when you sleep in it? What good is having a lot of interesting possessions if you never have the free time to enjoy them? Above all, what good is having a family if you seldom see them?

> We are always getting ready to live, but not really living.
>
> —Ralph Waldo Emerson

If you are working more than eight hours a day, perhaps you are in the wrong job—or you are doing it wrong. You may be fooling yourself when you think you are productive just because you have worked fourteen hours in a day. You will be a peak performer when you do the same amount of work in eight hours, and take the other six hours to enjoy the good things life has to offer.

Herein lies the difference between workaholics and peak performers. Workaholics aren't peak performers; workaholics are weak performers. The following chart points out the differences between workaholics and peak performers:

Workaholic	Peak Performer
➤ Works long hours	➤ Works regular hours
➤ Has no defined goals—works to be active	➤ Has defined goals—works toward a major objective
➤ Cannot delegate to others	➤ Delegates as much as possible
➤ No interests outside of work	➤ Many interests outside of work
➤ Misses vacations to work	➤ Takes and enjoys vacations
➤ Has shallow friendships developed at work	➤ Has deep friendships developed outside of work
➤ Always talks about work matters	➤ Minimizes talk about work matters
➤ Is always busy doing things	➤ Can enjoy "goofing off"
➤ Feels life is difficult	➤ Feels life is a celebration

According to psychologists who have conducted research in the area of work/life planning, workaholics generally are not strong individuals; rather, they are weak individuals who don't have the will to enjoy life more. Health and happiness seem unimportant to them. People overwork to avoid their inner growth, the experience of having fun, their families, social outings, and themselves.

Some experts go so far as to claim that workaholism is a serious disease. If not treated in time, workaholism can result in mental and physical health problems. According to Barbara Killinger, author of *Workaholics: The Respectable Addicts,* workaholics are emotional cripples. Their work obsession leads to ulcers, insomnia, depression, and heart attacks. For good measure, add an early death to the list.

In contrast, peak performers are much healthier and live longer because they enjoy both work and play. Moreover, they are more

Hard work is the soundest investment. It provides a neat security for your widow's next husband.

—Unknown wise person

effective workers. When needed, peak performers can turn on bursts of speed for a week or two. They can be lazy at times, though—and be proud of it. Life/work planning consultants advocate a balanced lifestyle that satisfies six human needs: intellectual, physical, family, social, spiritual, and financial. Because they seldom overwork, peak performers are able to fulfill all six needs.

Figure 4-1. Balancing Your Wheel of Life

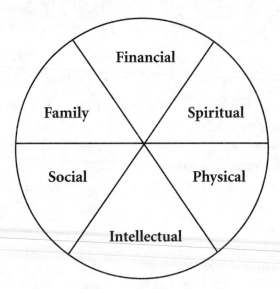

Contrary to popular belief, being a workaholic is nothing to be proud of. In addition to those shown on page 47, workaholics tend to exhibit the following five traits:

- The less a workaholic has to do, the longer it will take to get done.
- The workaholic will carry out any simple idea in the most complicated way imaginable.
- No problem is so small that a workaholic can't make it really big—or so big already that he can't make it even bigger.
- The peak performer's trivial task not worth pursuing is the workaholic's important task worth doing to excess.
- A workaholic often works toward solutions for a problem that was long ago forgotten by everyone else.

Although you may have been hardworking all your life, you can transform yourself to be lazy, intelligent, and productive all at the same time. While workaholics focus on the number of hours they put in, you should focus on the results. The difference can be remarkable in terms of the balanced lifestyle you are able to lead.

Clearly, everything in life has a price attached to it. There is a price for not working hard enough, and there can be an even larger price for working too hard. As a peak performer, you must know the moment in which to work diligently. Even more important, you must know the moment when you should *not* work, but relax and play instead. Not only will this benefit you immensely, it will also astonish your friends and colleagues.

Leisureholics Have More Fun

A great work/life balance can't be attained until work is put into its proper place. Although there are many positive benefits derived from work, there are just as many harmful effects that people tend to ignore. "One of the saddest things is that the only thing that a man can do for eight hours a day, day after day, is work," stated William Faulkner. "You can't eat eight hours a day nor drink for eight hours a day nor make love for eight hours—all you can do for eight hours is work. Which is the reason why man makes himself and everybody else so miserable and unhappy."

Above all, you must not allow yourself to think that workaholism is some intelligent and heroic state, even though at least 20 percent of the working population is addicted to work. Perfectionism, compulsiveness, and obsessiveness all complement the workaholic mentality. Because workaholics invest 100 percent of themselves in their jobs, they have nothing left for friends, family, and themselves.

No matter which way you look at it, salvation from a meaningless personal life can't ever be found in the workplace. Work should be a part of daily living, but not more important than family activities, exercise, solitude, and play. You must not put all your energy into a job; at the same time, you must learn to experience and appreciate leisure activities. Tapping into your leisure-related passions and talents early in life will make your professional life much richer and more satisfying.

As a leisureholic, not only will you have more fun, you will prepare yourself beforehand for the time when you could lose your job. Spare time handled in a leisurely way, besides making you happier while working, prepares you for a better life should you find yourself unemployed. In this regard, some retirement consultants suggest employees should start preparing and planning for their retirement when they are thirty-five or younger, not at sixty-five.

Figure 4-2. Before and after for a Workaholic

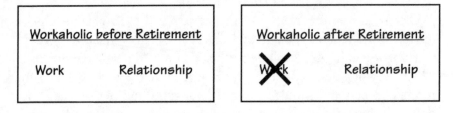

Figure 4-3. Before and after for a Leisureholic

Leisureholic before Retirement	Leisureholic after Retirement
Work Relationship	W̶o̶r̶k̶ Relationship
Golf Tennis Jogging	Golf Tennis Jogging
Stamp Collecting Church	Stamp Collecting Church
Reading Gardening	Reading Gardening
Volunteering Friends	Volunteering Friends

Figure 4-2 shows the effect of losing a job when you have no interests. If you have only your job and a relationship (marriage or otherwise) to keep you busy, your life will be narrowly focused once you lose your job. Without a job, you are limited to your relationship for things to keep you active. In contrast, Figure 4-3 shows the effect of losing your job if you have many interests and hobbies. As a leisureholic, you don't have to rely solely on your relationship for fulfillment, since you can shift your extra time to a range of activities and interests.

By working diligently (sometimes not so diligently) for forty years or more, many workers hope that one day they will cash in their chips for fifteen to twenty years of fruitful leisure. Upon reaching retirement, however, many people are unprepared because they didn't indulge in much leisure during their working years.

Sadly, many workaholics abstain from social and leisure activities because they don't know what to do with themselves outside of work—even if they are married and have children. Indeed, sociologist Arlie Hochschild, author of *The Time Bind: When Work Becomes Home and Home Becomes Work,* concludes that many dual-income couples spend long days at work not because their employers want them to, but because they want to escape the turmoil of family life. Some of them have been known to come to work even when they are sick, just to escape family life.

Unfortunately, most people don't change until they have to change. They wait until retirement is a reality, then desperately try to make the adjustment. For the unprepared, the adjustment is extremely difficult because of the drastic change in the amount of spare time. A gradual adjustment to more leisure while they were working would have been much easier to make. Moreover, interests and new skills not cultivated earlier in life are difficult to cultivate in retirement.

After two weeks of vacation, you finally have a smile on your face.

I can't wait to get back in the office to tell everyone what a great time I had, even though I didn't.

To be well prepared for retire- ment, you must start developing many interests and enjoying leisure while you are still in the workforce. It is in your best interests, particularly if you want to eventually live the Life of Riley, to have many interests unre- lated to your career. Indeed, leisure isn't something to be saved up until you are totally without work. Not only will you prepare yourself for retirement by indulging in a good measure of leisure, you will also live a balanced and happy life in the mean time.

For retirement to be enjoyable, breadth in interests is critical. Life can feel empty when your interests aren't varied. While you are in the work- force, you should develop many eclectic interests outside of your job. Just one interest, such as golfing, will not be enough to fill your retire- ment days. Ensure that you have a varied combination, from writing books to playing golf to visiting friends to taking a course unrelated to your job.

Leisure should be a quiet and enthusiastic absorption in things done for their own sake and unconnected to work in any way. Try to adopt the European approach to leisure rather than the North American approach. There is an important contrast between the philosophies behind the two approaches.

In North America, corporate values tend to rule employees' lives, even in leisure. Because America has a working tradition rather than a leisure tradition, to corporate America leisure is a time for relief and escape, to recharge one's batteries for the work ahead. In contrast, leisure in Europe is done for leisure's sake, not for work's sake. The main purpose of vacations is to enjoy leisurely activities, not to recharge. This is the result of a leisure-class tradition in Europe that has spanned many centuries.

The spirit in which you spend your spare time can actually make this time more stressful than work itself. For your leisure to be effective in helping you create a good work/life balance, ensure that you spend your spare time in a leisurely way and not in a competitive way. In North America, the traditional vacation is, more often than not, another tightly scheduled week with an itinerary resembling a week at the office. The week is spent at a spa, at a resort, on a road trip, visiting theme/amusement parks, or on a cruise, with little or no choice for spontaneity. A ski holiday in the Rockies or the Sierra is filled with so many activities that relaxation is nearly impossible.

> Few women and fewer men have enough character to be idle.
>
> —Ed Lucas

Squeezing as many leisure activities as possible into your personal time won't help you attain a balanced and relaxed lifestyle. Ironically, the activities that are supposed to help you relieve stress and enhance your health can actually have the reverse effect if you try to rush through them. Exercising in a hurry, for example, is liable to create more stress than it dissipates. In the same vein, you can't meditate effectively if you feel rushed. You are likely to regret having meditated at all when you realize you have wasted your time.

To add to the stresses of leisure, many vacationing employees keep in regular contact with the office. It is no wonder that the widely used Holmes and Rahe Social Readjustment Rating Scale for stress indicates that people find vacations more stressful than they find the Christmas season, although people experience quite a bit of stress before Christmas. Vacations can be much less stressful if people spend their time reading a book, getting to know the neighbors, or writing a novel just for the fun of it. Of course, more leisurely vacations are also a better way to prepare for retirement.

To be truly leisurely in North America, you must learn to take a rather unconventional approach to leisure. Don't be like the fast trackers in the corporate world who engage in their leisure with as much competitiveness as they show at the workplace—or more. They miss the whole point of leisure. Try taking a vacation at home; refuse to keep in contact with the office. Treat yourself to an unexpected day off to add some spontaneity to your life. When in between jobs, take a vacation for a month or two. The goal is to be as leisurely as you can be. You will be more relaxed during your work life and more prepared for your retirement years.

Don't forget to take it easy on weekends. A few years ago Elizabeth Custer, private-time editor for *Glamour* magazine, telephoned me from

New York to solicit my opinion on why the magazine's readers indicated in a survey that they are usually more exhausted on Sundays than they are on Fridays. Surprised by the survey's results, I had to give some thought to the question.

The answer, however, is straightforward: Because of the Protestant work ethic, these people feel anxiety or guilt when they try to relax. So they get busy doing things, such as repairing houses, mowing lawns, and attending to miscellaneous chores. As is to be expected, weekend busyness adds to the burnout already experienced during the workweek. No wonder these workers feel more exhausted on Sunday than they do on Friday.

The first half of life consists of the capacity to enjoy without the chance; the last half consists of the chance without the capacity.
—Mark Twain

Busyness is one of those bad habits sanctioned by organizations, educational institutions, and the media. In today's society, if you're not extremely busy and stressed out, you're not considered important. Mainstream society fails to consider, however, that being busy and being happy are entirely two different things. Contrary to popular belief, continually being busy doesn't lead to happiness and success. If this were the case, a lot more North Americans would be happy and feel successful. Clearly, the key to happiness and success is to be a peak performer at work and a leisureholic away from work.

In your search for happiness, above all, don't ever underestimate the value of increased leisure. Abundant leisure is indeed one of life's great treasures. Thus, the words of William Lyon Phelps: "Those who decide to use leisure as a means of mental development, who love good music, good books, good pictures, good plays, good company, good conversation—what are they? They are the happiest people in the world."

Fire Yourself If Your Employer Doesn't

In the nineteenth century, when asked to give a lecture for a large fee, Swiss naturalist Jean Louis Rodolphe Agassiz replied, "I cannot afford to waste my time making money." It's too bad that few people today have the same priorities. The world would be a better place if they did. To be sure, the nature of modern society dictates that we must work to earn a living. Unfortunately, when we overdo earning a living, we suffer the consequences of not having a relaxed, satisfying, and prosperous lifestyle.

As a matter of course, work can create imbalance in your life. Some jobs demand unending attention and won't give you the opportunity to

> There is something wrong with my eyesight. I can't see going to work.
> —Teddy Bergeron

have a great work/life balance. The results are often an unhappy spouse, undisciplined kids, no social life, and a miserable you. If you're getting about as much payoff from your job as you would from being the captain of the *Titanic,* then you may want to do something to change your state in life.

Here are some signals that your life is not in balance and you are probably in the wrong job:

- ➤ You take more than your share of mental-health days due to headaches, tension, and other stress-related complaints.
- ➤ You dread going to work practically every morning.
- ➤ You don't like your present job because you can't express your creative side.
- ➤ Your main interest in staying in your present job is to cope for another sixteen years until you can collect a good pension.
- ➤ You spend the first hour of work reading the boring sections of yesterday's newspaper.
- ➤ You're married to your job; your life is all work and no play.
- ➤ You can't remember when you last got excited about your job.
- ➤ Your job is undermining your health with problems of insomnia, excessive stress, and no time to relax.
- ➤ You daydream away over half of the workday and are just going through the motions the other half.
- ➤ You keep trying, but to no avail, to convince yourself and others that your work is stimulating.
- ➤ You have trouble concentrating and can't generate any new ideas for your projects and problems.
- ➤ When you think about your workplace, you get depressed.
- ➤ You long to be back in university or school, even though you didn't like attending either one.
- ➤ At 5:00 P.M. on Sunday afternoons, your stress level increases dramatically because of the thought that on Monday you have to go back to work.
- ➤ You have nothing good to say about your company, even though it recently made it to *Fortune* magazine's "100 Best Companies to Work for in America."

The first day your job does not nourish and enthuse you is the day you should consider leaving. Indeed, I advise you to quit. This may be the right thing to do even if you generally like your job. If it takes more than fifty hours a week from your life, and you are unhappy because of your unbalanced lifestyle, it is time for action. Particularly, if your spouse calls you a stranger, your kids are on drugs, and you are miserable, why not do something else? Fire yourself if your employer doesn't. You will do your spouse a big favor, your kids a big favor, your organization a big favor, and yourself a big, big favor.

Forget about these excuses—*I can't quit because I need the security, I need to make payments on my big house, I want to send the kids to college*—and all the other ones that arise. Don't wait for the right time to quit. Do it now. There is never a right time; waiting for the right time is another convenient excuse to justify procrastination.

> All paid jobs absorb and degrade the mind.
>
> —Aristotle

Regardless of how much money you earn, you will never be able to recover the forty hours or more you are putting into a job that doesn't enliven you. It is impossible to buy back enough enjoyment in retirement to make up for the pleasure you missed while working at a lousy job. Ask yourself, "What good is the money going to do if I lose my health?" Many rich people can't buy back the health that they lost due to overwork.

Many work with the same company until retirement, even if they don't like their job, because they don't want to give up their good salaries. Others hate what they are doing, but won't change careers because of the generous retirement benefits. Staying in an unpleasant job environment makes these people function at much less than optimum. They increase their chances for experiencing burnout before retirement, and they may not even live long enough to retire and collect those generous pensions.

> Work is the greatest thing in the world, so we should always save some of it for tomorrow.
>
> —Don Herold

You are imprisoned by the system if you are working just for the money. It is important to be growing in your job, doing what you like, and putting your favorite talents to use. Don't allow society's idea of financial security to dictate your life. Spending time at a job you hate just to make money will interfere with your ability to enjoy life. As odd as it seems, it will also interfere with your ability to make good money in the long term.

There is a common feeling that getting one's financial house in order will help put other needs in place; however, the opposite is frequently true. Studies confirm that individuals who do what they like generally end up making much more money than individuals who work just for the money in jobs they dislike.

It's not impossible to leave a job, just difficult. Don't trick yourself into thinking something is impossible when it is only hard. If you want to do something, and are committed to doing it, you can. There is a price to pay, but it will be worth it in the long run.

If you are afraid to quit your job, ask yourself, "What is the worst thing that can happen?" Pinpoint that, then ask yourself, "So what?" If the downside doesn't involve death or terminal illness, then say the heck with it.

In short, it's not the end of the world if things don't work out perfectly. Put things in proper perspective. First, you will still have your health and your creativity. Then, think about all your options. In North America, even without a job, you have more opportunity than millions of people can ever dream about having on this earth. As for worrying about security, there is no such thing as true security from holding on to a job. Knowing you have the ability and creativity to always make a living is the best financial security you can have.

Just imagine all the great activities in which you can participate between this job and the next one. You can sell everything you own, take the money, and travel as far as it will take you. You may want to go to China, Rio, or Mexico. Or go to Spain and paint. Write that book you've always wanted to write. Sleep in until ten every morning and feel sorry for all the workers who can't.

Of course, when it's time to go back to work, you may wind up with a much better job than you had before. After you fire yourself, you may not want another job if you can somehow avoid one without incurring severe financial hardships. Many people feel better about themselves when they quit corporate life. Even those who don't find something financially rewarding say they would have a hard time returning to their old corporation.

To be sure, there will always be some risk to leaving your job; everything worthwhile involves some risk. But with downsizing so prevalent in the twenty-first century, you may get fired sooner or later anyway. The odds are pretty high that your company will set you free whether you like it or not. By voluntarily leaving your job, you get to handle being without one. You will be more proficient at handling this situation should it surface again.

> Learn to pause . . . or nothing worthwhile will catch up to you.
> —Doug King

Since *The Joy of Not Working* was first published, several readers have written to happily inform me that they quit their jobs after reading the book. They said I was instrumental in helping them quit. While my feat is not exactly worthy of a Nobel Prize, it's gratifying that I have helped some people see the light. Les Oke from London, Ontario, was one of these individuals.

Dear Ernie:

I have just finished reading your book *The Joy of Not Working*. Your inspirational words have changed the way I now view my life. I always felt that working harder would eliminate my problems, but all it ever did was complicate my life and cause more problems. You have given me the courage to quit my job. I used to be a tax consultant. Now I'm a human being again.

That's right. I marched in this morning and told them I quit because my wife, my kids, and my health (both mental and physical) were more important. I've been seeking security through working more, but that's not the answer. There are so many things I've wanted to do but felt I couldn't. I love reading, and I've always felt writing would be a natural extension of my personality. If you have the time, I'd appreciate learning how you got started writing. I also failed first-year university English.

Thank you,

Les

If hanging on to your job keeps you in a tunnel with no cheese, the greatest risk is in *not* leaving it for something different, as was apparently true for Les. Les has written to me twice since the first letter. Happily, he was doing just fine the last time I heard from him.

If you cannot risk being fully alive, what can you risk? Going through the motions in your job means you spend eight to ten hours a day in a boring, joyless, and lackluster way. When your job is taking its toll on your body, mind, and spirit, it's time to leave, whether or not you have found another job. Your dignity and personal worth must come first. No job is worth the loss of freedom and other personal sacrifices that interfere with your enjoyment of life to the fullest.

Are You Listening to Your Calling?

One of the chief sources of happiness is having a special purpose or personal mission in life. The optimum is to have your overriding purpose or personal mission take the form of a job that expresses who you are—your true calling. Whether that involves being a teacher of some important knowledge to children, or being an inspired artist, your days will be filled with satisfaction and happiness. Finding and pursuing your true calling can make life a totally new experience.

> The deepest personal defeat suffered by human beings is constituted by the difference between what one was capable of becoming and what one has in fact become.
>
> —Ashley Montagu

If, instead, you neglect your ultimate purpose or personal mission, you can cause yourself much dissatisfaction. Even worse, avoiding what you love may result in emotional turmoil and physical ailments. People who suppress their true interests and desires are most likely to get addicted to alcohol, drugs, work, or television in a futile attempt to ease the pain and dissatisfaction in their lives.

So many baby boomers are suffering from midlife crises because they never pursued their passions. During the 1980s and 1990s, these individuals pursued the careers or jobs that paid the most money, so they could live a life of excessive materialism. They may have achieved career success as they defined the term: getting to the top of the corporate ladder and collecting material possessions. But they are experiencing great dissatisfaction, even emptiness, in their lives, mainly because they haven't found their ultimate purpose or personal mission. Many haven't found it because they haven't searched for it; others, because they don't know how to find it.

> It is not enough to be busy . . . the question is: what are we busy about?
>
> —Henry David Thoreau

Contrary to popular belief, everyone can discover a primary purpose for living. Your personal mission can be expressed through your career or avocation, but it doesn't necessarily have to involve your work. You can also express it through volunteer work, a pastime, a hobby, or some other leisure activity. What's more, your ultimate calling in life can be expressed through a combination of the various facets of your life, including your interests, your meaningful relationships, your work, and your leisure activities.

I sometimes lie here meditating a bit about my greater purpose in life, but most of the time I just fantasize about what I will do when I win a million dollars in a lottery.

Your true calling will surface when you are ready for it. Paradoxically, some individuals find their true life's calling just when life appears to be going downhill. It could be part-time volunteer work for a charity, or an assignment with a special-interest group, that becomes a full-time mission. It could also be a neglected hobby that turns into a full-time passion—or even an extremely profitable business.

In their book *Whistle While You Work: Heeding Your Life's Calling*, authors Richard J. Leider and David A. Shapiro suggest that people ask themselves three important questions:

1. What gift do I naturally give to others?
2. What gift do I most enjoy giving to others?
3. What gift have I most often given to others?

According to the authors, by answering these questions, people are likely to reveal to themselves their calling—and ultimately move toward new realms of success and fulfillment. The authors define calling as "the inner urge to give our gifts away in service to something we are passionate about in an environment that is consistent with our values."

Clearly, a job that you take for the sole purpose of making money or a leisure activity in which you participate to kill time is not a personal mission. Your personal mission is something that will make a difference in this world. If you have an overriding purpose in life, you know that humanity is benefiting from your efforts. A mission can be modest by other people's standards. For example, a friend's father is a school janitor; his mission is to create the cleanest school possible for the students and teachers.

Here are some other examples of personal missions:

➤ To make the world a better place to live by reducing pollution
➤ To raise money to help care for others in need
➤ To help children develop a special talent or skill, such as playing piano
➤ To write entertaining children's books that help young boys and girls discover the wonders of the world
➤ To give foreign travelers the best possible tour of the Rocky Mountains
➤ To create a committed relationship and keep it exciting and energizing

Although a true calling should be closely tied to your values and interests, it can also be determined by your strengths and weaknesses. Your personal mission will intimately connect you to who you are and to the world around you. Taking the time to answer the following questions may help reveal a personal mission that you would like to pursue.

> Music is my mistress and she plays second fiddle to no one.
> —Duke Ellington

1. **What are all your passions?** Discovering what turns you on is the most important element for recognizing your personal mission. Your passions give you great enjoyment; you seem

to have unlimited energy when pursuing your passions. Write down all the things you find enjoyable. Your list can include things as varied as fishing, horses, serving others, researching at the library, making people laugh, and traveling to other countries. Pay attention to the things that would get you out of bed an hour or two earlier than your usual time.

2. **What are your strengths?** Looking at your strengths says something about yourself and where you like to concentrate your energy. If you are artistic and able to go with the flow, you may want to create art or music or sculpture. Strengths normally support passions.

3. **Who are your heroes?** Spend some time thinking about your hero or heroes who would be good role models. Heroes can be people from the past or present you have admired, or even revered. They can be famous or obscure people who are doing something special or outstanding. If you were given the opportunity, which three role models would you choose to have dinner with? What have these people accomplished that you admire? Studying your heroes' qualities and actions will give you clues about your own aspirations.

> I never thought of achievement. I just did what came along for me to do—the thing that gave me the most pleasure.
>
> —Eleanor Roosevelt

4. **What do you want to discover or learn?** It is important to look at what stimulates your curiosity. Which topic or area would you like to explore more? Think about the courses or seminars you would select if a wealthy relative appeared out of nowhere and offered to finance two years of study anywhere in the world.

Answering the above questions should put you on the right track to discovering your true calling. Your personal mission is something special that comes from your soul; it is your essence and reason for being. Your personal mission is why you came into this world.

Remember, your personal mission has nothing to do with making money. Having a personal mission or purpose means utilizing your unique talents in a way that enhances conditions for humanity. Your life is also enhanced because of the satisfaction and happiness you experience. While utilizing your talents in pursuing your mission, several by-products may result; one by-product may be making a lot of money.

To sum up, a true calling can fulfill your inner needs more than money or other activities ever can. Above all, your true calling will help you become much more than you have ever been. "There comes a special moment in everyone's life, a moment for which that person was born," declared Winston Churchill. "That special opportunity, when he seizes it, will fulfill his mission—a mission for which he is uniquely qualified. In that moment, he finds his greatness. It is his finest hour."

Having Your Cake and Eating It Too

If you would like to work at an enjoyable job, but at the same time you want a more leisurely lifestyle, you are in the group of individuals who want to have their cake and eat it too. Here is some good news: contrary to popular belief, you *can* have your cake and eat it too. It's really quite simple: just get yourself two cakes. See? You are already ahead of all those workaholics and competitive fast-trackers, because they are too busy and hard-headed to ever think of this.

Although few people in the fast lane of corporate America have a great work/life balance, you can, if you put your mind to it. First, you must learn how to be a peak performer by working fewer hours. As stated earlier in this chapter, some of the greatest achievers in the history of humankind have been creative loafers. They were peak performers who got ahead by slowing down. Moreover, they enjoyed a lot more leisure time than the general population.

To be a peak performer, you must work smarter, not harder. How you can achieve this is beyond the scope of this book, but there are several books that do justice to this topic, such as *The 80/20 Principle: The Secret to Success by Achieving More with Less* (Doubleday, 1999) by Richard Koch and *The Lazy Person's Guide to Success: How to Get What You Want without Killing Yourself for It* (Ten Speed Press, 2002) by none other than yours truly. I can assure you that if you dare to follow the principles in these two books, you can become a more creative, more insightful, more productive, more playful, wealthier, and happier human being. All this by working less and enjoying life more.

> I would not exchange my leisure hours for all the wealth in the world.
>
> —Comte de Mirabeau

It is worth repeating that overwork, and the excessive stress that often accompanies it, can lead to serious deterioration of health. According to Dr. Ingrid Bacci, the author of *The Art of Effortless Living*, chronic illnesses such as arthritis and cancer can result. Due to overwork and excessive stress, Dr. Bacci herself developed a crippling illness that kept her in bed for three years. She eventually attained radiant health by following certain techniques for easing emotional and physical stress.

In her book, Dr. Bacci shows readers how to stop being compulsive performers and start leading lives of creativity, fulfillment, and health. She states that by doing less—by focusing on becoming peaceful and calm—you can actually achieve more, whether at work, in sports, or in your personal relationships.

I highly recommend Dr. Bacci's book if you are working hard and continually feeling anxious and frustrated. Dr. Bacci shows that the best way to handle stress, frustration, and creative blocks is by focusing on relaxing your mind and your body. With the help of Dr. Bacci's techniques, you can become more effective and productive while putting out less effort. This may seem too good to be true, but Dr. Bacci backs her theory with scientific evidence.

To be a peak performer, working efficiently is key, but you should also be working at what is right for you. Clearly, you won't excel in any field unless you enjoy what you are doing immensely. Do whatever you must to work at what's right for you, because a day of work you hate will seem like an eternity compared to a month of work you love.

Surprisingly, despite all the fancy job titles and corporate propaganda, workers in the United States are growing unhappier with their jobs. Even though most Americans continue to find their jobs interesting and are even satisfied with their commutes, only a thin majority like their jobs. A 2002 survey of 5,000 Americans found that only 51 percent were satisfied with their jobs, compared with 59 percent in 1995.

Today, far too many people work long hours at jobs they terribly dislike. These people are motivated to get up in the morning by a paycheck, and little else. An accountant who makes $45,000 a year in a dead-end job is experiencing a fulfillment deficit; so is a university professor who makes $150,000 a year but who dislikes lecturing to students. Both cases represent career failure of the highest order.

> If you have to support yourself, you had bloody well better find some way that is going to be interesting.
> —Katherine Hepburn

There must be more to your work—and life in general—than just earning a good living. You can only feel prosperous insofar as you experience happiness today and do not sacrifice everything for a joyful tomorrow that may never arrive. Because you need to spend so much of your life working, it's important to make your career satisfying and fulfilling.

By working at what you are most suited for, you will succeed with the least amount of stress and effort. This is the peak performer's way, attaining success in the healthiest, most relaxed way possible. You will know when you have the right job or career: overall, it won't seem like work to you; instead, it will be enjoyment for which you get well paid.

Here is another sure sign that you are in the right job: you would gladly do the work for free—even pay handsomely to do it—if you didn't have to earn a living.

To have your cake and eat it too, you must not only work smart at what you enjoy, you must also spend a lot of time relaxing. Making time for leisure should be a priority. The richest people in the world are those who have fun earning their living and at the same time have a healthy work-life balance.

According to popular belief, a rigid career track in North America offers little opportunity to properly enjoy and handle leisure because of the long working hours of the average worker. Estimates vary, but certain researchers claim leisure time shrank by as much as 37 percent from the 1970s to the start of the twenty-first century.

Other studies contradict these findings, however. One study indicates that, because of fewer children and less housework, the majority of North Americans have more free time—about five hours a week—now than in the recent past. The problem, according to the latter studies, is not one of insufficient leisure; rather, most people under-estimate the amount of leisure time they have available and don't use it constructively. For example, about 40 percent of free time in North America is spent (wasted, in my view) watching TV.

Regardless of what studies say, I am not convinced that the average North American has no control over the decrease in his or her leisure time. If you haven't enough time to catch a breath of air, let alone smell the roses, you are probably to blame. Practically everything in your life is a matter of choice. The lack of leisure time is mostly self-imposed. Those who have too little are likely either in the wrong job, doing it wrong, or simply not opting for free time.

A case in point is that some 21 percent of Americans don't take the vacation time they're entitled to. What makes this even more serious is that Americans aren't entitled to as much vacation time as the Australians, Germans, French, and Swedes. Yet those people would find it unthinkable, if not stupid and laughable, to pass up a single day of their five- and six-week vacation allotments.

Extensive breaks away from work provide present-day enjoyment; however, the benefits go far beyond short-term gratification. Vacations and sabbaticals also relax the body, unclog the brain for some real cre-ative thinking, and allow you to be much fresher and more motivated when you return to work. The health benefits of vacations are real—a 2002 study by the American Psychosomatic Society found that men age thirty-five to fifty-seven who took annual vacations were 21 percent less likely to die young than nonvacationers and 32 percent less likely to die of heart disease.

The most important point of this chapter is that you should be pursuing your leisure interests now; otherwise, you aren't winning at life. You may have to perform a remarkable balancing act to get a more balanced lifestyle—juggling your career, your debts, your possessions, and even your family—but it is a mistake to put aside physical exercise, travel, and personal pursuits because of a job and the desire to make more money than others. You can always squeeze in leisure activities if they're worth it. Just in terms of health alone, you cannot afford to discount creative loafing from your life.

To find that tunnel with lots of cheese, you must realize that the road to unhappiness is paved with the pursuit of things that matter little. It's a big mistake to pursue things that don't matter at the expense of the few things that do matter. Most of those things are, in fact, completely unnecessary and pointless. These include longer job titles, bigger houses, flashier cars, and trendier activities. After all is said and done, however, only a few things contribute significantly to happiness. You must learn to distinguish between the truly unimportant and the truly important. Eventually you may be considered not only a genius, but a messiah as well.

The Joy of Not Working Nine to Five

You should work less than the majority in society just for the health of it. The more you are out of step with society in regards to the nature of your work and the hours you have to put in, the greater your chances for self-discovery and adventure in this world. Moreover, you increase your chances for becoming healthier and happier than most human beings.

There is no better example than busker Ben Kerr of Toronto, Ontario. He is one of the most intriguing individuals that I—and thousands of other people—have ever met. You can often find Ben performing his songs before hundreds of people either at the St. Lawrence Market or at the corner of Yonge and Bloor, Toronto's busiest business and tourist district.

I first encountered Ben late on October 13, 1993, when he called the John Oakley radio talk show on which I was a guest, helping listeners enjoy being unemployed. After a few words with Ben, I promised to meet him in person on the corner of Yonge and Bloor the next day and give him a copy of *The Joy of Not Working*. In exchange, Ben agreed to sing his song "I Don't Want to Be the Richest Man in the Graveyard."

Here are some of the things that I have learned about Ben since I met him that lucky day: on March 31, 1981, when he was somewhere in his fifties, Ben retired from his executive position at the Toronto Harbour Commission because he wouldn't put up with the smoking-allowed policy the company had at that time. Soon after, he ran—physically— 3,000 miles from Toronto to Los Angeles to campaign for a no-smoking policy in office buildings.

Before he left for Los Angeles, Ben wrote and recorded a song for his crusade: "Fire on One End (Fool on the Other)." It was recorded on the Emphysema Label in the CBC studios in Toronto.

Upon his return home from Los Angeles, Ben pursued his passion— writing and singing songs. For over twenty years now, Ben has been a street musician, singing and playing his five-string guitar (the G string is missing). Toronto's harsh winter months haven't dissuaded Ben from singing outdoors—ballads about other people and songs about his own life. He claims that singing in the fresh, cold air exercises his lungs. Known to tens of thousands of people in his hometown, Ben is regularly voted "best busker" in a survey conducted by Toronto's *NOW* magazine.

Ben surmises that if he had decided to stay with the Toronto Harbour Commission until the traditional retirement age of sixty-five, he probably wouldn't be alive today. Yet, today, in the words of *Health Perspectives* magazine reporter Jerry Gillians, "Ben is as spry a senior as you will ever meet, with energy and enthusiasm abound."

When reporters ask Ben his age, he typically replies, "I am ageless, because age is a state of mind. I'm not too young or too old to do any-thing. When you are ageless, you never get sick, tired, or depressed."

Ben has run for mayor of Toronto every three years since 1985. He has never come close to winning, but he says he will win sooner or later because he plans to live forever. "The thing is, I'm going to win eventually," he declares.

When I met Ben, the first thing I noticed was that he is an extremely happy man. While he sings his songs throughout the afternoon, people from all walks of life happily greet him and give him money. Inspired by the first edition of this book, Ben wrote a song called "The Joy of Not Working Nine to Five." Here are the lyrics:

The Joy of Not Working Nine to Five

I know the joy of not working nine to five
Singing every day at Yonge and Bloor
Strumming my old five-string guitar
It's the joy of not working and that's for sure

People say that I'm a lucky guy
And they wish that they could be like me
To know the joy of not working from nine to five
To be footloose and fancy free

But they'll never lose the treadmill that they're on
And it's sad to see dejection in their eyes
The joy of not working could be there
But they're just too afraid to try

Ernie J. Zelinski wrote a book
The Joy of Not Working is its name
'Cause Ernie is a fellow just like me
And the joy of not working is his game

I know the joy of not working nine to five
Singing every day at Yonge and Bloor
Strumming my old five-string guitar
It's the joy of not working and that's for sure

Strumming my old five-string guitar at Yonge and Bloor
It's the joy of not working and that's for sure
The joy of not working and that's for sure

In June 2002, Ben told me, "When I was a young lad, I used to look at 'old' people and tell myself, 'When I get old, I'm not going to be like that.' I had a firm resolve in my mind back then that I would be happy, healthy, and financially independent in my golden years. And that's exactly what's happened. Today I can honestly say that I'm the happiest man in the world because I can do whatever I want when I want to do it."

I hope the story of this intriguing individual will challenge you to make a drastic change in your life, such as leaving a boring job, so that life becomes a lot more interesting and enjoyable. As you can see, Ben copped out of society's chorus long ago to sing his own songs, and he is much healthier and happier for it.

CHAPTER 5

Unemployed: The True Test of Who You Really Are

The Time of Your Life to Have the Time of Your Life

The purpose of this chapter is to help you make an easy and comfortable transition to more leisure. If you are like most people, you put many years of preparation into entering the world of work, but little or no preparation into leaving it. Provided you take the right approach, you can discover a whole new and exciting world out there without work. Being away from the workplace allows you to enjoy life in a way not available to you when you are working. It's the time of your life to have the time of your life, whether you are unemployed or retired.

The day you wind up with a great deal of spare time through retirement or unemployment is the day you get to test who you really are. Extra leisure time will be a gift from heaven, if you take the time to grow as a person and don't keep your identity tied to your former job. You get to experience everything through your own essence, instead of through the demands and directions of society, the business world, and the media.

If you are temporarily unemployed, it's just as beneficial for you to learn how to handle lots of spare time as it is for

> To be able to fill leisure intelligently is the best product of civilization.
> —Bertrand Russell

retired people. Career specialists say the general outlook is that people will have to rebuild their careers several times in a lifetime. The average time spent on one job is now only 3.6 years. Moreover, employees will be more vulnerable to firings and layoffs than ever before. In fact, the average forty-year-old white-collar worker can expect to change employers three times in his or her career, with at least one firing or layoff. Therefore, if you are in between jobs at this time, make the most of it.

This time, like all times, is a very good one, if we but know what to do with it.

—Ralph Waldo Emerson

Handling joblessness will make you more confident in handling it again when it happens in the future, including when you retire.

Many variables will affect how well you utilize your time; your attitude will be the most important one. To be sure, the transition to more leisure is not always easy. While you were working hard and trying to get rich and famous, you weren't learning how to handle leisure. You were learning how to work hard and how to try to become rich and famous. These habits are not easily forgotten. Even with lots of opportunity to relax and enjoy life, you may have a difficult time being happily unemployed.

Unemployment Is a Great Opportunity to Develop Some True Character

Virtually everyone who loses a job due to retirement or unemployment is affected in some significant way. Those who say they aren't are either crazy or lying. Being fired, laid off, or retired is initially hard to handle. Although throughout my adult life I have been known as more of a slacker than a hard worker, even I found out that handling leisure is *not* as easy as shooting fish in a barrel or rolling off a log.

The degree to which individuals have identified with their jobs will determine how much difficulty they experience handling a life of total leisure. The greatest loss of identity is experienced by people who have totally immersed themselves in their work. For these people, grieving the loss of their jobs takes some time. As is to be expected, managers and executives normally experience a harder time during unemployment and retirement than blue-collar workers. After all, white-collar workers identify more with what they do.

Most of us rely on outside forces—such as the business media, universities, and corporations—to provide a script for leading what society considers a successful work life. Unfortunately, society's institutions haven't drafted another script for handling a life of total leisure. All of us, therefore, need to put effort into writing our own script for leading a worthwhile and satisfying life when we find ourselves unemployed or retired.

Although many people nearing retirement have a fear of diminished purpose and activity, the good news is that, sooner or later, most of them successfully make the transition to a life of leisure. Unfortunately, some people have been so rigidly socialized with Puritan values that they find being without a job difficult, distasteful, and depressing. Because of their unhealthy attitudes and unwillingness to change, such individuals may experience a total loss of self-esteem, as demonstrated by the suicide rate for American men, which is four times higher in retirement than in any other stage in life.

According to researchers, the transition from work to retirement can seriously affect one in five individuals, leaving them in a state of mild to severe depression. Marilyn J. Sorenson, a clinical psychologist and author of *Breaking the Chain of Low Self-Esteem,* claims that low self-esteem is often the cause of postretirement depression. "Many people with low self-esteem become overachievers," she says. "Driven to prove their adequacy, they throw themselves into their work."

In my view, people who find it extremely difficult or impossible to have a worthwhile life without work have no individuality. They are, for all intents and purposes, admitting that their basis for existence is entirely externally oriented, and that their personalities are extremely shallow. Perhaps a complete personality transplant is the only solution.

> Work is the refuge of people who have nothing better to do.
> —Oscar Wilde

A period of unemployment, whether in between jobs or during traditional retirement, is a great opportunity to show or develop some true character. It's safe for me to assume that you aren't so rigidly socialized that there isn't any hope for you to be happily unemployed. Rigid people don't normally read books like this one. Moreover, I will assume that you are willing to write a new script for your life and live it better than you did while employed.

However, if you have strongly identified with your job, don't expect instant breakthroughs. Allow the process to take some time—after all, you are remaking your self-image. You may initially feel like a loser, but this will change as your self-image improves. Rest assured that, in time, your self-image will change to that of a winner.

Being Unemployed Means Being a Winner

As I have said, for most people the end of a job or career means the end of their main source of identity. If there is no new job or career to replace the old, leisure must satisfy the human needs that the job satisfied before. In making the transition to a life of total leisure, people find the first few days or weeks the most difficult. Some experience fright and panic. Others feel the situation is completely unnatural. Still others, particularly those who hated their jobs, have mild discomfort, but take at least some delight in their newfound freedom.

If people really liked to work, we'd still be plowing the land with sticks and transporting goods on our backs.
—William Feather

There's no doubt being unemployed can be harmful to the well-being of those who do not psychologically adapt. There are many negative aspects of unemployment: financial insecurity, less social contact, fewer goals to pursue, and reduced opportunities for satisfaction from achieving something worthwhile. Studies show that the best way for people to fight boredom and dejection is to get involved in constructive leisure activities. The worst thing a person can do is sit in front of a television set and dwell on how bad unemployment is.

An important step in making a transition to more leisure is the discovery of your true essence. If you have been totally obsessed and absorbed by your work, you may have had little in the way of the leisurely life. In fact, you may barely have had a life, period.

Your career may have determined most of your identity. Over the years, through the demands and nature of your job, you may have allowed your career to transform you. What was dear to your company may have been ingrained in you instead of what is dear to you—your essence, your true self.

Rediscovering your essence—what is truly important to you—can take a little time. You will have to do some digging around—mainly within yourself—to find out what makes you tick. Moreover, you must be committed to learning how to grow and learn in this new situation. Once you have discovered your true essence, you won't require the trappings of a job to define who you are.

Productive work certainly has its place, but there are many leisure activities that are equally valuable, challenging, and rewarding. Whether it's painting a picture, volunteering at a charity, playing an intense game of tennis, or traveling with a purpose, a constructive leisure activity can provide the same satisfaction as work can. If you find yourself unemployed, though, you must be in the proper frame of mind to accept this.

To be at ease is better than to be at business.
—Baltasar Gracián

Above all, you must remain positive about your position in life. Indeed, not only will you feel better while unemployed, but you will also find another job a lot quicker. This is supported by a recent study conducted by Gary Latham of the University of Toronto.

Working with twenty-eight ex-managers who had been jobless for at least thirteen months, Latham separated them into two groups. He taught the first group self-guidance and positive talk. The second group received no training. Nine months after the sessions, half of the first group had found employment within $10,000 (plus or minus) of their former salaries. Only 12 percent of the second group had found a job. "For training that takes only fourteen hours of someone's life," declared Latham, "these are pretty positive results."

In regards to retirement, there is scholarly evidence that with time most people adjust to being without a job and find life to be as satisfying as, or even more satisfying than, it was with a job. Morris M. Schnore, a former professor of psychology at the University of Western Ontario, conducted an extensive research study on the well-being of retirees. His findings, presented in his book *Retirement: Bane or Blessing,* support the notion that people don't need a job for happiness and satisfaction in life.

The formula for complete happiness is to be very busy with the unimportant.

—A. Edward Newton

According to Schnore, shortly after leaving work a majority of retirees find life to be fulfilling. Only a small minority suffer from a prolonged identity crisis. For 10 percent, retirement causes a serious maladjustment. Schnore concluded, however, that satisfaction in life among most retirees is as high as or higher than it is among most younger adults.

What's more, contrary to the negative myths about retirement, retirees are happier and more satisfied with their lives than middle-aged workers. Some retirees even find retirement better than they expected. According to Schnore, several factors contribute to effective adjustment to retirement:

➤ Striving for goals that are attainable

➤ Developing an appreciation for what one has

➤ Confidence that one can cope with problems as they arise

If you are presently making a transition to a life without work, no doubt there are going to be important changes in your life. As you shift from work to more leisure, you can't help but re-create your true essence. There is no reason to feel incompetent or worthless, despite your not having a job. Once you find inherent value in leisure, you should have little trouble coming up with new ways to keep yourself challenged—with or without external influences.

Keep in mind that you can feel just as successful without a job as you can with a job. Success, as peddled by society, means a well-paid career, a big home, and a luxury car. Clearly, this isn't the only way to define success. If you want to feel successful between jobs or during retirement, simply follow Ralph Waldo Emerson's definition of success:

What Is Success?

To laugh often and love much;
To win the respect of intelligent persons and the affection of children;
To earn the approval of honest critics and endure the betrayal of false friends;
To appreciate beauty;
To find the best in others;
To give of one's self without the slightest thought of return;
To leave the world a bit better, whether by a healthy child, a rescued soul, a garden patch or a redeemed social condition;
To have played and laughed with enthusiasm and sung with exaltation;
To know that even one life has breathed easier because you have lived;
This is to have succeeded.

Clearly, all aspects of Emerson's definition of success are attainable away from the workplace. Indeed, contrary to popular belief, joblessness doesn't have to mean being unproductive or being a loser. You are a loser only if you see yourself as one. As mentioned in chapter 2, perception is everything. Perceive the world more positively, and you will realize that being unemployed means being a winner. You can see yourself as a winner simply because you have unlimited leisure time to engage in the productive pursuit of self-actualization. After all, not many people in the history of humankind have had this privilege.

We Often Miss the Good Old Days That Never Were

One key factor for being happy when we are unemployed or retired is to overcome whatever nostalgia we may experience for our last job. The problem is that the further we get away from an event, the more selective our memories become. Indeed, some of us even reminisce about great things that never happened. With jobs, we remember the few things we liked and forget the many things we disliked. As someone once put it, we often miss the good old days that never were.

Allow me to share how I was able to overcome nostalgia for a job. Several years ago, I quit a part-time instructor's job at a private vocational school because of conflicts with the academic director. Despite my previous success in handling extended periods of unemployment, and despite the fact that I had been working only sixteen hours a week, I still had some difficulty in making the transition to more leisure. In the mornings, I was raring to go, but there was just one slight problem—no place to go. Weirdly, I started missing some of the things that the job had offered. At the same time, I realized that I had lost my ability to handle being without a job.

> As lousy as things are now, tomorrow they will be somebody's good old days.
> —Gerald Barzan

Although totally out of character for me, for the first two or three days I had misgivings about having resigned from the job. Around the fourth day, however, I was back in the groove. My feeling of prosperity returned. I started feeling sorry for people who had to go to jobs that they didn't like. What's more, I even felt sorry for those who liked their jobs. They couldn't possibly be as happy as I was.

My success in being happily unemployed was due in part to my thinking about the things that I disliked about working in the private vocational school, as well as in other

> Nostalgia isn't what it used to be.
> —Unknown wise person

organizations. This quickly put unemployment into proper perspective. Happily, whatever nostalgia I had experienced was quickly put to rest.

Exercise 5-1. Telling the Truth about Your Last Job

Be honest about your last job. List the things you didn't like about your boss, the organization, or the daily events associated with going to work.

Based on the organizations where I have toiled away in at least some degree of misery, I compiled my own list of things that I disliked about most workplaces. This list gives you twenty-five good reasons for feeling fortunate to be retired or unemployed.

Twenty-Five Reasons to Dislike the Typical Workplace

- ➤ An excessive workload as a result of corporate downsizing
- ➤ Being confined in the office all day when the sun is shining
- ➤ No opportunity for advancement for at least fifteen years because the baby boomers holding senior positions are not moving anywhere
- ➤ Having to work with jerks and incompetents who should have been fired ten years ago

- ➤ Power struggles within the office involving fierce competition, backstabbing, and pasted-on smiles
- ➤ Receiving less pay than someone who is much less productive but who has been around longer
- ➤ Commuting for an hour or two each way, every day, in the jungle of traffic
- ➤ Unnatural inactivity such as being restricted to a desk all day
- ➤ Constant interruptions and no time to think because of the daily pressure
- ➤ Paperwork—memos that mean nothing and reports no one ever really reads
- ➤ No cooperation from other departments
- ➤ Double-talk—even triple-talk—from superiors
- ➤ Regular two-hour, or longer, meetings that go nowhere fast
- ➤ Having to work with repulsive workaholics who refuse to take vacations even when they are encouraged to do so by their boss
- ➤ Overly rigid vacation schedules that make it impossible to take vacations at the best times (the months whose names don't have an "r")
- ➤ The organization's asking employees not to take full vacation entitlements because of too much work

SOMEDAY I'M GOING TO LEARN HOW TO USE THESE THINGS AND FIGHT MY WAY OUT OF THIS DEAD-END JOB.

- ➤ Supervisors taking credit for others' work and ideas
- ➤ Lack of good parking for employees (except for overpaid executives)
- ➤ Having to stay the full workday even if you are twice as productive as someone else and get your work done ahead of schedule
- ➤ Bureaucracy, red tape, foolish rules, illogical procedures, and unmotivated people specializing in dynamic inaction

➤ Discrimination on the basis of race, sex, physical features, or single status

➤ Organizations that advertise themselves as being innovative but don't support innovative people

➤ Office air-conditioning that functions properly only in winter

➤ No recognition or acknowledgment for excellence in work

➤ Working with repulsive yes-men and yes-women who prostitute themselves for salary increases and promotions

Given that the situations just described are par for the course in most North American organizations, it's no wonder many people consider the workplace demeaning to the human spirit. Regardless of your present employment status, this list should have some effect on you. If you are unemployed, reviewing it should have put things in proper perspective and brought a smile to your face in no time flat. If you are presently employed, however, any smile you had to start with has probably disappeared.

Three Needs to Satisfy at Your Leisure That Jobs Inadvertently Fill

Unemployment can negatively affect people's well-being and self-esteem through the stress that can arise from the lack of predictability, lack of control, and lack of social contact. Some unemployed individuals become so lost that they have been known to start missing jobs that they passionately hated and colleagues who used to drive them berserk.

Clearly, these people don't actually miss that distasteful work and their obnoxious former coworkers; they miss other aspects of the workplace. Although most people don't realize this, a job is more than a means for getting an income. Particularly if they have a supervisory or management position, employees receive many rewards: self-worth, status, achievement, recognition, room for growth, and power. Upon leaving the workplace, they lose these rewards.

In addition, there are three important human needs that most jobs inadvertently fill: structure and associated routines, a sense of purpose, and a sense of community. Even if people work at a job that is low status or undesirable, the workplace generally provides them with the means for satisfying these needs. To be happy and successful, the unemployed must satisfy all three needs through other sources.

Three Important Needs

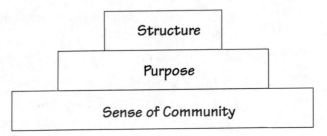

1. Creating New Structures

For better or worse, structure and associated routines are set for us by society from the time we are children until we retire. Tasks—such as getting an education, working at a job, getting married, and raising a family—all have ready-made routines associated with them. A problem arises when we find ourselves away from the workplace, with substantial free time on our hands. Upon retirement or job loss, the structure and routines we had in our jobs abruptly disappear.

Losing workplace structure and the associated routines can create much havoc, particularly for rigid people. Time must be filled to pass the days, but empty time can end up being the rule instead of the exception. Empty time results in boredom and joyless living. Rigid people may even withdraw from society and lead a life of desperation because they refuse to adjust to an existence in which they have personal freedom to do what they want. In extreme cases, mental and physical capabilities rapidly deteriorate.

Initially, the loss of ready-made structures and associated routines can sound great to most people: no need to get up early in the morning, no need to rush breakfast, no meetings to attend on time, and no commuting in rush-hour traffic. In other words, the clock no longer rules us. The problem is that most of us, no matter how creative, like at least some structure and routine in our lives. Being creatures of habit, we get addicted to structure. There is a great deal of comfort from the routines. And, of course, we all like comfort.

To lose workplace structure and routines can end up being unnerving. If you are independent, creative, and motivated, however, the loss will be a blessing rather than a curse. This is the time to enjoy your freedom and to create your own new structures and routines in your life. You can do this in various ways.

For example, after I semiretired many years ago, I had to create my own routines to replace those provided by the organizations where I had worked. Exercising twice a day to keep fit puts routine and structure in my days. I do stretch exercises for about fifty minutes soon after I get up. Later in the afternoon, I exercise for up to one and a half hours with a combination of cycling, running, walking, and playing tennis. Besides all the other great benefits I get from exercising, I create over two hours of routine every day.

I also add more structure to my days with activities such as regularly visiting coffee bars to have coffee, chat with the regulars, and read three different newspapers. Setting regular time slots to write this book, as well as ten others, has provided me with even more structure. Here are a few other ways to put routine and structure into your life:

> *I'm trying to arrange my life so I don't even have to be present.*
>
> *—Unknown wise person*

- ➤ Take courses at your local college or university
- ➤ Jingle your car keys at four o'clock each afternoon
- ➤ Join the boards of charities that meet regularly
- ➤ Take part in a sport—such as tennis, golf, hockey, or soccer—that you can do on a regular basis
- ➤ Work as a volunteer

If you have developed as a person, your interests should be so varied that the lack of routine and structure is not a problem. Your most powerful inner resource is your creativity. The big advantage of being creative is you get to design your routines and schedule around your leisure time, your friendships, and your relationships with the world. This ensures a lifestyle that is truly your own.

2. Being on Purpose

For the retired and unemployed, having a purpose can be a matter of life or death. After all, people without a purpose don't seem to live as long as those with a purpose. Studies indicate that retired people without a purpose in their lives aren't known for breaking many records for longevity. Seven in ten of such people die within two years; of these, on average they receive only thirteen Social Security checks before checking out of this world for good.

Moreover, studies show that there are significant differences between retirees who feel retirement is easy and those who find it difficult or have mixed feelings. The more purpose and meaning people have in their lives, the easier they find retirement. As is to be expected, retirees' personal and emotional lives are greatly enhanced when there are purpose and meaning to their existence. No doubt the same applies for the unemployed.

"Leisure," advised Benjamin Franklin, "is time for doing something useful." Unless you put some purpose into daily activities, you may end up constantly questioning the meaning of life. This invariably leads to depression, which some unemployed and retired people regularly experience. An overriding purpose is a great antidote for depression because people feel useful, committed, and productive.

Purpose in retirement involves pursuing activities that express our true selves. Clearly, it's not easy for all of us to discover a purpose that is our own. Ingrid Bacci, in her book *The Art of Effortless Living*, states, "For all our culture's so-called individualism, most people have very little true sense of themselves, or of a purpose to their lives that they can eagerly espouse. It is no wonder that, if we focus on externals and find our validation primarily in what we do and in what we get for what we do, we will never find ourselves."

GLASBERGEN

Don't feel bad about being unemployed, Dad. I've been unemployed my whole life, and it's fun!

Put another way, many individuals (I use the term loosely in this case) don't have an important purpose because their focus has been on superficial pursuits, such as material possessions, status, competition, and wasteful consumption. They have been so programmed to work hard and earn a lot of money that they have totally forgotten who they are.

You too may have allowed yourself to become so engrossed in your career and in amassing material possessions that you have forgotten what makes you feel fulfilled and truly alive. Indeed, work and the pursuit of material things may have estranged you from who you really are. Therefore, one of the most important aspects of defining a purpose for your retirement is to find out who you really are.

Discovering who you really are is essential, because purpose is created from within. Again, I refer to purpose as an important mission, a true calling, or a passionate pursuit. Your purpose in life won't appear on its own. If you haven't found your purpose, it's important to take some time—a few days or weeks or even months—to explore your deeper self. Otherwise, you may never find your true purpose in life.

Years ago, after I was fired from my job as an engineer, my purpose for the next two years was fully enjoying life without working at a job or attending an educational institution. I developed a passion for leisure and lived happy, wild, and free, even though many capable and intelligent people would have gone bonkers under the same circumstances. I could lay claim to going two years without a job and enjoying practically every minute. Needless to say, this gave me great satisfaction and a sense of accomplishment.

> The secret of success is constancy of purpose.
> —Benjamin Disraeli

A good way to find an overriding purpose is to fill in the blanks in these self-discovery statements:

To change the world I would like to _____.

Wouldn't it be great if I could _____?

Someone with purpose whom I admire is _____.

At the age of ninety I would like to look back and say this is what I have accomplished: _____.

I would get satisfaction in my life if I could _____.

There is no end to the scope and variety of activities that can constitute an important purpose when you are unemployed or retired. It depends on your interests and values. Here are several examples of pursuits that others have found worthwhile:

- ➤ Make a difference in other people's lives
- ➤ Make a contribution—for example, community work
- ➤ Experience creative expression
- ➤ Take part in discovery and challenge
- ➤ Help preserve the environment
- ➤ Show other people how to enjoy life
- ➤ Accomplish some challenging task
- ➤ Improve health and well-being
- ➤ Create personal happiness and satisfaction

Don't ever underestimate the power of having an overriding purpose, or several of them, while you are retired or unemployed. A life without purpose can lead to disassociation from life; a life with an interesting purpose can lead to an incredible love of life. Being involved in activities with a major purpose will not only keep you mentally and physically active, it will also reward you with emotional and spiritual fulfillment.

3. Generating a Sense of Community

Beyond being an arena of business, accomplishment, and power, the office has become a community center. Increasingly the office is also where friends are made and after-work activities are arranged. An important component of employees' happiness is their sense of making a contribution to a community. Jobs can make individuals feel appreciated, valued, and cared for by co-workers. What's more, for some employees the workplace is the only place where they have a sense of being loved.

> I don't care to belong to any club that will accept me as a member.
> —Groucho Marx

Today, the only companionship and socializing that many people get while pursuing their careers is at the workplace. In fact, over the years some workers become totally reliant on the company for social intercourse—so much so that they have no skills with which to develop new friendships away from the workplace. After they retire or get laid off, these people become social misfits. They no longer have the corporate social haven that provided them with familiarity and a sense of security.

Unfortunately, with the loss of a job, some people also lose what they feel is their best opportunity to make new friends. If you have recently retired or been laid off and you want to meet new friends, you can't wait at home to be discovered. Nor are you going to meet new friends if you pursue your interests alone. If you watch TV or work on a solitary hobby all day long, you can rest assured that no new friends will come your way. Making new friends requires that you place yourself in communal and social situations where you can share yourself with others.

Where you go and don't go to meet others is important. Like-minded people are drawn to each other, much more so than people who have little or nothing in common. Indeed, when it comes to making friends, there's a lot to be said for bingo halls, raunchy nightclubs, and seedy bars: these places attract—and remove from other places—a lot of people with whom you wouldn't want to associate under any circumstances.

> Don't stay away from church because there are so many hypocrites. There's always room for one more.
> —Unknown wise person

On a slightly more serious note, given that you want to meet quality people, you must go where quality people hang out. Don't expect to meet artists where Hell's Angels are known to hang out. Similarly, if discussing philosophy is important to you, you probably won't experience this at a donut shop, where regular customers normally discuss sports, TV shows, and little else. Perhaps the art gallery, museum, or planetarium doesn't seem like a good place to meet others; nonetheless, you are more likely to meet a like-minded person at one of these places than at the local pub.

Try to get involved with a group—large or small—that has a defined purpose related to one of your interests. The organization can be community-oriented or related to church, hobbies, or current affairs. You will establish not only new social bonds, but also your own purpose and the opportunity to attain recognition.

Learning from others is an effective way to gain wisdom about how to be happy without a job. It makes good sense to seek the company of creative individuals who are good at handling leisure and living life to the fullest. Try to befriend unemployed and retired individuals who are having a ball away from the workplace; study what they are doing.

Making a Career Out of Leisure

The day you wind up retired or temporarily unemployed is the day you must look at leisure as a career. The rewards from this new career are satisfaction, self-actualization, and achievement of meaningful goals. You shouldn't feel worthless because you don't have a job. Look at yourself as making an incredible contribution to society by being able to handle being without a job.

> If hard work was such a wonderful thing, the rich would have kept it all to themselves.
>
> —Lane Kirkland

Karen Hall of Toronto wrote to me to share her thoughts about the opportunities and freedom that being unemployed offered her.

Dear Ernie:

I have just finished reading your book *The Joy of Not Working* for a second time and felt compelled to write a letter of thanks.

This past July I quit a job that was both frustrating and extremely stressful. It was taking a toll on my health. At that time I saw you on CBC-TV and read your book. Everything that I had been feeling for quite some time was in the book. It was so refreshing to know that someone else viewed the world of work the same way as myself.

For six wonderful months I have lived the Life of Riley, which has been both exciting and relaxing. I had the chance to travel to eastern Canada and to Thailand, as well as reading a ton of books and magazines. I got to know my family and friends again. And most importantly, I got to know myself. Of course, others were extremely envious of my position—which actually equates to FREEDOM.

Unfortunately, I am not in the financial situation to live independent of a regular full-time job. Alas, I have obtained a new job and will start this January. The important change has been in my attitude, in that I now realize it's okay not to be a workaholic, and I am determined to again live the Life of Riley (semiretirement at least).

Sincerely yours,

Karen Hall

Being unemployed is a privilege to Karen. It should be the same for you. Your time can be filled with infinite possibilities. Without the confines of the workplace, you gain certain freedoms: freedom to think, freedom to reflect, and freedom to act. In short, being without a job is the true test of who you really are—and an incredible opportunity to become who you truly want to be.

CHAPTER 6

Somebody Is Boring Me; I Think It Is Me

An Extremely Boring Disease to Have

Two gentlemen of leisure, a North American and a European, were discussing the joys of life when the European nonchalantly stated that he knew one hundred different ways to make love. The North American, somewhat in awe of what he had just heard, replied that he knew only one. The European asked which one it was. The North American described the most natural and conventional way. The European then replied to the North American: "Most interesting, I never would have thought of that! Thanks a million. Now I know a hundred and one ways."

He was known for ignorance; for he had only one idea, and that was wrong.

—Benjamin Disraeli

Are you like the North American or the European? Do you see only one way of doing things, or do you look for many? The habit of looking for one way—and the most conventional one, at that—will set you up for the disease described in the following exercise.

Exercise 6-1. Don't Get This Disease

This disease afflicts over twenty million North Americans. It can give you a headache or a backache. It can give you insomnia or make you impotent. It has been labeled as a cause of gambling, overeating, and hypochondria. What is this ailment?

If you, at this moment, have a headache, are reading this book because you can't sleep, and are deeply craving a giant five-decker

CALVIN AND HOBBES © Watterson. Dist. by UNIVERSAL PRESS SYNDICATE. Reprinted with permission. All rights reserved.

sandwich after having just eaten one, it's likely you are bored. The ailment described above is none other than boredom.

Now recognized as one of North America's most serious health problems, boredom is at the root of many psychological disorders and physical problems. Some of the common physical symptoms associated with boredom include shortness of breath, headaches, excessive sleeping, skin rashes, dizziness, menstrual problems, and sexual dysfunction.

Moreover, boredom deprives people of the meaning of life and undermines their zest for living. Although it would seem to specifically affect those who are idle and jobless, boredom often afflicts people in the workplace.

People who are chronically bored tend to have the following traits:

> ➤ They are anxious for security and material things.
> ➤ They are highly sensitive to criticism.
> ➤ They are conformists.
> ➤ They are worriers.
> ➤ They lack self-confidence.
> ➤ They are not very creative.

Clearly, boredom is most likely to hit people who choose the safer, no-risk path. Because they take no risks, bored people seldom reap the payoffs of accomplishment, contentment, and satisfaction.

People who, on the other hand, choose the path of variety and stimulation are rarely stricken with boredom. To these creative individuals, who look for many things to do and many ways of doing them, life is tremendously exciting and fun. Just ask the European who now knows at least 101 ways to make love, if you ever run into him.

The Real Cause of Boredom

Most of us get bored to some degree at various stages of our lives. Ironically, many of the things we strive for can end up boring us. For some people, a new job becomes boring over time. An exciting relationship may become dull. And leisure time once deemed precious may turn into dead time.

When we get bored, we can place the blame on many things: society, friends, relatives, dull TV programs, an uninteresting city, a depressed economy, the neighbor's stupid dog, or a gloomy day. Putting the blame on external forces is the easiest way to react because then we don't have to take responsibility for our boredom. Placing blame elsewhere, however, is as effective as a screen door on a submarine.

> Any idiot can face a crisis—it's day-to-day living that wears you out.
> —Anton Chekhov

To overcome boredom, we can look to psychologists for guidance. They cite the following causes for this affliction:

> ➤ Unfulfilled expectations
> ➤ Boring jobs that have no challenge to them
> ➤ Lack of physical activity
> ➤ Being too often a spectator and too seldom a participant

Clearly, we are responsible for our lack of physical activity, unfulfilled expectations, remaining in boring jobs, or being a spectator instead of a participant. We end up being bored because we allow these factors to manifest themselves in our lives. In short, we are the ultimate authors of our boredom.

"Somebody is boring me," declared Dylan Thomas. "I think it is me." If you get bored often, it behooves you to post Thomas's words where you can regularly read them. After all, whenever you are experiencing boredom, you have chosen it. The question you have to answer is: why?

> Boredom flourishes too, when you feel safe. It's a symptom of security.
> —Eugène Ionesco

Perhaps the words of Leo Buscaglia may come in handy. "If you are bored," stated Buscaglia, "it's because you are boring."

Life can be fulfilling and rewarding, or it can be boring and disappointing. Richard Bach warned us with these important words: "In order to live free and happily, you must sacrifice boredom. It is not always an easy sacrifice." Overcoming boredom does require giving up the safe and familiar. It is well worth it, however. Particularly if you have wasted the first part of your adult life on boring work, you certainly don't want to be like so many individuals who waste the second part of their adult lives on a boring retirement.

Retirement Is Boring Only If You Retire from Life

Not long ago, while shooting the PBS documentary *My Retirement Dreams*, filmmaker Marian Marzynski explored a Miami Beach retirement community and the way its residents were growing older. Marzynski formed relationships with several retirees and got to know their dreams, their enjoyments, and their struggles. As the retirees pondered the meaning of their lives, Marzynski discovered that many held onto the past and some missed their productive years of work.

> Is not life a hundred times too short for us to bore ourselves?
>
> —Friedrich Nietzsche

Marzynski made a few more observations. As is to be expected, he found some retirees were bored, some were physically active, a few were expanding their minds, and many were waiting for destiny to show them the way. Marzynski concluded that what makes the difference for a happy retirement has little to do with age or education. Just as significant was his conclusion that a happy retirement had little to do with level of income.

Happiness in retirement, as in all stages of life, doesn't care how you get there. Not only does happiness not care how you get there, it doesn't even care whether you get there at all. And you are sure not to get there in your retirement years if you rely solely on money, as do so many people in western society. You are also sure not to attain true happiness if you wait for destiny or others to show you the way. If nothing else, you'll end up extremely bored and lacking satisfaction and inner peace.

Although boredom in itself doesn't appear to be a serious problem, it's at the root of many psychological afflictions that the unemployed and retirees experience. Surprisingly, boredom can actually be more of a problem to retirees—and to the unemployed, for that matter—than poor physical health.

David Evans, a professor of clinical psychology at the University of Western Ontario, and Terry Lynn Gall, a professor in the Faculty of Human Sciences at Saint Paul University, found that although health plays a role in quality of life, just as important—if not more so—are the mental pressures of coping after leaving the work force. Evans and Gall concluded that symptoms associated with boredom—such as being unhappy, depressed, or lonely—can be more bothersome on a daily basis for people than physical symptoms.

Do you think I'm boring?

I know we've met, but who the heck are you?

You can add an early death sentence to the serious symptoms that accompany boredom—even for those bored retirees who are still alive. In the eighteenth century, the English statesman Lord Chesterfield lamented his friends' and his own dilemma after the two had retired. "Lord Tyrawley and I have been dead these two years," stated Chesterfield, "but we don't choose to have it known."

Yet for individuals in the right psychological state of mind, even a traditional retirement—one without part-time work or a major passionate pursuit—doesn't have to be boring. Betty Sullivan, sixty-nine at the time, was one of the Miami Beach retirees featured in *My Retirement Dreams*. Unlike many individuals, Sullivan didn't find traditional retirement a major disappointment in her life.

Before Sullivan retired, she was an administrator at the Department of Animal Pathology at the University of Miami for seventeen years. Prior to this, she and her husband owned an appliance and sewing machine store in Amherst, Massachusetts. To Sullivan, retirement was liberation from years of tedious responsibilities associated with work and family.

"Before I left," Sullivan stated, "some of my co-workers had warned and joked about the perils of retirement: boredom, imaginary health problems, lack of purpose, and possible depression. None of these things has happened to me. Why? I exchanged a grueling nine-to-five routine for a well-earned casual and carefree lifestyle."

Betty Sullivan retired happy, wild, and free. Like other self-actualized retirees, Sullivan found that retirement is at least as exciting and interesting as her work life was.

The cure for boredom is curiosity. There is no cure for curiosity.

—Ellen Parr

"Do I miss the challenge of the workplace that had once been so much a part of my persona? Heavens, no," she declared. "My days are filled with healthy activities—swimming, working out at the gym, shopping, bicycling, and taking classes such as writing, art, and yoga. In the evenings there are movies, concerts, and dining and dancing. Soon, I may do a little traveling. And you know what? If I don't feel like doing anything at all except lounge around my apartment, I'll do that too."

Clearly, retirement is boring only if you retire from life. Betty Sullivan found that the world of retirement is overflowing with opportunity. Retirees can experience many different events, things, people, and places. Indeed, the incredible variety available to active retirees offers endless possibilities for enjoyment and satisfaction, ensuring that boredom is not part of their vocabulary.

Abolish Boredom with the Easy Rule of Life

Whether retired, unemployed, or gainfully employed, people afflicted with boredom violate the Easy Rule of Life. "What the heck is the Easy Rule of Life?" you may ask. It's a basic principle of the universe and a very powerful one. The degree to which you follow the Easy Rule of Life will determine how much satisfaction and happiness you achieve throughout your whole life. Indeed, the principle is so important that I recently wrote an inspirational fable on it, called *Look Ma, Life's Easy*.

The Easy Rule of Life is represented in diagram form in figure 6-1. The essence of the Easy Rule of Life is straightforward: if we do the easy and comfortable, life ends up being difficult. Ninety percent of us immediately choose this route because short-term comfort seems more appealing than the alternative. But one problem with a comfortable life is that it gets boring in no time.

Figure 6-1. The Easy Rule of Life

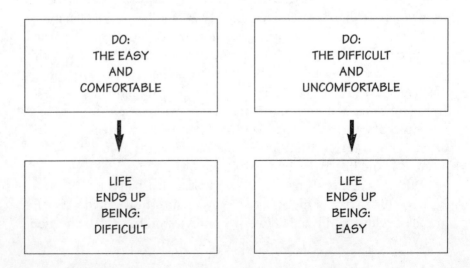

Unfortunately, most of us gravitate toward less pain and more pleasure. Choosing the easy way, however—the one with lots of comfort and pleasure—ensures that we wind up in a rut. And the only difference between a rut and a grave is the dimensions. In the rut we get to join the living-dead, and in the grave we get to join the dead-dead. Joining the living-dead is a surefire way to have a lot of boredom in our lives.

If we do the difficult and uncomfortable, however, life ends up being easy. Ten percent of us immediately take this route because we know we must experience short-term discomfort for long-term gains. By undertaking difficult and uncomfortable activities, we experience satisfaction and accomplishment in our lives. This means being truly alive, with little or no room for boredom.

Let me warn you that the Easy Rule of Life is something like the law of gravity. Mess around with the law of gravity by walking off the top of a building and see what happens to you. It knocks you on your butt. The same thing applies with the Easy Rule of Life. Mess around with it by taking the easy way, and you wind up on your butt as well. Believe me, it works every time.

The Easy Rule of Life had a bit of an influence on Lynn Tillon of New York. Lynn sent me the following letter after she read the first edition of this book:

Dear Ernie,

In the last few minutes I've followed some of your suggestions from *The Joy of Not Working*:

1) Wanting to write to you—and actually doing it

2) Doing the "difficult" now so that life will be easy

3) Breaking the rules of writing to a "stranger"—only using a business-letter form

4) Writing a letter—which I haven't done in ages (though constantly promising myself that I will)

I teach juvenile delinquents in a NYS Division for Youth Facility. I made copies of the Easy Rule of Life. The kids were interested and enthused and came up with parallels in their own lives that amazed me: e.g., easy money selling drugs leads to family pain, danger, death, jail. If I had tried to bring these things up, it would have been preachy.

Personally, I want out of the job and the lifestyle of driving over three hours a day—leaving precious time for leisure—to say nothing of the stress. Your book has given me hope and many tools to free myself for living and also to enjoy the present more until I decide to change.

Sincerely,

Lynn Tillon

Given that juvenile delinquents in Lynn Tillon's class saw the relevance of the Easy Rule of Life in many areas of their lives, adults should be able to do the same. For some reason, however, many people violate the Easy Rule of Life throughout their adult lives. Boredom is just one of the many consequences. On the other hand, other people follow the Easy Rule of Life throughout their adult lives. These individuals are seldom, if ever, bored.

> To do the same thing over and over again is not only boredom; it is to be controlled by rather than to control what you do.
>
> —Heraclitus

The Easy Rule of Life influences every area of our lives, including success at work, financial gain, quality of friendships, quality of family life, parenting, love, health, and satisfaction from leisure activities. For example, if you are presently a smoker, the easy and comfortable way is to keep smoking because you don't think you have what it takes to quit. Conversely, the difficult and uncomfortable way is to challenge yourself and realize that if others can quit, then so can you.

When you eventually quit smoking, you will consider this as one of your greatest life accomplishments. It will give you incredible satisfaction and elevate your self-esteem a few notches. Of course, we can't forget all the other benefits of quitting smoking—such as more energy, less coughing, fewer colds, fewer respiratory problems, and reduced risk of lung cancer and heart disease—not to mention all the money that will stay in your hands instead of the tobacco companies' coffers. These benefits will make your life a lot easier and more comfortable in the long term, including being able to be more effective at work or play.

Clearly, if all of us applied the Easy Rule of Life more, we would have far fewer lingering problems, attain much more success, and be much more effective in using our leisure time. Moreover, we would abolish boredom in our lives.

If you are presently working and your job is primarily composed of tasks that you consider extremely boring, you should consider making changes in your job or leaving your job, either for another job or by retiring. You must make the Easy Rule of Life work for you. Only by doing the difficult and uncomfortable can you make your life more interesting and fulfilling.

Interestingly, the Easy Rule of Life even applies to workaholics who erroneously think that they are taking the difficult and uncomfortable route by working harder and longer than the mass of humanity. Perhaps you yourself are a workaholic and think that you are well on your way to eventually finding fulfillment when you attain more knowledge and power than everyone else. A few months of therapy should put an end to your illusion.

Workaholics are in fact doing the easy and comfortable by choosing work as an escape from other aspects of life. Workaholics work long hours to avoid job loss, criticism, bad marriages, debt, and loneliness. Peak performers, on the other hand, work for praise, satisfaction, self-respect, challenge, and fun. Regardless of the positive aspects of their jobs, peak performers indulge themselves in many of life's other great pleasures. This is why they work as hard as they have to for a comfortable living, and as little as they can get away with.

Workaholics' lives end up difficult not only because of boredom, but because they don't find the contentment and peace of mind that peak performers find. For workaholics who want to

> I had a boring office job. I cleaned the windows in the envelopes.
> —Rita Rudner

overcome boredom and have an interesting life instead, the difficult and uncomfortable task is indulging in more leisure time. Only then can they get a life that leads to fulfillment.

If You Do Boring, Stupid, Monotonous Work, Chances Are You'll End Up Boring, Stupid, and Monotonous

In much of the developed world, working at something that is extremely boring—even if the activity has absolutely no purpose to it—is viewed as much more noble and productive than taking it easy and enjoying one's life. How sad indeed! Ironically, this happens in societies that consider themselves the most intelligent and advanced ever.

Weird as it may seem, the inability to conquer boredom in their personal lives is why many people shun retirement and continue to work at the most boring jobs imaginable. British-born American writer and critic W. H. Auden stated, "A tremendous number of people in America work very hard at something that bores them. Even a rich man thinks he has to go down to the office every day. Not because he likes it but because he can't think of anything else to do."

> All work and no play makes Jack a dull boy—and Jill a wealthy widow.
> —Evan Esar

No doubt there will always be people who display impressive talent in the work world, but aspire no higher. They have no inclination to develop themselves as more rounded human beings by getting immersed in the world of leisure. These people will probably want to work at their boring jobs until they drop dead or they can no longer work due to ill health.

Unlike people who want to work, and do nothing else, until they drop dead, you no doubt have constructive leisure activities and other dreams that you have wanted to pursue for some time. These may have been suppressed because you have become too obsessed with making as much money as possible and obtaining more possessions than your neighbors and friends. Fame, as a way of attaining immortality, may also be one of your career objectives.

In your quest for fame and fortune, however, don't ever forget this important message from Michael Pritchard: "No matter how rich you become, how famous or powerful, when you die the size of your funeral will still pretty much depend on the weather."

Ashley Montagu also had an important message: "The deepest personal defeat suffered by human beings is constituted by the difference between what one was capable of becoming and what one has in fact become." To put it another way, it's not what you become, but what you don't become that will hurt most in the end.

If you are stuck in your career, leaving a less-than-mediocre job won't be easy. You may need the money and not have time to look for another job. If you have some opportunity to leave a boring and dehumanizing job, however, you must do it now for your long-term health and happiness. Making too many compromises to your lifestyle for the sake of your job makes for a bored (and possibly a boring) you.

In his essay "Abolish Work: Workers of the World, Relax," Bob Black offers some food for thought. "You are what you do," states Black. "If you do boring, stupid, monotonous work, chances are you'll end up boring, stupid, and monotonous."

Yet it is in our idleness, in our dreams, that the submerged truth sometimes comes to the top.

—Virginia Woolf

Here is a test for the true value of your present job: If your two favorite times at work are lunch time and quitting time, the message is clear as could be: It's time to move on. Clearly, you won't have a complete life until you have work that really matters to you. It may be difficult to leave a well-established job for a new, interesting, and challenging occupation, but not impossible. Millions have done it; so can you.

Alternatively, after focusing on the negatives of the typical workplace long enough, you may start looking at alternatives. The prospect of taking a long sabbatical or early retirement may appear highly promising. It will be easy to fantasize about the wonderful things that you could do—

go on a cruise in the Caribbean, spend a lot of time with your children, spend a year in a monastery, or live in Costa Rica for a year. If this is actually happening to you now, perhaps it's time to tell your boss, "I'm outta here."

After giving some serious thought to the quality of their lives, many people decide to pull the plug on their employers in search of something better. Ian Hammond of Montrose, in the county of Angus, Scotland, is an example of someone who was itching to leave his job and did so at an opportune time. After reading *The Joy of Not Working*, Hammond decided to take early retirement. A plan of action helped him achieve his goal of doing something more productive with his life than merely working for a living.

> People who know how to employ themselves always find leisure moments, while those who do nothing are forever in a hurry.
> —Jeanne-Marie Roland

Ian drafted his notice of resignation more than a year before he actually left his job. The letter was posted in his electronic calendar manager as an "out-of-office reminder." Ian showed this notice of resignation to his boss and his co-workers several months before his exit. Following is Ian's notice of resignation, which he kindly allowed me to use in this edition of the book:

I will terminate my employment on the 30th of September, to pursue a more rewarding lifestyle which I intend to enjoy for at least the next several years. The technical content of the job for which I believe I show an aptitude and commitment has diminished; this change is due to a corresponding increase in administrative duties, for which I am entirely unsuited and which are of little interest. The performance system places too high a reliance on managerial ability in what should be a technically based environment, and as a graduate, there is an expectation that I will move through the company system and become "Dilbertized" along with all the others; unfortunately I refuse to prostitute myself in this way and prefer to collect a modest salary based on my intellectual achievements, demonstrating ability rather than visibility. The time wasted in this job, whether in circular arguments, writing unread reports, or performing substandard work due to inadequate resources and poorly trained staff, is worth more to me than the recognition and reward that the company sees fit to deny me. It is with much pleasure that I announce that, after spending some time with my dad in Cornwall and with friends in France, I will overwinter in New Zealand for four months, camping and cycling. On my return I intend to pursue several interests:

- Study for an astronomy degree
- Speak Spanish and German fluently
- Write and publish a travelogue, short stories, and poetry
- Read all the "classics"
- Volunteer as an overseas science/French/English teacher
- Study for an electronics degree
- Cycle around the world
- Compete in an international chess tournament
- Play classical guitar to concert standard
- Learn tourist Italian and Portuguese
- Paint watercolors
- Do ten things I haven't thought of doing yet!

If I achieve a third of these aims, I will consider my time well-spent. The corporate work ethic and its success depend on the uncritical thinking of those who believe that they are making a difference and are being recognized for it.

Best wishes for your future, if you want one.

Ian, May 26, 1997

> Success is important only to the extent that it puts one in a position to do more things one likes to do.
> —Sarah Caldwell

I don't know about you, but I found Ian's notice of resignation inspiring. I suggest that you use Ian's list of interests as a model for creating your own list to pursue on a sabbatical or in retirement. Ian did, in fact, retire on September 30, 1998. He wrote to me on April 28, 2000, at which time he included the above notice of resignation. Here is what he had to say:

Dear Ernie,

I have just read *The Joy of Not Working* for the third time, so it is about time that I congratulated you on such a sensible book; it states the obvious, which isn't to most people.

I came across the book while browsing one rainy day waiting for a bus. I bought it after reading the first two chapters—and missing the bus—since it confirmed that there was at least one other madman who thought like me. This is quite an achievement on your part; although I'm an avid reader, your book was the only book I bought in 1997 or since, because I use my own town library.

Your book reinforced what I have thought for many years about work and society, the purpose of life, solitude, money, and motivation. My final job was as an analytical chemist for a large company here in Montrose, which is about to be merged into a much larger company. I'm only a shareholder now and not an employee, what with all the downsizing that will inevitably result. The folks at work don't smile much anyway.

I've enclosed an "out of office" reminder from my electronic calendar manager which could be viewed for over a year before I finally left. I'm sure you've received similar stories from other technical people who could only progress as managers. My boss came across it one day appropriately enough while he was booking me for my annual appraisal! He ended up borrowing your book, and later we had a long chat during which he glumly handed it back, saying it was all true. It felt good to give the company I worked for effectively a year's notice instead of the statutory one month, and the reception I received from everyone (except the upper echelons, of course) was genuine; it started a waiting list for your book! The last six months were wonderful: others were given my modest managerial responsibilities, and I was sidelined from new fast-track projects, instead becoming an expert trainer/troubleshooter on call to anyone. It was almost a job worth living for.

It was a good job, but my life since has been better. I biked and camped around New Zealand, but for six months, not four, because the scenery, climate, and, most importantly, people were fantastic (as a fellow cyclist I can recommend it to you as better than anywhere else that I've visited so far). I've also done similar two-month trips to the American Midwest and the Canary Islands, learning Spanish before the latter. I've done several watercolors from my New Zealand photographs, surprised myself with the results, and this year will attempt pastels too. I've seen more of my family and friends even though I've been travelling for half of my new life.

> If you are losing your leisure, look out! You are losing your soul.
> —*Logan Pearsall Smith*

This summer I'm doing a two-monther around Ireland, studying electronics for the first time in a quarter-century, and seeing long-lost friends in Sydney, then biking around Australia for six months this winter. I don't know how I'd fit in work now!

All this on £6,000 a year, which is the income from my investments. What you say about money and the environment is very true, and I recycle or (better) reuse everything. My fruit and vegetable garden is not only a source of pleasure, but a way to help support my chosen lifestyle. I haven't put the dustbin out since I "retired"; maybe I should claim for a rebate.

If you ever come to Britain, let me know, because I'd like to attend one of your talks. Failing that, I may travel in Canada one day, and we could go for a bike ride. I'd even buy you that meal!

Keep in touch, and thank you once more.

Ian

As you can see from Ian's experience, even leaving a good job can result in a more interesting and fulfilling lifestyle. It takes doing the difficult and uncomfortable, which is to muster enough courage to walk away from a job, regardless of what your co-workers, friends, or family may think of your decision.

> If you burn the candle at both ends, you are not as bright as you think.
> —Unknown wise person

Perhaps you are married and will quickly point out, "Ian Hammond is obviously single, and married people can't possibly quit their jobs like Ian did." Then go back to page 57 and reread the letter that Les Oke wrote to me. You will note that Les was married with children when he quit his job. Need I say more? Case closed!

One of the realities of modern life is that we all have many interesting things we would like to pursue, but limited time for pursuing them. We have to make decisions as to how we spend our time, not only in how much we work, but also in how we pursue the interesting and challenging things life has to offer. Irrespective of our income and net worth, we can be truly prosperous only if we get involved in a myriad of activities away from the world of work.

Clearly, being successful at work is irrelevant if you are a failure at life in general. Indeed, it's possible to be a huge success at work and miss out on life completely. You shouldn't be sacrificing present joy, happiness, and satisfaction for a few extra lousy bucks, especially if you are going to spend the money frivolously on some gadgets that won't enhance your life significantly. Day-to-day life will be boring and have little meaning if your main reason for going to work is to pay for all those possessions you don't have time to use.

What's the point of being well-off financially if there's no time to truly live, only enough to exist? Constructive leisure activities are at least half of what you need for a life of purpose and accomplishment. Friends, family, adventure, walking, meditating, creative loafing, and spiritual fulfillment—not working long and hard hours—are the things that make life worth living.

If you find yourself focusing on business and financial issues to the detriment and exclusion of everything else, you have a clear case of poverty consciousness—more so than many people who have much less money than you, but nevertheless get to enjoy many constructive leisure activities. Money and possessions are important to a certain extent, but not important enough to put them ahead of everything else. If you are leading a boring life to earn big money, you are poor no matter how much you earn.

The best way for us to get rid of our boredom is to take some risks in our lives. By subjecting ourselves to the chance of failure, we put our boredom at risk.

Moe Roseb put his boredom at risk. After purchasing my first book, Moe called me from San Diego to talk about the power of creativity. In our conversation we discussed the whole idea of taking risks in life.

He talked about how his friends, many of whom he had known for years, were rather boring. Some were having midlife crises. Friends still saw Moe and his wife as being the same as they were fifteen years ago, even though both of them had continued to grow and develop as individuals. Moe felt that his relationships with these friends had stagnated.

So did Moe continue to blame his friends for his situation? No. He put his boredom at risk and did something about it. At forty-six, with the children gone, Moe moved to from Toronto to California to new friends, new surroundings, and a new life. Moe looked at it this way: "Many of my friends are having midlife crises. I am going to have a midlife adventure instead."

> Perpetual devotion to what a man calls his business, is only to be sustained by perpetual neglect of many other things.
> —Robert Louis Stevenson

Many people immersed in a sea of boredom during their working lives take refuge in visions of a full, adventurous, satisfying, and happy life sometime later, when they will be able to slow down and start enjoying themselves. They are waiting for the day they finally acquire a sufficient sum of money, or the day that they retire on Social Security, to really start living. Unfortunately, this day rarely comes. People either die first or don't have the mental or physical capacity to enjoy themselves when they eventually have enough money and time.

You won't be prosperous until you sleep enough, eat well, exercise regularly, spend sufficient time with friends and family, and have plenty of time left over to pursue interesting and challenging leisure activities. Not surprisingly, researchers have found that individuals who find the time to do the things they enjoy are much happier and live longer than people who just plod on with their work and regular routines at the expense of personal life.

To sum up: boredom is something you experience because you invite it into your life. The best way to overcome boredom is to do something about it. To repeat the words of Leo Buscaglia, if you are bored, it's because you are boring. The only person who can help you overcome this is you.

CHAPTER 7

Lighting Your Own Fire Rather than Being Warmed by Someone Else's

Dancing the Motivation Dance

Many years ago a young man mustered enough courage to ask a young woman to dance. After he danced with her for a few minutes, the woman told him that he was a lousy dancer. She complained that he danced like a truck driver.

To be sure, this bad experience would be enough for most people to quit dancing for good. Watching television or sitting around being bored would be more appealing than dancing again. Yet this man developed a passion for dancing and continued to dance for many decades.

In fact, this man became known as one of the great dancers of modern times. By the early nineties, when he died, he had 500 dance schools named after him. At one time, he had been on television for eleven years straight, showing people from all walks of life—including truck drivers—how to dance.

I could dance with you till the cows come home. On second thought I'd rather dance with the cows till you come home.
—Groucho Marx

No doubt by now you have guessed that this man was none other than the late Arthur Murray. His story underscores the importance of motivation and direction for getting what we want in life. Murray became a great dancer because he was self-motivated enough to actually pursue what he wanted. Equally important, he knew what he wanted. Unfortunately, not only are a lot of us not that motivated to get what we want, we don't even know what we want.

It's Difficult to Experience Pleasure from Reminiscing about Things You Haven't Done

If you were to walk in a clockwise direction on the walls of the object depicted in the figure below, you would think you were going up. For some time, you would be certain that you were destined for greater heights.

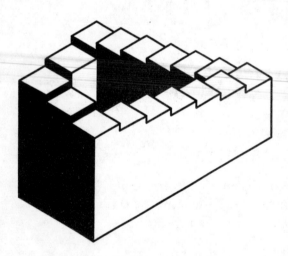

In time, however, you would realize that you were back at the same level at which you started. No matter how much energy you put into walking up the steps, higher levels would just be illusions. Your unfocused activity would leave you without any accomplishment, satisfaction, or happiness.

Such is the illusion of activity without goals and dreams. Indeed, many people misconstrue their unplanned activity for direction. Even if they put substantial energy into their activity, they still end up getting nowhere, staying where they don't want to be. Activity is necessary for reaching greater heights, but, even in leisure time, greater heights only come with defined goals. If we are to arrive at new and worthwhile destinations, first we must define these destinations. After all, the journey has direction once the destination is known.

Defined leisure goals give us something to pursue that we otherwise wouldn't pursue—they give us purpose. When we have purpose and direction, we have reasons for being innovative and creative. Once we have established our leisure goals, more effort and discipline are required for trying to achieve these goals.

If we have defined our leisure goals, sooner or later they will change. Some goals will have been reached, and some activities will no longer turn us on. This will necessitate a revision of our leisure goals. It follows that we should review our goals regularly—as often as every few months.

In short, it's just as hard to attain satisfaction and success from attaining goals we don't have as it is to get pleasure from reminiscing about things we haven't done. Thus, we must be clear about the type of leisure success we would like and how we are going to get there. And being clear about the success we would like to attain is dependent on our knowing exactly what we want in life.

Do You Want What You Think You Want?

Whether you are retired, unemployed, or working, in order to live a well-balanced life—relaxed, laid-back, productive, and successful all at the same time—you must be motivated. First, you must be motivated to contemplate and decide what's important to you. Second, you must be motivated to do the important things with excellence. Third, you must be motivated to stop doing the unimportant things. Last, you must be motivated to take it easy and enjoy life for all it is worth.

> Learning is finding out what you already know. Doing is demonstrating that you know it.
> —Richard Bach

Perhaps you are successful by society's standards, yet yearn for something much different. The one thing that can be more disappointing than failure is success itself, because it doesn't always bring us what we thought it would. To have achieved the success that you have always dreamed about can seem quite silly once you have attained it—especially if you have dedicated most of your life to being successful at the expense of life itself.

A research study conducted in 2001 by Florida's Nova Southeastern University observed "successful" Wall Street stockbrokers who were, in fact, not all that successful. These individuals, all men between the ages of twenty-two and thirty-two, worked an average of ten to twelve hours a day. Sure, these men were making $300,000 to $1,000,000 a year, but to what end? Over 38 percent were suffering from subclinical depression. Even worse, 28 percent were suffering from clinical depression. This compares with 5 percent of men in the general population who suffer from clinical depression.

> It is the superfluous things for which men sweat.
> —Seneca

Clearly, it's pretty hard to be happy in life while continually clinically or subclinically depressed. These stockbrokers should be evidence enough that working in a job that doesn't provide self-fulfillment can be seriously detrimental to one's emotional well-being, even if it provides great monetary rewards. You have to wonder why the depressed stockbrokers don't quit and work at something more suited for them, or take more time off work. They certainly are not getting everything they want out of life. Moreover, their success is dubious at best.

Success at experiencing a deeper meaning in life is far different from success as defined in the modern world. Financial success is shallow if fulfillment, virtue, and true happiness are missing. Today many people, like the stockbrokers just described, are successful in that they are materially wealthy, but they don't have any real purpose and meaning. This is partly because they don't create the time to pursue a more holistic and spiritual lifestyle. The consequences are frustration, stress, and burnout, which further lead to bad nerves, tics, twitching, strokes, and heart attacks.

It's all too easy to get too intoxicated with the dream of what conventional success is going to do for our happiness. Yet conventional success and happiness are two entirely different things. Conventional success—

Motivated Tennis Player

a big house, a beach cabin, two or three fancy cars, an attractive spouse, and a high-powered job—hardly serves any purpose other than to make life extremely difficult for most people.

My point is this: success is what we say it is, nothing more and nothing less. What success is, of course, varies from person to person. Two people can have accomplished similar things in their lives, yet those who are optimists will see themselves as successful, whereas those who are pessimists will see themselves as failures. Moreover, a particular individual will see success differently at different times.

The hardest way to achieve success is to have someone else define it for you. Let friends, relatives, society, the media, and advertisers tell you what success is, and you are headed for big trouble. You will end up feeling a lot of pressure to do it all—have an extremely attractive mate, raise a perfect family, have a well-paid job, take exotic vacations, live in a stately mansion, drive an overpriced, flashy car, and still save a million for retirement. Attaining all of these things may be possible, but highly improbable. Even attaining all these things can leave you feeling unsuccessful in the event these aren't the things that you truly want out of life.

As a rational human being, you should always be alert to creative shortcuts to success. In this regard, the most creative shortcut to success is to think more about it. Put another way, you must redefine what success means to you. Ultimately, you will make yourself successful or unsuccessful just by the way you define success.

> Argue for your limitations, and sure enough, they are yours.
>
> —Richard Bach

Not long ago I received a letter from Joy Barlow of Red Deer, Alberta, who shared her views about success.

Dear Mr. Zelinski,

I recently finished your book *The Joy of Not Working* and just wanted to tell you how much I enjoyed it.

Approximately a year and a half ago, I was laid off from my job and was what I thought very devastated. This lasted about two weeks. I then realized for the first time in several years I had time to visit my friends and family, play tennis, and do the many other things I have always enjoyed, but due to being the "dedicated worker" never seemed to have time to do.

In the past year I have started a business and set up a second company as well—something I have always wanted to do but never had the guts to do until this layoff. I do a lot of public speaking, and one of the groups I speak regularly to are people starting their own businesses.

One question I get asked a lot is "Are you successful?" So I ask them what they classify as being successful. Lots of money in the bank? Etc. I always say I am successful even though I am still struggling to make my mark in business. I have good clients established, I have helped them meet safety needs, and I am happy and have the time to do the things in life that I want. Do I have a lot of money in the bank? No! But I base my success on the customers I help. So I found the piece in your book on success to be very interesting as people feel money is the only grounds for success and I have always put it last.

Anyway, thanks for writing a great book. I will be passing this title on to others I know who need to get some leisure in their lives.

Yours truly,

Joy Barlow

To attain true success, above all, we must clarify what we want in life. The biggest problem isn't so much that we can't get what we think we want. The biggest problem is when we get what we think we want, it isn't what we truly want. Indeed, what will keep us from getting what we truly want is not knowing exactly what it is.

My life is filled with many obstacles. The greatest obstacle is me.

—Jack Parr

Only with effort and action can you start getting what you want in life. Filling your time with just any activity— such as being a stockbroker—when it may not have much meaning to you, isn't the route to a satisfying life.

The degree to which you are able to attain the success you would like is dependent upon your ability to determine what your wants are and how you can best satisfy them. The following exercise is a good way to begin.

Exercise 7-1. Another Simple Question

What do you really want in life?

"The simplest questions," stated well-known author Richard Bach, "are the most profound." The above question is a simple one, but it has profound implications. It isn't an easy question to answer.

Let's say, without realizing it, deep down you really want to stay at home for your next summer vacation. All you want, for a change, is some rest, a lot of local sunshine, the time to read some good books, the coziness of your own home, and a daily visit to your bistro for a great cup of cappuccino with your spouse. Unfortunately, you haven't gotten in touch with your true wants. Instead, you listen to what other people think you should want.

Only the shallow know themselves.

—Oscar Wilde

Your parents suggest that you go to Florida, where they went for a vacation. To convince you to go would validate that it was a good place for them to have gone in the first place, even though they didn't enjoy it all that much. Your friends Bob and Alice want you to go to the Rocky Mountains because that is where they are going. It would be nice for them to have someone accompany them to dinner, because their conversation is extremely boring when they are by themselves.

What's more, your travel agent wants you to choose an exotic place such as Aruba, Martinique, Bermuda, Puerto Vallarta, or Morocco. Your agent says she wants you to have the best possible vacation; actually, she wants to make the biggest possible commission so she can have the most exotic vacation later in the year. Eventually, the travel agent convinces you to go to Martinique for two weeks. Besides, everybody who is anybody is going to Martinique, and advertisers have convinced you that it is important to show the world you are a successful somebody.

Four days after arriving in Martinique, you realize that you have seen all there is to see. You and your spouse lie on the beach all day, bored from watching all the other people being bored, who are in turn watching you being bored. You only brought one good book with you, which you have already read, and there is nowhere to purchase good books. Even worse, it is impossible to get a cappuccino at the hotel where you are staying. You stick it out for the entire two weeks, all the time wishing you were back at work, even though you hate your job.

After ten years of traveling to exotic, faraway places I realized I just wanted to vacation in my backyard.

The flight back is tiring. When you finally get home, in your heart you realize that you didn't get what you wanted out of your vacation; you are more tired than when you left, and you feel unfulfilled because you didn't get the vacation you really wanted. You realize how much you were influenced by others to pursue a vacation that you didn't really want.

The moral: to get what you want out of life, you'd better be clear about what you want. Granted, one of life's most difficult processes is discovering what we really want as individuals. Most of us don't know what we really want because we haven't taken the time to find out. Instead, we let the expectations of others define our personal wants and successes.

In *Escape from Freedom*, Eric Fromm wrote: "Modern man lives under the illusion that he knows what he wants, while he actually wants what he is supposed to want." Indeed, in today's consumer society, advertisers and the media dictate what people are supposed to want. Many people consume this programming greedily instead of stopping to question what will truly make them happy. After all, it is much easier to try to fit in with the majority than to question what the majority is doing and then do something different.

Given that societal standards have become more important than our own unique needs, it is no wonder we don't get what we want. We pay too much attention to what others want us to want. Society wants us to want. Advertisers want us to want. Our family wants us to want. Friends want us to want. Many others, such as newspaper reporters, radio announcers, and self-serving travel agents, want us to want. All told, everyone wants us to want so much that most of us have forgotten what we want.

To further complicate matters, our wants have a habit of shifting with the winds. Our desires are shaped by hidden needs and reshaped by mysterious forces. Sometimes even when we get something that we truly wanted in the past, we don't want it anymore.

> Work is what they try to con you to do so that you will have the money to be able to buy what they try to con you to think you want.
>
> —Unknown wise person

Finding out whether you are the source of your wants, or they are something you were told you wanted, is key to knowing what you truly want. As you become more aware of which wants are your own and which you were conditioned to accept, you will be better prepared to pursue your genuine interests. Perhaps you will find all of your wants were there only because you were told you should have them or because you thought you should want them, but really didn't.

It follows that you have to look harder to discover your true wants. Don't shy away from this task, or you may waste the rest of your life doing what everyone else wants you to do. Ensure that you aren't chasing after what your mother or your best friend or Madison Avenue wants you to want. This will not contribute to a fulfilling and happy life.

> Man is a creation of desire, not a creation of need.
>
> —Gaston Bachelard

Pursuing our true wants may mean that we have to make some important changes in our lives. After Gilles Gagnon of Dundas, Ontario, and his wife, Annette, got in touch with their true wants, they realized that they didn't need to work hard and pursue conventional success. Gilles and Annette decided to work less so that they could enjoy life more. Gilles wrote to let me know how the changes they made had improved their lives.

Hello Ernie,

I do hope this letter reaches you. This is just a short note to let you know that your book *The Joy of Not Working* has been very beneficial. I recently left a company I had been with for eight years to become a self-employed consultant. I now provide my services to the company (Andrés Wines Ltd.) but only three days per week. The rest of the time? . . . Active leisure!!!!

I am thirty-six years old, married (for eleven years now), with no children. My wife, Annette, is a registered nurse who left the medical profession three years ago. After much soul searching she concluded that nursing was not what she had hoped it to be. It appears that politics comes before patient care. It was difficult for her to put nursing behind as she had spent four years in university for a nursing degree. She now follows her passion, fiber arts. As an artist in development, she does not bring in an income.

Therefore, for me to reduce my workweek by 40 to 50 percent, with the associated reduction in income, was something we had to really think about. It has been only two months now, and so far so good. It has taken me some two years to make the move. By the way, I'm a network analyst. I first read your book when I borrowed it from the local library. A year or so later, when I needed some re-affirmation that I was on the correct path, I had to have my own copy.

Shortly after the purchase of TJONW is when I took the plunge and proposed my new work schedule and arrangement to my employer. It's too early to tell how we will fare financially, but after some calculations, we don't believe it will be a problem. Neither of us have ever been on the consumerism bandwagon everyone seems to be on these days. We get *much* joy out of very simple things in life. One of my favorite quotes of all time (I believe it's in TJONW) is "That man is richest, whose pleasures are cheapest." One of our most favorite activities is to walk in the woods.

More challenges will be coming my way as I believe that I would like to change my profession. To what remains a mystery (to me) at this time. The additional free time I have will provide a source for more time for introspection, reading, self-discovery, and research.

Thank you for your inspiration!!!

Gilles

Having the courage to do their own thing was key to Gilles and Annette making important changes in their lives. You should do the same. The more you are out of step with society, the greater your chances for self-discovery, adventure, and happiness in this world. To get what you want out of life, you must be motivated enough to light your own fire rather than being warmed by someone else's.

> One of the strongest characteristics of genius is the power of lighting its own fire.
>
> —John Foster

Following the majority of people as they look for happiness in all the wrong places is pointless. Why waste time, energy, and money chasing after something you don't really want and may not enjoy for even one second? Some things are important; others are not. Some things appear to be important because people have been brainwashed by society, educational institutions, and advertisers to believe that they are important. Upon close scrutiny, most of these

Tell me something! Now that I have made it to the top of the heap, what more do I have to do to be happy?

things have no relevance whatsoever to leading a happy and healthy lifestyle.

The more attention you pay to what the masses are doing, the more you will realize that the everybody-else-is-doing-it approach isn't the way to lead a balanced life. While it's tempting to join the masses, always remember that you have meaningful dreams and more important things to pursue.

Probably the hardest thing about living a satisfying and prosperous life is to be true to our own fancies and refrain from going along with the masses. To be sure, following our hearts is difficult when our rational minds, along with our not-so-rational minds, are subject to so many outside influences. Some people do follow their hearts, however. After making changes to her life by moving from the United States to Europe, Aida Hudson wrote to me from Århus, Denmark.

> Dear Mr. Zelinski,
>
> I just wanted to let you know how much I enjoyed and appreciated *The Joy of Not Working*. Last summer I quit a miserable job with a large consulting firm in Washington, D.C.—with no prospects for another job or project. Six months later, I am happily married and living in Europe, studying Danish and writing.
>
> Until recently I had always been a pessimist and over-achiever; but now I know that if you follow your heart, things will work out. Your book makes perfect sense to me.
>
> Well done!
>
> Sincerely,
>
> Aida J. Hudson

Only you can decide whether you have your priorities right and are living according to them. You have to be completely clear about the type and quality of life you want to live. The degree to which you put time and effort into the things that really matter will determine your overall happiness and satisfaction.

It is possible to have a lifestyle that coincides with your deepest values if you really want it. Taking control of your life starts with you—not with your employer, the government, your spouse, or society. You can choose whether you want to opt out of excessive work and material-ism for a life that includes more leisure activities, time to relax, more time with your kids, and more rewarding work.

Life is a progress from want to want, not from enjoyment to enjoyment.
—Samuel Johnson

Although making life-altering changes to create a balanced lifestyle isn't easy, millions have shown it is possible. They have gotten their emotional acts together and accomplished what most have not. It is no wonder that these people live happier and fuller lives by spending more time with family, connecting with nature and the community, and enjoying the many simple plea-sures that they had forgotten in pursuit of the good life. And even if only 2 percent of people in the western world can lead a full, relaxed, happy, and satisfying life, you can make the choice to be in this group. It's a matter of paying the price—à la the Easy Rule of Life—to get there.

It doesn't matter so much what you do for a living, or how much fame and fortune you attain, as whether you enjoy peace, health, and love. If you don't have these, what can replace them? Don't lose sight of the fact that happiness is not a desti-nation, but a journey, a by-product of living fully. To live fully, in my view, you must enjoy an abundance of leisure time.

You are never given a wish without also being given the power to make it true. You may have to work for it however.
—Richard Bach

Summing up, if there is anything that will keep you from getting what you want, it is not knowing exactly what you want. Reaching your ideal destination is highly unlikely if you don't know what that destination is. You must do some soul-searching and really understand yourself before you can determine what your wants are. Only then can you proceed toward getting what you want out of life.

It's Time to Plant Your Get-a-Life Tree

Few of us derive our greatest joys in life from money, power, or prestige. Joy comes from the satisfaction of total immersion in doing something worthwhile. Instead of money, or something derived from it, a worth-while activity—whether work-related or leisure-related—becomes its own reward.

Work-related duties are easy enough to follow since these activities are normally laid out for us. It's the leisure activities that can be somewhat of a problem. Knowing what we want to do in our leisure, however, is as important as knowing what we want to do in our workplace.

Exercise 7-2. What Have You Always Wanted to Do?

Assume that you wind up on your deathbed in the next month. You say to God, "Please, give me one more shot, and I will give it all I've got." God replies, "Okay, you can have five more years of healthy living for doing what you have always wanted to do. All your activities must be leisure-related, however. Put another way, I want you to 'get a life.'"

The million-dollar question is: how would you spend those five years to make your life happy and fulfilling?

Even if you haven't been presented with this challenge from the Almighty, making a list of the leisure activities that you would pursue if you only had five years to live is a worthwhile exercise, regardless of whether you are retired, unemployed, or working. This list should be an important motivator for you. Even more valuable than such a list is a tool called the Get-a-Life Tree: a variation of what is commonly known as a mind map, spoke diagram, thought web, or clustering diagram.

The Get-a-Life Tree is simple, but powerful indeed. It is a creative approach that allows us to generate a large variety of activities for a full life. Because our memories are not as good as we think they are, it is important to write all our ideas down before we select those activities that we are going to pursue.

If you are like most people, you normally use a list to record ideas. A list is better than nothing, but it may limit the number of ideas you generate. The Get-a-Life Tree is more effective in this regard.

> Life is a banquet and most poor fools are starving to death.
>
> —"Auntie Mame"

A Get-a-Life Tree is started at the center of a blank page by recording the goal, theme, or objective. In figure 7-1 on page 111, "Options for My Leisure" appears at the center, with branch lines radiating from it. Each is identified with a primary category of leisure activity.

There are three primary categories that you should use to generate leisure activities that you may want to pursue (we'll get to the fourth and fifth branches of our example tree soon):

1. Activities that turn you on now
2. Activities that turned you on in the past (but you have stopped doing)
3. New activities you have thought of doing (but haven't done yet)

Figure 7-1. The Get-a-Life Tree

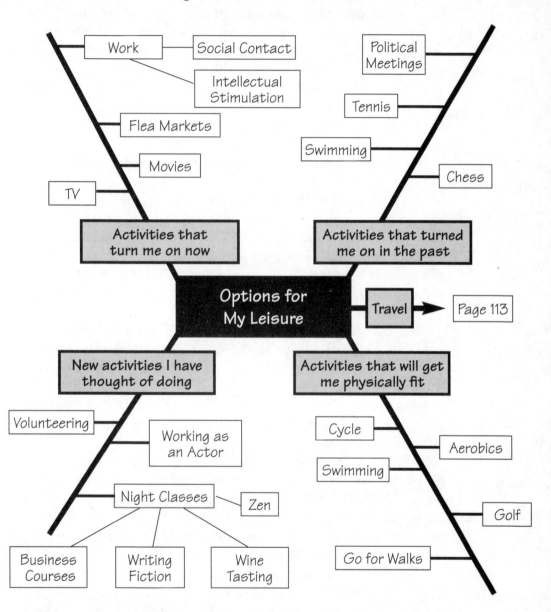

On secondary branches from the primary ones, you should add the various activities relating to the category. As indicated in figure 7-1, for the primary idea, "New activities I have thought of doing," you can add "Working as an Actor," "Volunteering," and "Night Classes." You can add more branches off the secondary ones to record a third level of ideas; for example, for the general activity "Night Classes" there are specific classes: "Zen," "Wine Tasting," "Writing Fiction," and "Business Courses." You could even add a fourth level: for example, "Marketing" and "Accounting" (not shown) from the "Business Courses" branch.

Now is the time to plant your own Get-a-Life Tree, using figure 7-1 as a guide. Utilizing the first three primary categories, make sure you generate a total of at least fifty things that you truly like to do now, have liked doing in the past, or have thought about but never gotten around to doing. Record every idea, no matter how frivolous it seems. Don't judge your ideas here. You must get at least fifty even if it takes you two days; forty-nine won't do!

If you have additional categories of activities you want to actively pursue, you can add them to your tree. For example, you may be particularly interested in getting fit and traveling. Then, as in figure 7-1, you can record the primary categories "Activities that will get me physically fit" on one primary branch and "Travel" on another. Note that if you run out of room you can expand the Get-a-Life Tree to another page, as this one has been for ideas on travel—in fact, in figure 7-2 "Travel" appears as a tree in its own right, with six primary branches, each with its own specific activities.

It's fine for the same idea to appear in more than one category. In fact, if this happens, you've identified a leisure activity that may be a priority in your life. In figure 7-1, "Swimming" appears in the categories "Activities that turned me on in the past," "Activities that will get me physically fit," and "Travel." If this were your actual Get-a-Life Tree, swimming would have to be one of the first activities that you would pursue immediately.

Let's look at the benefits of using the Get-a-Life Tree as an idea-generating tool: First, it is compact—many ideas can be listed on one page. If needed, the Get-a-Life Tree can be expanded to additional pages. Second, your activity ideas are assigned to categories and thus are easier to group. Moreover, you can expand on your existing ideas to generate many new ideas.

> I'll try anything once, even Limburger cheese.
>
> —Thomas Edison

Still another advantage of the Get-a-Life Tree is that it can be used as a long-term tool. After setting it aside for a while, you can come back and generate a batch of fresh ideas. In fact, you should update it on a regular basis to ensure that you can choose from an endless number of leisure activities.

Color and images make for a more creative Get-a-Life Tree and at the same time enhance our ability to remember what's on it. The images used in the enhanced Get-a-Life Tree in figure 7-2 make it a lot more interesting and useful than a conventional list.

Figure 7-2. Enhanced Get-a-Life Tree

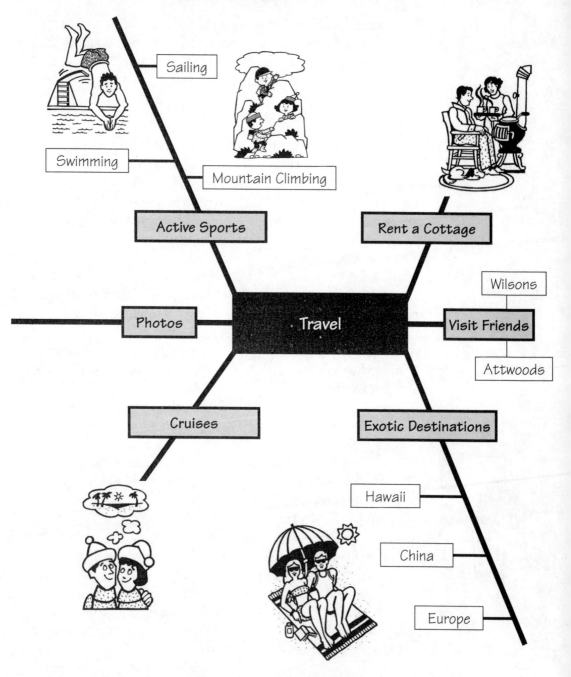

After you expand your Get-a-Life Tree to five or six pages, you are in a position to choose from a vast number of different activities. If you have any zest for living, you should be able to record enough activities to keep you busy not just for five years, but for five lifetimes.

There's So Much to Do

Finding the right set of activities for a full life is a personal matter. But it's easy to overlook many possible activities. To help you add to those you have already placed in your Get-a-Life Tree, I have listed over 300 activities below.

Activities for Your Get-a-Life Tree

Spend a lot more time with your children or grandchildren

Climb the mountain you have always wanted to climb

Take up golf for the first time

Go to a baseball game on a Wednesday afternoon

Play tennis again

Go to Mardi Gras in New Orleans

Teach English as a second language

Phone an old boyfriend or girl-friend just for the fun of it

Walk barefoot through a mountain stream

Type your name in an Internet search engine and see what comes up

Skip rocks on the water

Start a new business for the enjoyment, not for the money

Attempt a form of writing, such as a song or a poem, that you have never tried before

Join a club such as the Lions or Kinsmen

Go on a cruise to the Caribbean

Record the history of your hometown

Treat yourself to a massage

Learn to be a child again

Play the guitar that has been sitting in the closet for twenty-six years

Write the novel that you tell everyone you are capable of writing—now's the time to walk the talk

Paint a self-portrait—if it doesn't turn out well, you can always blame the subject

Teach children of low-income parents to read

Write your autobiography

Play an instrument

Learn how to play an instrument

Walk

Run

Volunteer

Choose a person you've been angry with; write a letter of forgiveness

Join a discussion group

Sit on the beach and contemplate the ocean

Choose someone famous in your hometown whom you admire and would like to have dinner with—ask this person to dinner

Write a letter to yourself listing the goals you expect to accomplish within the next five years—seal it and open it in five years

Learn to play the piano

Become a movie critic

Surprise a good friend

Prepare a meal for yourself

Learn how to cook

Create a new recipe

Visit present friends

Visit old friends

Try to meet new friends

Go hiking

Write letters to celebrities

Take a survey

Sleep

Meditate

Drive around in the city

Drive in the country

Count the items in this list to see if there are really over 300

Read books

Listen to the radio

Watch television

Listen to the stereo

Travel

Go to the movies

Make a movie

Learn computing

Write a computer program

Paint your house

Golf

Fish

Walk through a jungle

Go camping

Climb a mountain

Become involved in politics

Attend a poetry reading

Write your own poem about your experience of a poetry reading

Take part in a poetry reading

Start an underground newspaper

Have a heart-to-heart conversation with a friend in which there is no planned ending time—let it end when it ends

Research your ancestors

Create a drawing of your family tree

Write a book about how your ancestors have affected your life

Become a connoisseur of inexpensive restaurants

Have a latté while reading the newspaper in the outside patio of a coffee bar on a weekday morning

Ride a bicycle

Ride a motorcycle

Invite friends to your home

Invent a new board game

Go to the library

Play with children

Appear on a talk show

Offer to work for nothing

Play billiards

Dance alone for relaxation

Dance with someone else

Take dancing lessons

Restore an old car

Restore a piece of furniture

Renovate your house

Clean your house

Telephone old friends

Write a book

Write in your diary
Create a new cartoon
Write someone's biography
Make a dress, hat, or other
    apparel
Try to create an interesting
    wardrobe for only fifty dollars
Start a collection of . . .
Pan for gold
    Sunbathe

    Swim
    Have sex
    Go to church
    Dive into the water
    Go scuba diving
    Go snorkeling
    Get a pilot's license
    Take up photography
    Develop a photo album
    Find out what a rebus is and
    create ten of your own
Find out what was happen-
    ing the day you were born
Have a garage sale
Rearrange your living-room
    furniture
Take up acting
Write a play
Fly a kite
Learn to run backward
Learn to impersonate someone
    famous
Plant a garden
Ride a horse
Pick some flowers
Write poetry
Write a letter to a friend
Attempt a record for running
    backward
Learn how to sing
Write a song

Memorize a poem
Join an encounter group
Learn famous quotations
Memorize a song
Gaze at the stars
Truly experience a sunset
Watch the moon
Learn about new religions
Build a house
Design a unique house
Go live in another country
Go sailing
Play hockey
Build a boat
Watch interesting court cases
    at the courthouse
Learn more about the stock
    market
Invent a better mousetrap
Start a new club
Window shop
Learn how to repair your car
Throw a dinner party for a
    variety of people
See how many strangers will say
    hello to you
Dance in the rain
Do a rain dance to make it rain
Adopt a new identity and try to
    live the whole day with it
Approach strangers on the
    street and ask them to tell
    you their life story
Take a walk through the rough
    part of town just for the fun
    of it
Go to the library and leaf
    through old magazines to
    remind you what life was like
    in your teens

Reminisce about your favorite childhood pastimes—then choose one to relive today

Take up woodworking

Write a hand-written letter to an old friend

Have a long conversation with a child to see what you can learn

Research the Green Tortoise bus tours on the Internet and choose one for your next out-of-town trip

Photograph nature while enjoying the outdoors

Shop for clothes

Watch people in public

Roller skate

Play cards

Telephone a talk show to voice your opinion

Have a candlelight dinner with someone

Join a club to improve your public speaking

Join a wine-tasting club to learn about wine

Go back to university or college to get a degree

Take up skydiving

Learn all about health and fitness

Pick fruit in an orchard

Visit local tourist sights

Take up a new hobby

Create your own palindrome

Help fight pollution

Go to a flea market

Take a catnap

Go to garage sales

Help an environmental group preserve a rain forest

Use the Internet to search for former classmates

Test your memory by seeing if you can name all your schoolteachers from grade school to senior high

Prepare a collage of all the things you want to do in retirement

Create your own file of jokes and graffiti and see if you can get it published

Start a pirate radio station

Record a CD

Sponsor a foster child in Haiti

Go visit your foster child in Haiti

Start your own personal web page with your favorite quotations and other things that others may find interesting

Choose somewhere exotic in Europe or elsewhere that you would like to visit—then take a part-time job to earn the extra money so that you can go

Climb a tree

Go to the horse races with ten dollars

Ride public transit for fun

Start a newsletter

Write a letter to a pen pal in another country

Walk in the wilderness

Do crossword puzzles

Start and operate a bed and breakfast

Build a swimming pool

Daydream
Attend a sports event
Travel to old haunts
Go white-water rafting
Go up in a hot-air balloon
Be a big sister/brother
Go to your favorite restaurant
Try a new restaurant
Go to a tennis ranch to improve
    your tennis
Teach your dog new tricks
Learn a new trick to show your
    dog
Attend live theater
Attend the symphony

Go to a retreat to
    relax
Truly communicate
    with someone
    special today
Enter your favorite
    recipe in a
    contest
Play with your pet
Train your mind to be creative
Run for political office
Visit a zoo
Make your own wine
Kick the television habit
Raise your vocabulary
Learn how to read financial
    statements
Learn how to judge personalities
    better
Improve your personality
End the evening by reflecting
    on your day
Start a new charity
Study clouds
Make a list of all the successes
    in your life

Play a prank on a friend
Dream up new pranks
Take twice as much time as
    usual to eat
Go bird watching
Create a new comic strip
Try doing nothing
Visit a museum
Join a new club
Go play bingo
Check this list to see whether
    any activities are repeated
Fly a kite
Skip rope
Start an argument
Watch someone work
Lie on a beach
Wash and polish your car
Start a hobby farm
Help fight crime
Learn about solar energy
Write a book on leisure
Learn how to hypnotize yourself
Have your palm read
Do a jigsaw puzzle
Visit a craft show
Learn a magic act
Cook a lousy meal for someone
    not to enjoy
Learn to speak French, Spanish,
    or another language
Care for someone ill
Be a philosopher
Be nasty to politicians
Write down five of your great-
    est faults or weaknesses and
    then choose one to overcome
    over the next year
Compile a to-do list for the rest
    of your life
Write a fairy tale

Truly enjoy the atmosphere of the present season by looking out of your front window for a few minutes

Organize a protest group for your political pet peeve

Compile a not-to-do list for the rest of your life

Take stock of all the material things you don't want or need; sell these and use the money to throw a big party for your friends

Visit a cemetery and find the most interesting epitaph

Also look for the funniest epitaph

Imagine what your epitaph will say

Teach a lifelong hobby to others at a night school

Research a certain era of your country's history that keenly interests you

Trade homes for a month with a friend who lives in another city or country

Put something unusual in your will so that your heirs will have to earn their money in a fun way

Invent a new service, product, gadget, or the like

Choose a town within fifty miles of your home and spend the afternoon there

Go to a park and sit in silence for thirty minutes to absorb the sounds of nature

Celebrate your adventurous spirit by . . .

Reconnect with a hobby from your youth

Expand this list to 500 activities to outdo me

Rate each activity according to whether it (1) turns you on now, (2) has turned you on in the past, (3) is a new activity that you would consider doing, or (4) does not interest you at all.

Obviously, activities in categories 1, 2, and 3 interest you and belong in your Get-a-Life Tree. As you add these activities to your Get-a-Life Tree, they may trigger new ideas that you will also want to put on the tree. In no time your Get-a-Life Tree should have enough activities to keep you from getting bored for a long time. Instead of risking later regret that you have not pursued the important things in life, you should be pursuing a number of these activities now.

Karen Mangan of Ukiah, California, wrote to me about how she was using the Get-a-Life Tree (called the Leisure Tree in previous editions) to light her own fire and create a fuller life in the process.

Dear Ernie,

Congratulations on your book *The Joy of Not Working,* which I've read many times, often referring to it for inspiration and amusement. I am forty-two years old, and in my peak earning years, working for one of the better companies out here, a large winery in beautiful Mendocino County, California. (Hint—our wines can be found all over Canada, and one of our brands is "Bonterra.") If I had the inclination, I could continue to climb the corporate ladder and make more and more money over the next fifteen to twenty years. However, it is not to be. Although I have what many would consider an enviable position, I am, in fact, looking forward to NOT WORKING.

At this point, I have a three-year plan to pay down the mortgage and quit my current job to live simply on less, and explore other interests. Like a lot of Americans these days, my boyfriend and I are opting to work hard now, make and save money, and then voluntarily downsize. I have created a leisure [Get-a-Life] tree with high priority given to running, tennis, reading, hiking, travel, photography, sex, music, and volunteer work (not necessarily in that order, of course). As you point out, it's not about getting more stuff, it's about getting more life!

It is amazing how few people have figured this out and think that they are doomed to toil until they are sixty-five at a less than satisfactory job, working on someone else's agenda. The key to happiness, as I see it, lies in pulling your own strings and becoming the architect of your own life, not its victim.

If you ever get to the wine country, please look us up.

Sincerely,

Karen

CHAPTER 8

Dynamic Inaction Will Get You Nowhere

You May Be Living, but Are You Alive?

One evening a regular patron of a neighborhood pub, who spent five hours a day there drinking and watching TV, ordered another drink. "Make me a zombie!" he said to the bartender. The bartender facetiously replied, "I can't—God beat me to it!"

Many people are not very different from this TV-addicted bar patron. They also spend all their leisure time passively. Because of their relative inactivity, they are not really alive; neither are they dead. In fact, they are somewhere in between—zombies at best.

> Action may not always bring happiness; but there is no happiness without action.
>
> —Benjamin Disraeli

Just because people have leisure time doesn't mean they know how to use it properly—just as their own-ing a car doesn't mean they know how to drive it properly. Unfortunately, after forty or fifty years of boring leisure, many people are still in the same tunnel—without any cheese—wondering when the plots in their life stories will thicken. Truth be known, more interesting leisure pursuits would do the trick.

North Americans have become a nation of spectators rather than a nation of doers. Over the years, the pleasures of urban populations have become largely passive: watching DVDs or videos at home; watching football, baseball, basketball, and hockey games on TV; and listening to the radio. In the past there was a reason for people to pursue passive leisure: active energies during the industrial revolution were fully expended in manual work. However, this isn't a valid reason for most working people today—the vast majority of them don't work at physical tasks anymore. Moreover, people who still do manual work don't have to work as hard because they use labor-saving tools and machines.

Most of us are passive in our leisure simply because we are lazy. Even in the 1930s, when people were employed in more physical work, they were much more active in their leisure than we are today. For example, people back then spent more time reading, going outside the home to movies, and dancing than we do. Today, the vast majority of North Americans spend their leisure time watching a lot of TV or pursuing other activities that require little physical effort. The less physical and thought-provoking the leisure activity, it seems, the more attractive it is to them.

> Leisure may prove to be a curse rather than a blessing, unless education teaches a flippant world leisure is not a synonym for entertainment.
> —William J. Bogan

Indeed, researchers claim that about 90 percent of North Americans today choose passive activities over active ones. This group spends ten times more time at home in activities such as watching television than outside the home pursuing more active leisure activities. Moreover, when people make it out of the home, they aren't necessarily more active—given that, after the home and the workplace, shopping malls are the number-one place where people spend their spare time.

What's wrong with passive activities? They seldom, if ever, give us the mental highs that conquer boredom. These activities are typified by no challenge, no purpose, low arousal, monotony, and lack of novelty. Although these predictable activities are safe and secure, they provide us with little satisfaction and self-fulfillment.

Recently a group of psychologists separated happiness into two types: feel-good happiness and value-based happiness. Watching a hockey game on TV is feel-good happiness—which is, unfortunately, ruled by the law of diminishing returns. With time—sometimes in minutes, rarely in more than a matter of hours—the satisfaction from the activity decreases until it reaches zero.

Value-based happiness, on the other hand, comes from meaningful activities that serve some higher purpose than just plain pleasure. Ultimately, value-based happiness stems from attaining a sense of satisfaction. And that satisfaction is attained from fulfilling some deeper purpose in tune with our values. The activities contributing to value-based happiness are not normally ruled by the law of diminishing returns. If they are, the time to reach zero satisfaction is normally a lot longer than for activities that provide pleasure-based happiness.

He did nothing in particular, and did it very well.

—W. S. Gilbert

Only by being physically, intellectually, and creatively challenged can individuals find satisfaction and fulfillment in their leisure activities. Following are a few examples of passive leisure activities that provide little satisfaction and fulfillment:

- ➤ Watching television
- ➤ Getting drunk or stoned
- ➤ Junking out on food
- ➤ Going for a drive
- ➤ Shopping
- ➤ Spending money
- ➤ Gambling
- ➤ Spectator sports

Note that passive activities need not be avoided altogether. There are a time and place for some passive activities. For example, spontaneously goofing off with no particular purpose in mind can be healthy for the body and mind, to some degree. Nonetheless, passive activities should be done in moderation, and they should complement a contingent of active activities.

Activity, after all, is essential to happiness and longevity. At this time it's worthwhile to go back to chapter 6 and review the Easy Rule of Life. Note again how it applies to leisure. When people get involved wholly in passive activities, they are, in fact, doing the easy and comfortable; as a result, life turns out difficult, if for no other reason than that life is boring. Conversely, when people get involved in a host of active, challenging

I always wanted to be an artist in my spare time. Now if I could only remember if I'm supposed to use my right brain or left brain.

leisure activities, they are doing the difficult and uncomfortable; as a result, life turns out easy, because it is adventurous and exciting.

Activities that mentally and/or physically engage people, such as bowling or writing a novel, are much more exciting and satisfying than passive activities such as watching TV. Moreover, there is scholarly evidence that adults who partake in the more active leisure activities are more likely to exhibit higher states of physical and psychological well-being. Even daydreaming, meditation, reflection, and fantasizing are more active in nature than watching TV and contribute more to general well-being.

Following are a few examples of active leisure activities:

> Writing
> Reading
> Exercising
> Walking in the park
> Painting a picture
> Playing music
> Dancing
> Taking a course

Contrary to popular belief, a satisfying life is not attainable if we are free from all duty and responsibility. Indeed, a life filled with nothing but passive leisure and pleasure soon becomes an extremely boring life. Undoubtedly, if you have read this book thus far, you don't want to end like up the average North American, looking for as much recreation, entertainment, and cheap thrills as you can get at the expense of doing something that is challenging and exciting.

And when I get real, real bored, I like to drive downtown and get a great parking spot, then sit in my car and count how many people ask me if I'm leaving.
—Steven Wright

We can't achieve enduring happiness from pleasure alone. In fact, if life were all pleasure and nothing else, there would be no happiness. In *Henry IV,* Part I, William Shakespeare wrote, "If all the year were playing holidays, to sport would be as tedious as to work." And the nineteenth-century American humorist and lecturer Josh Billings warned us, "Don't mistake pleasure for happiness. They are a different breed of dog." Total pleasure and comfort can become detrimental to our well-being.

It should go without saying that dynamic inaction will get you nowhere. There are two types of people: participants and spectators. Some people spend most of their time making things happen; others spend most of their time watching what happens. If you spend most of your time watching what is happening, it won't be long before your life is over and you will be wondering what happened.

Once you accept that your attitude and motivation determine the quality of your life, you should have no difficulty creating the events and situations that help you live life to the fullest. As a creatively alive and action-oriented person, you will overcome the inertia that stops the majority from pursuing satisfying leisure activities. "Action is eloquence," declared William Shakespeare.

Active leisure activities play a much bigger role in eliminating depression, anxiety, and stress than passive ones. Study healthy and happy retirees and no doubt you will notice active individuals undertaking challenging activities that provide a good measure of satisfaction. When retiree Frank Kaiser is asked by his friends why he and his wife take hot-air balloon rides, fly motorless gliders, and sky dive, he answers, "I suppose part of it is that we don't want to become like so many old farts, sitting around, dead, and not knowing it."

What sort of interests and active activities would make *your* life much more challenging and well worth living? Perhaps accomplishment is important to you. You can achieve this in many ways. For example, running five miles every day when you are sixty years old may be challenging and difficult, considering that the majority of sixty-year-old retirees have a hard time running twenty feet. Achieving this is sure to leave you feeling good about yourself.

> Time is what we want most, but . . . what we use worst.
>
> —William Penn

It is worthwhile to develop a bank of leisure activities and options that are worth pursuing in case you get bored with your original choices. This is where the Get-a-Life Tree can play a big role. A wide variety of activities—both physical and mental—will go a long way toward conquering boredom. Best of all, you won't have to watch television—or pretend to enjoy watching it with others—ever again!

Take the time to discover the types of leisure activities that you can be passionate about. Start by making a list of your favorite college courses, cities, countries, resorts, sports, games, exercise, songs, artists, authors, and artistic pursuits. Incorporate these in as many active leisure activities as you can. These activities will contribute to personal growth, higher self-esteem, less stress, improved health, excitement and adventure, more satisfaction, more happiness, and an overall higher quality of life.

Watching Television Can Get You Killed

Despite the many negative things said about it, television is North America's most time-consuming pastime. Surveys indicate that North Americans spend over 40 percent of their leisure time watching television. No doubt these are the same people who claim life is boring or bemoan the shortage of leisure time for doing interesting things such as exercising, visiting friends, and watching sunsets.

Watching TV is, like most activities, harmless in moderation. But most people are not moderate in their viewing. Indeed, research indicates that today's full-time North American retiree watches an average of twenty-six hours of TV a week. That's almost four hours a day, on average. Yet many active full-time retirees have a hard time fitting in four hours of TV in a complete spring and summer; some don't even own a TV. Given that the active retirees bring down the average, it follows that many retirees are watching TV eight or more hours a day.

Yet when asked to rate the degree of enjoyment and satisfaction provided by each of twenty-two different leisure activities, Americans rated TV viewing seventeenth. (Interestingly, reading was rated ninth.) Despite this, each week the average North American adult

Harold, you can't solve all your problems by watching reruns of All in the Family *and adopting the philosophy of Archie Bunker.*

between eighteen and sixty-five spends sixteen of his forty hours of spare time in front of the tube—an activity that offers little real enjoyment and satisfaction. In comparison, on average only two hours are spent reading and four hours are spent talking to relatives, friends, and acquaintances.

If a man watches three football games in a row, he should be declared legally dead.
—Erma Bombeck

Perhaps you have joined the unfulfilled individuals who spend most of their time watching TV and the rest of their time contemplating why life is so weird, stale, and boring. Not to worry; there's medication available to help you conquer boredom. Well, not really. There is good news, nonetheless: you can do something about the problem.

TV-Free America (TVFA) is a national organization based in Washington, D.C., dedicated to raising awareness of the harmful effects of excessive television watching. The organization recommends that, instead of watching television, we should spend our time in more productive activities, such as contemplating life, playing sports, attending community events, and volunteering.

When you have had as much as you can take of yourself, you find it easier to face reality. Watching a lot of television is a choice you make and not a great way to spend the bulk of your spare time. If you are still in the workforce and spend most of your leisure time in front of the TV set, this is certainly not good training for an active retirement.

Like workaholism, excessive television watching is an addiction that will do you virtually no good. Indeed, because of its harmful effects, television was billed *The Plug-In Drug* by writer Marie Winn. Watching television is definitely a passive activity, not an active one. The mind is seldom challenged when watching television. Besides the inherent passivity associated with television, it is harmful for other reasons. Many programs and commercials depict life in a way that isn't real. This contributes to distorted pictures of the world and fantasies about life that can't be realized.

Equally harmful is watching TV as a substitute for spending time in personal encounters with real human beings. In early 2000, David Campbell and other members of a Harvard research team reported that television viewing has a corrosive effect on social and public life. People who adopt TV as their primary form of entertainment are significantly less likely to attend dinner parties, visit friends, entertain at home, go on picnics, give blood, and send greeting cards—all activities that could add a lot to their satisfaction and happiness in life

> I find television very educating. Every time somebody turns on the set I go into the other room and read a book.
> —Groucho Marx

Moreover, these same researchers have discovered that chronic TV viewing corresponds with, in their words, "the jerk-type personality." Being somewhat deficient in character, chronic TV viewers are more likely to give you the finger in traffic than occasional viewers. The researchers did not comment on whether the jerk-type personality is caused by excessive TV watching or the jerk-type personality is prone to watching way too much TV.

> Give a man a fish and he eats for a day. Teach him how to fish and you get rid of him for the whole weekend.
> —Zenna Schaffer

Excessive TV watching can even get you killed. In the early 1990s, the UPI news service reported that a Florida man's family confessed to trying to shoot him several times before actually succeeding. They eventually shot him dead because he was a miserable, grouchy man who spent all his spare time lying on the couch watching television. "He'd come home from work and all he'd do is lay on the couch and watch TV," stated the man's daughter. "That's all he did. Like, he never did anything."

If you watch television excessively, cutting down on your viewing hours is key to having a full and interesting life. I can't tell you how much television is the right amount for you. It's your leisure time, and it's your life. If, however, you watch a lot of television and you haven't been enjoying life lately, then doing something more challenging and fulfilling is surely the answer.

Getting off the couch and branching out in new directions will do wonders to relieve your boredom. Indeed, creative and constructive use of your time will leave little desire to watch TV. Even activities promoted by the Institute of Totally Useless Skills—feather balancing, paper-airplane making, napkin stunts, pen bouncing, creative beer-can crushing, or generating symptoms of false physical self-abuse— will be more interesting and do you more good than watching most television programs.

Don't Wait Too Long to Control Your Weight

No person is an island, but some people come pretty close with their constant nibbling on chips, nachos, peanuts, grass, trees, and anything else they can get their hands on and quickly put into their mouths. Junking out on food is a passive activity in which many people indulge quite actively. Overeating goes hand in hand with excessive television watching. Both are passive activities that can lead people to an early death.

> I went on a diet, swore off drinking and heavy eating, and in fourteen days I lost two weeks.
> —Joe E. Lewis

Life is too good in North America—that is why far too many people are overweight. According to Statistics Canada, 48 percent of Canadians are overweight, including the 13 percent who are obese (dangerously overweight). Not to be outdone by Canadians, 61 percent of Americans are over-weight, including 20 percent who are obese. Even worse, researchers say that people tend to underreport their weight. Thus, these figures may be considered somewhat conservative.

The obesity problem is not confined to North America. Even in France, once thought to be a slim nation, obesity is reaching epidemic proportions. A French government report found that although the rate of obesity is still lower than in Britain and the United States, the num-ber of obese French people has risen by 17 percent in three years to 4.2 million. In fact, the World Health Organization has declared obesity to be a worldwide epidemic. Ironically, there are now about 1.1 billion

overweight people in the world, the same as the number of malnour-
ished ones.

Although obesity is more common than it has ever been, this is no
reason for it to affect you as well. Your best bet is to avoid it if you can.
Being overweight will interfere with your ability to enjoy
many great pleasures in life. There are many excuses for
putting on those extra pounds—and with all those excuses,
the battle against the bulge is easily lost. Although gaining
a pound or two with age may be unavoidable for some
people, most people can control their weight through
exercise and diet. You can also select a healthy weight and maintain it
for decades if you commit yourself to it. I have designated 163 pounds
as the weight I am comfortable with and have worked hard to maintain
it at this level for almost three decades.

*I am not going to starve
to death just so I can
live a little longer.*
—Irene Peter

Many experts now agree that waistlines should not automatically
expand with age. In fact, recent U.S. government guidelines indicate that
gaining weight with age is avoidable. Guidelines jointly issued by the
U.S. Department of Agriculture and the U.S.
Health and Human Services Department no
longer make age-related weight distinctions
for adults. The guidelines state that people
should not gain more than ten pounds after
they reach their adult height, which generally
occurs by age twenty-one.

As is to be expected, some other experts
take issue with these guidelines—probably
those who themselves are overweight. It's a
lot easier to be in denial that they are overweight than to do something about it.
Unfortunately, being in denial about
important health issues doesn't keep people
healthy.

It's always easier to stay out of trouble
than to get out of trouble. This is what exercise is supposed to do. Exercise by itself,
however, won't prevent obesity. Along with
lack of adequate exercise, the two primary

*If I had known I was going to live this long,
I would have taken better care of myself.*

reasons for obesity are overeating and eating the wrong foods. In the
early 1600s, George Herbert declared, "Gluttony kills more than the
sword." Things haven't changed much over the years.

If you presently have a weight problem, you can borrow a technique
from the elders on the Japanese island of Okinawa. Researchers consider

these elders the healthiest and slimmest on earth. The elders practice a habit called *hara hachi bu*. This means "stop eating when you are 80 percent full." Consequently, these Japanese elders take in 10 to 40 percent fewer calories than Americans do.

If you still have a weight problem after practicing *hara hachi bu*, try giving your problem away. Two days a week, have only one small meal a day and donate the money you save from your food bill to some of the many charities that help starving people in Third World countries. Not only will you end up thinner, you will have contributed to the health of people a lot less fortunate than yourself. Both of these results will make you feel good about yourself. Of course, how you feel about yourself is just as important to your overall well-being as your general physical health.

Are You Exercising All Your Excuses for Not Exercising?

Perhaps you know several people in their seventies and beyond who are in excellent mental and physical condition. They are living life with more vigor and joy than most people in midlife. They play tennis or baseball, run, walk, hike, dance, communicate, and debate with the same amount of energy as they had in their thirties or forties.

On the other hand, you undoubtedly know many people only in their forties or fifties who appear lazy, tired, and unenthusiastic. For them, getting out of bed in the morning, twisting a bottle cap, or turning on the TV set is a major project. Not only is their physical well-being significantly compromised in their midlife, their mental well-being is far from what it used to be. They are negative, complain a lot, and never seem to learn anything new. To add to their woes, their spiritual health leaves a lot to be desired.

> I like long walks, especially when they are taken by people who annoy me.
> —Fred Allen

The $64,000 question is: what degree of physical, mental, and spiritual fitness would you like to have? Undoubtedly, like everyone else, you want to wind up among the active people with an incredible joie de vivre. Now the million-dollar question is: what are you doing about it today? This question applies whether you are presently in your late thirties and working at a full-time job or in your sixties and fully retired.

Although some retirees with poor physical health, but great mental health, can still experience a good measure of happiness, it doesn't come easy. Staying physically and mentally active is the easiest way to retire happy, wild, and free. The degree to which we maintain our mental and physical fitness, before and after retirement, will determine in large part how fulfilling our retirement years will turn out.

Of course, adopting a healthy lifestyle is something you should do as early in life as possible. This improves your chances of reaching retirement and enhances your ability to enjoy retirement once you get there. In the event that you are less healthy than you should be, you should be putting a lot more time and energy into improving your health than into increasing the size of your retirement portfolio. Retiring rich, but unhealthy, won't do you much good. Without good health you can never be truly rich.

Some people are able to stay healthy for a fairly long time without having to exercise, eat healthy foods, or stop smoking. They think that they are invincible, and that "those health nuts" are wasting their time and money on exercise and good nutrition. One day, much to their surprise, they realize that their health is far from what it used to be. They also realize that they could have done a lot more to prevent their health from deteriorating.

If the television, the couch, and the fridge have become your three best friends, you must take action now. Establish a fitness program and stick to it. Exercise will keep you healthy and in a better mood—and better able—to be more active in other activities.

Individuals with good health are likely to pursue active leisure, while people with bad health are likely to pursue passive leisure. Exercising regularly and becoming fit will have a profound impact on your happiness and well-being. Your physical skills and abilities will be maintained far longer if you get out and exercise your body on a regular basis.

You have probably read about the benefits of regular physical exercise more than once. It's worthwhile, nonetheless, to mention them again, since all of us have a tendency to forget what is good for us. Various research studies conclude that exercise helps us lose weight, experience less anxiety, conquer depression, reduce the urge to eat, and sleep better. It also decreases the risk of colon cancer, breast cancer, heart disease, strokes, high blood pressure, prostate problems, and diabetes.

Those who do not find time for exercise will have to find time for illness.

—Unknown wise person

In the long term, physical activity contributes to robust health, long life, physical attractiveness, and happiness. Dr. Roy Shephard, in his article "Exercise and Aging" (featured in the May 2002 issue of *Geriatrics* magazine), claims that retirees who regularly indulge in moderate exercise can expect to avoid requiring institutional health care for ten to twenty years longer than people who don't exercise.

It's always easy to find an excuse for not exercising. Yet knowing that you have to exercise regularly for good health, and still not doing it, can cause you to feel lousy and disgusted with yourself. This is a big energy drain that can further negatively affect your health.

There are many other excuses that you can use to avoid exercise. Excuses are just that—excuses and nothing else. "A thousand and one excuses," stated Mark Twain, "and no good reasons." Being an adult, you should have noticed by now that making excuses is always an exercise in tedium with no results to show for it.

Richard Simmons, America's eccentric—but wise—fitness guru, told *USA Today*, "For twenty-four years, I've been telling people, 'Please exercise, I beg you to exercise.' They have the time to see a movie. They have the time to go shopping. They have the time to go out and eat. But, they buy a piece of exercise equipment and it ends up in the closet."

The important point about exercising is getting out there and doing it. The times that you don't feel like exercising are the times you need it most. Motivation is crucial. You must consciously force yourself to overcome any excuses.

The first ten minutes of any physical activity are always the hardest. More often than not, I must force myself to go. Once I am out there running or cycling, it feels great. When I am finished, I am always grateful that I went. In fact, I wonder whose voice it was inside my head that was trying to persuade me not to exercise.

As it turns out, the shortcut to being truly fit and trim is long-term vigorous action. The nineteenth-century French journalist Pierre-Joseph Proudhon stated, "The chief condition on which life, health, and vigor depend on, is action. It is by action that an organism develops its faculties, increases its energy, and attains the fulfillment of its destiny."

You aren't going to get fit by casually riding a bicycle at five miles per hour or going for a fifteen-minute walk while window shopping. Researchers at Harvard University have concluded that vigorous activity sustained for longer periods is essential for physical fitness. The researchers, who linked vigorous exercise to longevity, indicated that playing a standard round of golf can't be considered a vigorous workout. Similarly, gardening for a half hour is better than nothing; however, this won't get you fit. The physical benefit is minimal—a little better than nothing!

A British research study, reported in the May 2002 edition of the *Journal of Epidemiology and Community Health,* found that brisk walking is a much healthier option and a better way to keep fit and lose weight than mopping floors, dusting, and cleaning windows, particularly for older women between the ages of sixty and seventy-nine. "Older women need to be doing more physical activity. Housework probably does not cut the mustard," proclaimed Dr. Shah Ebrahim, an epidemiologist and expert on aging at the University of Bristol in southwestern England.

A drive in the country isn't too exciting.

This will be. The country is Mexico.

What will get you in shape, and add to your longevity, is speed-walking at four to five miles an hour for forty-five minutes at a time. Moreover, you must do this several times a week. The only way to get fit is to get your cardiovascular system going. A half-hour of intense walking, jogging, swimming, dancing, hiking, or cycling should be the minimum. You will know you are getting some benefit from your workout if you end up perspiring for at least twenty minutes straight.

Resist being like most baby boomers, who are inclined to choose those activities that require the least effort. A recent newspaper article stated that baby boomers were going for more "relaxed exercise." If ever a term came close to being an oxymoron, without actually becoming one, "relaxed exercise" is it. No one is going to get truly fit with relaxed exercise. Watching TV is the ultimate in relaxed exercise. Unfortunately, instead of enhancing your health, TV harms it.

There are 168 hours in every week. A rule of thumb is that you should devote at least five of those hours to rigorous physical exercise. For optimal fitness, the American College of Sports Medicine recommends twenty to sixty minutes of continuous aerobic exercise—running, brisk walking, swimming, or dancing will do—three or more times a week. The guidelines also recommend weight training twice a week. Lifting weights helps to improve balance and posture and to keep muscles and bones strong.

A fit and trim body commands the respect of others. More important, it commands self-respect. No doubt, if you are overweight and out of shape, creating weight loss and attaining fitness won't happen overnight. You must invest the time and energy in strenuous exercise. The return on your investment, however, is well worth it. You will be the person with a spring in your step while other people your age show their age, or look considerably older than they really are.

People who don't know how to keep themselves healthy ought to have the decency to get themselves buried, and not waste time about it.

—Henrik Ibsen

Not Writing a Book Can Be More Difficult than Writing It

Like many people, you may have always wanted to be a writer. Deep down, there has always been something about the Starbucks cappuccino-and-laptop-computer crowd that appealed to you. If you have thought intuitively for a long time that you should have been a writer, you should give it some serious consideration. Indeed, if deep down you have always wanted to write, *not* writing a book can be more difficult than writing it.

Perhaps, in response to a best-selling book on the *New York Times*, you have declared to yourself or others, "I could have written a book better than this one." Yes, you probably could have. So, why don't you? This also applies to any other person's creative accomplishment that you are capable of duplicating or surpassing. Particularly if you have always wanted to achieve in a certain area, you are selling yourself short by sitting back and talking about it.

I have decided to devote quite a bit of space to what it takes to write a book simply because there are so many people who would like to do so. Writing a book can be the principal expression for your mind and creative talent. Many options and opportunities await you if you look for them. Whether it's writing a novel, a self-help book, or a travel guide, you must choose the genre that will give you the most interesting challenge and satisfaction.

When one has no particular talent for anything, one takes to the pen.

—Honoré de Balzac

To be sure, not everything about writing a book is easy. Richard Bach, author of the best-selling *Jonathan Livingston Seagull*, admitted that it was tough for him to write his next best-seller, *Illusions*. Ernest Hemingway stated, "I read my own books sometimes to cheer me when it is hard to write and then I remember that it was always difficult and how nearly impossible it was sometimes." Joseph Heller, author of *Catch-22*, summed it up very well when he stated that all great writers have difficulty writing.

No doubt some people are born with more talent than others. This superior talent gives them greater potential to excel at certain things, including becoming an accomplished author. Nevertheless, writing a book is largely dependent upon commitment and perseverance.

Take me, for example. I know my limitations as a writer. My writing abilities will never approach those of George Bernard Shaw or of any other Nobel Prize winner. Indeed, giving me the Nobel Prize in literature would spark one of the biggest controversies ever in the world's literary community.

On the other hand, I won't allow my limitations to stop me from writing the books I am capable of writing. What I realized some time ago is that I can't write a book on the same level as William Shakespeare, but I can write a book by me. Truth be known, by the time I realized how bad a writer I really was, I was too successful to quit.

A week doesn't pass by in which I don't meet someone much smarter and literarily more capable than I am, who desperately wants to write a book, but hasn't gotten around to it. Notwithstanding my having failed a first-year university English course three times in a row, I know that I can accomplish more as a writer than millions of people who have three times my ability. I realize that most talented people who want to write are too afraid of failure or too distracted with life's frivolities to attempt a book.

Above all, my writing accomplishments are the result of my agreement with myself to write a minimum of three hours a day. I try to write four pages during this time. These pages don't have to be masterpieces. Sometimes they contain some pretty pathetic writing, but at least I have four pages to work with. Even if I break my agreement to write three hours a day, and instead write for only fifteen minutes, I am still closer to completing a book than people who talk for ten hours about writing one, but never get around to it.

You can take a course on writing books, but it's not necessary for many people. Indeed, most famous writers never took a creative writing course. As the Nike slogan advises, "Just Do It." Put another way, do the difficult and uncomfortable and start writing. The Easy Rule of Life ensures that you will be rewarded for your efforts. Conversely, you may have noticed that it seems to take eternity to complete something you aren't working on.

There is no question that being an author offers one of the few opportunities to make a great deal of money in a short period of time. There are far greater payoffs, however—adventure, personal satisfaction, and acknowledgment from readers. Most accomplished writers profess that the biggest reward isn't financial. It's the thrill of sharing their views of the world with others, and having others tell them that they experienced pleasure—even spiritual fulfillment—from reading their books.

Write without pay until somebody offers pay. If nobody offers within three years, the candidate may look upon this circumstance with the most implicit confidence as the sign that sawing wood is what he was intended for.

—Mark Twain

You can also share in these benefits if you are prepared to do all the difficult things that are necessary to write a book and make it a bestseller. If you can't find a publisher once you have written a book, publish it on your own if you believe in it. Many books that went on to be best-sellers were self-published. But don't equate success with producing a best-seller. If your book is enjoyed by one person other than yourself, it's a success—anything over and above this is a bonus.

Be content to act, and leave the talking to others.

—Baltasar Gracián

Whether you have recently retired, been laid off, or started enjoying a better work/life balance, you now have the opportunity to reclaim your creative spirit. More leisure time gives you the freedom to write the book that you have always wanted to write. You will put more life into your life by being more creative. This is what happened to Neil Kornberger of Winnipeg, Manitoba, after reading this section in a previous edition of the book.

Mr. Zelinski,

Your book pinpointed many of the things that are wrong with our society, such as materialism and the crazy attitude we have toward work. But what impressed me the most was how you stressed that people should use their creativity and imagination to get more out of life.

After reading the book I began to look at my life in a much different way. To my surprise I found a creative side of me that I never knew existed. I just spent the last year writing a book and have never felt so good about accomplishing something. So good that I just had to write you. Throughout the writing my motto has always been from [page 136]: "If your book is enjoyed by one person other than yourself, it's a success; anything over and above this is a bonus."

Congratulations for having written such an inspiring book. A book that has put LIFE back in my life. Well done!

Respectfully,

Neil Kornberger

CHAPTER 9

Zen There Was the Now

Now—and Only Now— Can You Experience the Now

No longer forward nor behind
I look in hope or fear;
But, grateful, take the good I find,
The best of now and here.
—John Greenleaf Whittier

Out of 500 people surveyed by *World Tennis* magazine in a sex/tennis poll, 54 percent said they think about sex while playing tennis. So what does this mean? It could mean a number of things: Perhaps these people find tennis boring. Perhaps they are playing with, or against, really sexy partners. How about a Freudian explanation? They are so obsessed with sex that they think about it all the time, whether they are playing tennis, eating a meal, sewing a dress, or riding a horse.

No doubt Zen masters would say that these tennis players just haven't learned how to live in the now and can't be present, regardless of what they are doing. It's too bad the magazine didn't conduct a more comprehensive poll. No doubt these same tennis players think about tennis while having sex. Moreover, members of a symphony orchestra playing Beethoven's Symphony no. 5 in C Minor likely think about playing tennis, having sex, or a myriad of other things.

Many of us, like these tennis players, have a hard time living the moment. We live in either the "before" or the "later" in place of the "now."

The day is of infinite length for him who knows how to appreciate and use it.

—Johann Wolfgang von Goethe

The more we are focused on the past or the future, the more we miss the now. Sadly, we miss most of life's precious moments because we are so preoccupied with the past and the future.

The value of living in the now isn't an overly profound concept, yet few of us do it. Most of us, in fact, walk around awake, yet asleep, paying little attention to what is going on around us. Some philosophers go so far as to say that most of us are unconscious most of the time; some of us are even unconscious all of the time.

The way to join the conscious minority is to accept that now—and only now—can you ever experience the now. Being in the now is crucial for living happily, because the present moment is all that you really have. There is nothing you can ever experience, except the present moment. Being in the now means accepting that you can never experience past or future moments.

CALVIN AND HOBBES © Watterson. Dist. by UNIVERSAL PRESS SYNDICATE. Reprinted with permission. All rights reserved.

In short, *this is it!* Believe it or not, the now is all you that you have and all that you will ever have. Don't be discouraged, however. The now holds the key to freedom and peace of mind.

Mastering the Moment

In some cultures, a moment can last the entire afternoon. Activities have natural starting and ending times not dictated by the clock. People don't limit their conversations to fifteen or thirty minutes. Conversations start when they start and end when they end, regardless of the number of clocks in the immediate vicinity.

Sadly, many North Americans haven't had a truly leisurely conversation with any of their relatives, friends, or neighbors for years. Given that a research study found that most couples spend about eighteen minutes a week in real conversation, most people probably haven't had a leisurely conversation with their spouse for as long as they can remember.

Happily, I am able to have truly leisurely conversations with at least one of my friends. His name is Mij Relge. We often meet at a local diner for lunch. When we agree to meet at 11:30 A.M., it is understood that this means plus or minus half an hour. After we connect at the diner, our conversations can go on for hours. Sometimes we talk from around 11:45 A.M. to around 5:30 P.M., with neither of us having to look at our watches. In my view, this is truly being in the now.

> Lost, yesterday, somewhere between sunrise and sunset, two golden hours, each set with sixty diamond minutes. No reward is offered, for they are gone forever.
> —Horace Mann

Being in the now is simply enjoying the present moment for all it is worth. Indeed, this is what Mij has been able to do for years in all areas of his life, not just in conversations with his friends. At the age of forty-three, Mij quit his job as a university professor to do some soul-searching and to grow as a person. Out of curiosity, I asked Mij, after he had been jobless for about two years, what he was doing with his free time. Mij indicated that he wasn't having any trouble at all with his work-free life, simply because he was "mastering the moment."

Mastering the moment is important for enjoying leisure—and enjoying life in general. The degree to which you can get totally involved in your leisure activities will determine the quality of your life. Unless you can get totally involved, you won't get much satisfaction from whatever you are doing. This is true whether you are playing chess, talking to a friend, wading through a stream, or watching a sunset. Learn to spend all your leisure activities in the now and you will experience freedom and a sense of peace with the world.

> Time is nature's way of keeping everything from happening at once.
> —Unknown wise person

Being in the now is the essence of Zen, an Eastern discipline that has personal enlightenment as its goal. The following Zen story illustrates the importance of mastering the moment:

A student of Zen asked his teacher, "Master, what is Zen?" The master replied, "Zen is sweeping the floors when you sweep the floors, eating when you eat, and sleeping when you sleep." The student responded with, "Master, that is so simple." "Of course," said the master. "But so few people ever do it."

In Zen terms, most people probably don't have sex when they are having sex, just as most people don't play tennis when they are playing tennis. Put another way, they are not fully conscious of what they are doing. It follows that they are missing out on life.

In contrast, fully alive individuals experience the here and now because they get totally immersed in an activity. Their concentration is so deep that they lose all sense of time. Because they totally immerse themselves in the activity, they have few, if any, distracting thoughts. They enjoy the moment for what it is and don't worry about what is going to happen next.

> The shortest way to do many things is to do only one thing at once.
> —Samuel Smiles

To live life fully, you must also be in the moment. This applies not only to leisure activities, but also to any routine activity. To be fully present, give the activity, which you normally look at as a means to an end, your fullest attention, so that the activity becomes an end in itself. For example, when you have a shower, pay close attention to the sound and feel of the water, as well as the scent of the soap. Moreover, truly feel the sensations in your body as the water connects with it as one. When you feel satisfaction and peace of mind, you are truly experiencing the shower.

Learning to do one thing at a time, instead of two or three, is crucial for mastering the moment. Doing something physically and thinking about something else at the same time are contradictory. You aren't fully taking part in the activity if you are thinking about something else. Key to mastering the moment is sticking with an activity, instead of quitting halfway through. Any activity or task should be worthy of your total attention, and completion, if it is worth doing at all.

Have you ever been so possessed by energy that it carried you away from your normal concerns into a state of indescribable bliss? If you have, you were mastering the moment, and undoubtedly you experienced many feelings that you don't normally experience in everyday life. Howard E. A. Tinsley and Diane J. Tinsley, professors of psychology as Southern Illinois University, concluded that individuals experiencing leisure activities to the fullest experience:

> ➤ A feeling of freedom
> ➤ Total absorption in the activity at hand
> ➤ Lack of focus on self
> ➤ Enhanced perception of objects and events
> ➤ Little awareness of the passage of time
> ➤ Increased sensitivity to body sensations
> ➤ Increased sensitivity to emotions

Cam Gase from San Diego, California, sent me the following letter. Obviously, Cam has learned to enjoy the moment more than most people in western society.

Must be nice to cruise around in a Porsche.

Must be nice to just goof off for the afternoon.

Dear Ernie,

I really enjoyed your book. I read it while on "watch" last night, midnight to eight A.M. I am an able seaman on a ship in the Indian Ocean, now anchored in a lagoon. As I came across the idea of enjoying sunsets and full moons, I was looking at a full moon, then shortly thereafter a beautiful sunrise. I guess leisurely people don't get up for sunrises. We are on the same wavelength. I self-published a small book of quotations, and I see many of them in your book.

Being a seaman, I enjoy and do a lot of traveling. A few years ago I took my girlfriend to Hong Kong and Bangkok. Then last year we went to London, Amsterdam, Munich, Venice, Switzerland, and Paris. We are going on a Caribbean cruise in January.

People working on these ships work hard seven days a week—especially holidays and weekends, due to the higher pay. Anyway, I took the day off and went to the beach to go swimming and write a few letters. People were astounded that I would loaf on a "premium pay" day. Tomorrow is Sunday, and I'm going to do the same. I have so many things to do in my leisure time: read, write, swim, etc. I don't watch TV, but I do watch some videos and films.

Your concept of living like you had six months left is one I picked up while studying Ninja philosophy and art. Living in the now is described as "being there: totally concentrating on the moment at hand." Yoga and Zen training used the idea of concentrating on a simple object as you described.

I truly enjoy my solitude too. It's just great when I read a book and agree with every page. I am surprised that someone put all the ideas and concepts in one book.

Sincerely,

Cam

Cam's secret to enjoying life is to master the moment while participating in interesting and challenging leisure activities. Learn to master the moment to the degree Cam does and you too will be carried away by experiences that are extraordinarily joyous, fulfilling, and meaningful.

Mastering the moment means happily spending a whole afternoon at the library browsing without a definite purpose in mind, or handwriting a letter that flows for five more pages of creative thoughts than you had originally intended. Mastering the moment is doing something with so much fascination and enjoyment that you lose all sense of time and place. You will know that you are mastering the moment if you get so immersed in a leisure activity that you forget who you are.

Half of our life is spent trying to find something to do with the time we have rushed through life trying to save.
—Will Rogers

Leo Tolstoy asked three questions:

1. When is the best time to heed? Now.
2. Who are the most esteemed people? He with whom you are.
3. What important pursuits are to be undertaken first? That which does good to him.

Tolstoy's answers to these three questions emphasize the importance of being in the now. He was underscoring the importance of focusing on the process at hand and not on the end result. By focusing on the process, we get to enjoy both the process and the end result.

Living in the moment means we get more enjoyment and satisfaction from our efforts than from actually reaching the goal. Satisfaction from reaching a goal, no matter how significant, is short-lived. "To travel hopefully," stated Robert Louis Stevenson, "is better than to arrive."

If you want to travel on a happy journey, learn to cultivate a higher appreciation for what is around you—sunsets, music, and other wonderful things. Don't take life for granted, because you'll miss it. Keep in mind that every sunset is different from all other sunsets, just as every snowflake is different from all other snowflakes. Wake up and listen to the birds sing, smell the flowers, and feel the texture of the trees.

Try to find something to enjoy every minute of the day. Look for the positive in all situations. Start and live each day with a task in mind. In your field of consciousness, practice the idea of enjoying your day. Act with presence of mind and experience each moment by being in the now. Remember that there is no other moment than this one; you can live only one moment at a time. Ultimately, you are the moment.

If You Must Hurry, Then Hurry Slowly

> If you're not served in 5 minutes
> you'll get served in 8 or 9 . . .
> Maybe 12 minutes
> RELAX!
>
> —*On menu of Ritz Diner, Edmonton*

In the modern world, most people are in a mad rush to get somewhere, but most probably don't have the slightest notion why they are in such a hurry or, even worse, where exactly they are heading. The only thing some people accomplish by hurrying to their destination is getting to wait longer once they get there.

What is your hurry in life? When was the last time you had a heart-to-heart conversation with a friend? Have you ever stopped to consider why you are rushing around? Do you rush to the phone when there is no need to do so? You can allow it to ring another ring without anything serious happening.

If you must hurry, then hurry slowly. Speed kills—in more ways than one. People suffering from hurry sickness tend to have many health problems, including a high mortality rate from heart disease. Physiological characteristics of people consumed by time include increased heart rate, high blood pressure, gastric problems, and muscle tension. In a rush to do it all, time-driven people can develop serious illnesses that lead to early deaths.

The world is ruled by letting things take their course. It cannot be ruled by interfering.

—Lao-tzu

"The feeling of being hurried is not usually the result of living a full life and having no time," stated the late American philosopher Eric Hoffer. "It is, on the contrary, born of a vague fear that we are wasting our life. When we do not do the one thing we ought to do, we have no time for anything else—we are the busiest people in the world."

Wisely and slowly. They stumble that run fast.

—William Shakespeare

The wise people in this world tell us that only fools are in a hurry to get to anywhere worth going. Regardless of what we are trying to accomplish, we will do ourselves great good to remember the words of Thomas Shadwell: "The haste of a fool is the slowest thing in the world." Rushing about in desperation will only push away from us what we are really after: satisfaction, health, peace of mind, and happiness.

Contrary to popular belief, the fastest way to any destination is to slow down and take it easy. Moreover, we must learn to give up the need to control how things are going to turn out. The need for control can be self-defeating.

No man who is in a hurry is quite civilized.

—Will Durant

If you have ever ridden a horse, you know that it is much easier to ride it in the direction in which it wants to go. Getting through life in this world is also easier if you ride with the world in the direction in which it's going. This means giving up the need to control the way everything is going to turn out. The following analogy is useful in illustrating the importance of giving up control in life:

Assume you are on a raft floating down a fast-moving, highly treacherous river. The raft happens to capsize, and you fall into the rapidly flowing water. You can do one of two things: You can try to take control and fight the river—if you do, you are liable to end up injured as a result of being thrown against the rocks. Or, you can give up total control—and the moment you do, you will be in control. You are now going with the flow. The water doesn't flow into the rocks; the water flows around the rocks.

Life is a fast-moving river; the best way to get through it with a minimum of scrapes and bruises is to slow down and learn how to go with the flow. This means being able to surrender and give up control. Try as we may to control life by planning everything, there are too many factors beyond our control that can destroy the best-laid plans.

True success, which contributes to satisfaction, peace of mind, and happiness, requires action, but also patience. Impatient people seldom arrive where they want to go—and if they do, it normally takes them much longer than it takes patient people.

Focusing on the goal itself, instead of the process by which you earn it, isn't the surest way to attain it. What seems urgent seldom is. By slowing down, you will be able to tap your creativity and come up with ideas that can make a difference in the lives of others, and to the world as a whole. This will put you in a position to implement your ideas and attain most of your goals. Paradoxically, when you become less preoccupied with attaining success itself and with attaining it in a hurry, success comes more easily and quickly.

The most important thing is not the prize, but the journey and your commitment to enjoying the journey. Have some fun and adventure along the way. Slowing down and tapping into your imagination allow you to come up with money-making projects that people in a hurry to get rich will never see. Not being in a hurry also means having the time to observe what's happening around you in the present moment. That's where life is—and always will be.

To be more successful at work or play, choose to be the smart tortoise instead of the foolish hare. The foolish hare rushes around in an attempt to cover as much territory as possible. In a mad frenzy, the hare tries to get to that ultimate destination called happiness.

In contrast, the tortoise doesn't have to try to cover as much territory as the hare; it knows this won't make it happy. The smart tortoise doesn't hurry, because it's already arrived at that destination called happiness; it's experiencing peace and satisfaction wherever it is.

Like the hare, everyone today seems to be in a hurry to get to somewhere they aren't. Choose to be exactly where you are right now and you will be happier than 90 percent of humankind.

Ultimately Nothing Matters— and So What if It Did?

Like constant hurry, constant worry robs people of the now. According to a study by Pennsylvania State University, about 15 percent of the U.S. public spends at least 50 percent of each day worrying. Moreover, other researchers say worrying is so rampant that approximately one out of three North Americans has serious mental problems as a result. Some people are so used to worrying that they worry if they don't have anything to worry about. If you are addicted to worry and don't have enough things to worry about, you can use some items from the following list. I generated this list when I suggested that we have obsession readings at one of my favorite coffee bars instead of poetry readings. As with all the great ideas I used to propose when I was an engineer, this idea wasn't immediately adopted and probably never will be.

> *I am an old man and have known a great many troubles, but most of them never happened.*
> —*Mark Twain*

Some More Things to Worry About

- ➤ What will happen to me and this world if I get overmotivated?
- ➤ Who keeps stealing my socks?
- ➤ What will I wear if I am invited as a guest on Oprah?
- ➤ Who invented socks?
- ➤ Will someone else be reincarnated as me?
- ➤ How come all the crazy guys at the coffee bar know me?

- Is my neighbor's cat dysfunctional?
- Why didn't Celine Dion marry me instead?
- What type of car should I buy if I win the lottery?
- Why am I the only customer in this coffee shop?
- What happened to all the crazy guys?
- Do dyslexics appreciate palindromes?
- Is my purpose in life to be a warning for others?
- Who is that intriguing blond over there?
- Do I actually have more fun with blonds?
- If I marry a blond, will I end up liking brunettes more?
- Why don't people put fender skirts on cars anymore?
- Can a perfectionist like me have a paradigm shift?
- Am I the only one who hasn't had a paradigm shift?
- Will someone steal this list and sell it to David Letterman for a big fortune?
- Will they lock me up for having prepared this list?

To put worrying in the right perspective, let's consider another story told by Zen masters:

Two monks, Eanzan and Tekido, were walking along a muddy road when they came upon a beautiful woman who was unable to cross the road without getting her silk shoes muddy. Without saying a word, Eanzan picked up the woman and carried her across the road, leaving her on the other side. Then the two monks continued walking without talking until the end of the day. When they reached their destination, Tekido said, "You know monks are supposed to avoid women. Why did you pick up that woman this morning?" Eanzan replied, "I left her on the side of the road. Why are you at this time still carrying her?"

This story points out that we should not burden ourselves with events from the past. Yet many of us repeatedly focus on the past with deep regret. Of course, the past can't be changed, so any negative thoughts directed at the past are useless. Moreover, these thoughts distract us from enjoying the present moment.

Worrying about the future also distracts us from enjoying the present moment. A lot of what we say, think, or do is actually influenced by the fear of problems that the future will bring. Yet if we were to focus on the present we would forget about these problems. Indeed, we should forget these problems because they are imaginary and don't exist in the present.

In *The Power of Now*, Ekhart Tolle suggests that all worry and other negative thoughts are the result of not being in the now. Tolle states, "Unease, anxiety, tension, stress, worry—all forms of fear—are caused by too much future and not enough presence. Guilt, regret, resentment, grievances, sadness, bitterness, and all forms of nonforgiveness are caused by too much past, and not enough presence."

Are you spending too much time worrying and missing out on today? Can you concentrate and be in the here and now? Spending too much time worrying about losing, failing, or making mistakes will make you tense and anxious. Too much worrying will predispose you to stress, headaches, panic attacks, ulcers, and other related ailments. Most worry is self-inflicted and has no benefit to you. Just consider the following chart based on research conducted by psychologists:

> It isn't the experience of today that drives men mad. It is the remorse for something that happened yesterday, and the dread of what tomorrow may disclose.
>
> —Robert Jones Burdette

Wasted Worries

40 percent of worries are about events that will never happen
30 percent of worries are about events that already happened
22 percent of worries are about trivial events
4 percent of worries are about events we cannot change
4 percent of worries are about real events on which we can act

---

The first four items in the above chart comprise 96 percent of the things we worry about. These are things that we cannot control. It follows that all this worry is wasted. Moreover, the time we spend worrying about the other 4 percent of things is wasted as well, because we can control these things.

So, time spent worrying about things we *can't* control is wasted because we can't control them, and time spent worrying about things we *can* control is wasted because we can control them. One hundred percent of our worrying time is wasted time. (Now you can worry about all the time you have wasted by worrying!)

To overcome the worry trap, it's best to adopt this motto: ultimately nothing matters—and so what if it did? If you can live by this motto, you will live in the present moment a lot more.

Time Is Worth More than Money; Spend It Wisely

Time is supposed to be money. In fact, time is worth more than money. If you lose your money, you can replace it with much more money. Doing the same with time is impossible, however. "Lost time," declared Benjamin Franklin, "is never found again." In this regard, money is unlimited; time isn't. Unfortunately, some people act as if the opposite were true.

Clearly, in today's fast-paced, stressed-out western world, time is more precious than ever before. Time is, in fact, our scarcest resource. It is a finite resource on which we place infinite demands by trying to do too much.

If you want to have time on your side, you can't always fight it. Indeed, to fight time is as asinine as to fight the law of gravity and the Easy Rule of Life. Try to fight them all, and the three will sooner or later put you six feet under.

Nothing indicates more surely that you are fighting time than the fact that you are always hurried. Always feeling rushed is no way for a prosperity-minded individual to live. The objective of life is not to get through it as fast as possible.

Perhaps you aren't concerned about the rapid pace of your life. What you *should* be concerned about, however, is the abrupt stop at the end of it, much earlier than you expected. And you are going to reach the end of life at a much younger age if you don't learn to slow down.

It's also important to quit worrying about what the future will bring. If you want the future to be better than the present, you must live mostly in the present instead of trying to live in the future. Stop to enjoy what you already have but haven't been enjoying. Take stock of the valuables, treasures, and talents—the good books, true friendships, artistic pursuits, hobbies, passions, and personal dreams—that you have misplaced, lost, or forgotten due to your hurried lifestyle.

The best way to achieve long-term happiness is to experience perpetual short-term happiness. It's important to have a good balance between work and play in the present. Putting off having a happy work-life balance until years down the road is tantamount to putting off sex until after you retire from your job. In either case, it ain't gonna work.

Your mind can be your greatest asset, but it can play tricks on you. One such nasty trick is making you believe that you

My goals in life are to be happy, live every moment for all it's worth, and learn to do one thing at a time.

don't have sufficient time to do your work and still have time to lead a satisfying, balanced lifestyle that includes time for relaxation, social engagements, and other leisure activities. Perhaps you should think again! Each day you have 1,440 minutes, or 86,400 seconds. That's the same amount of time that everyone else on Earth has, including people who have a full, relaxed, happy, and satisfying lifestyle.

Having more time for the good things in life is actually quite easy. Whenever you feel short on time for those good things, you must create more time by making better use of it. A recent research study at Penn State University indicated that what we perceive as a time crunch is, in large measure, just an erroneous perception. We all have enough time to do the important and enjoyable things, but we squander it. If we would make excellent use of just 30 or 40 percent of our time, we wouldn't have any shortage.

> The time to relax is when you don't have time for it.
> —Sydney J. Harris

It may appear that the way to have more time in your life is to rush more during the day and try to do as many things as possible in the shortest time. You may have tried this many times and discovered that you always feel even more time-deprived. No wonder that an old Dutch saying contends, "The hurrier we go, the behinder we get."

You can transcend time by doing your own thing at your own speed. Again, forget about what the masses are doing. Even if practically everyone else seems to increase the pace of life every day, you don't have to try to keep up. Take control of your physical and psychic space instead of allowing the distractions of the modern world to influence your lifestyle.

To make your days longer, don't rush; slow down instead. In a somewhat magical way, you will have more time when you start living every moment for all it is worth. Once you slow down, you will no longer fight time; you will master it. Full involvement in and appreciation of any activity—whether writing your first novel, walking in the park, talking to your neighbor, or taking a shower—will make the whole world slow down for you.

> The most wasted day of all is that on which we have not laughed.
> —Sébastien Roch Nicolas Chamfort

The next time you think that you don't have time to enjoy a sunset, think about it a little more. You will realize that the most important time to enjoy a sunset is when you don't have time for it. Taking ten minutes to watch the sun go down will do more to help you catch up with the world than rushing around for several hours. To your surprise, the world will actually slow down for you.

The more sunsets you stop to enjoy, the more relaxed and less rushed life will be. Moreover, you will realize the importance of reducing the quantity of your other activities so that you get more quality in those that you pursue. You don't have to apologize to anyone for slowing down and enjoying life. If someone asks what has gotten to you, tell them you read *The Joy of Not Working*. Not everyone will approve of your behavior, but this will add to your satisfaction.

Following are some reminders that will help you better manage your time so you have more of it for the important things in life:

Ways to Slow Down and Really Live

- ➤ To create more time for enjoying that mysterious and unpredictable phenomenon called life, minimize your search for the secret to it. You don't need to fully understand life to enjoy it.

- ➤ Don't waste precious time by taking more than a minute to make insignificant decisions, such as which flavor of ice cream to buy. If you have a hard time making a decision, flip a coin.

- ➤ Don't spend any time looking at what your neighbors are up to. Do something interesting and empowering, instead, so they waste their time pondering what you are up to.

- ➤ Remember that regardless of how little time and effort it takes someone to perform a tedious task, there has to be a more efficient and effective way to perform it.

- ➤ Choose one of these three ways to handle a task fast: do it yourself, hire an expert to handle it for you, or decide that it isn't worth doing and strike it off your to-do list.

- ➤ Watch at least one less hour of TV per day for the next year. This will give you 365 extra hours, or the equivalent of fifteen twenty-four-hour days, to pursue more worthwhile activities.

- ➤ Be creative as well as selective. Choose your activities wisely. Spend your time and energy on the important few instead of the significant many. Putting outstanding effort into two or three important things will give you much more joy and satisfaction than putting average effort into many things.

- ➤ One of the greatest time-wasters is associating with the wrong people.

I asked the boss for a four-day work week. He told me I am already have one, but it takes me five days to complete it.

Yet many people spend time with people they don't even like. Spend time with the people you like most and totally avoid the people you like least.

➤ Keep in mind that the more things you buy, the less time you have to enjoy the things you already have.

➤ If excellence is your theme, then let moderation be your song. There is no perfect way to complete any project; therefore, stop trying to find it. Whatever is worth doing well is definitely not worth overdoing.

➤ Learn to distinguish between these three: Some things need doing better than you or anyone has ever done them before. Some just need doing to get by. Some are not necessary; they don't need doing and are best left to the misfits of this world to pursue.

➤ Several times a week, relax by not doing anything in particular for an hour or two. Author Scott Peck, who has a full and busy life, is often asked, "How can you do all that you do?" His normal reply is, "Because I spend at least two hours a day doing nothing."

➤ When you are doing something difficult, tedious, or extremely time-consuming, ask yourself what would happen if you didn't do it. If the answer is nothing, or next to nothing, stop doing it.

➤ Of three precious resources in life—time, money, and creativity—the only unlimited one is your creativity. Make creativity your number-one resource, and time and money won't be as scarce.

➤ When you have a cup of coffee, live the moment. Drink the coffee slowly and with great concentration, as if the whole world had stopped to help you enjoy the coffee.

➤ Avoid driving your car as if your journey is the only one on earth that is going to save the universe. Stop and think about it and you will realize that your journey is rather insignificant in the higher order of things.

➤ Have thirty minutes or so of some unstructured time every day to do something spontaneous and different.

➤ Spend time alone for an hour or two every day and let the telephone answering machine take your calls.

➤ Truly watch a sunset in the evening, for the amount of time it takes for the sun to go down.

➤ Have a real conversation with your neighbor during which you have a natural starting time and finishing time not dictated by the clock.

➤ Experience your shower in the morning for as long as it takes you to truly experience it.

➤ In a culture addicted to materialism, workaholism, and speed, the battle cry is "time is money." It's best that we reject the notion of measuring time solely in terms of money, simply because time is worth much more than money. The proper adage is "time is happiness." People who live by this adage are healthier and better off because of it.

The road is better than the inn.

—Miguel de Cervantes

➤ Keep in mind that you can't earn more time, no matter how hard you work. And you can't buy it, no matter how much money you have. So spend it wisely, much more so than you spend money.

➤ Above all, enjoy today as if it were your last day—because it just may be. With this in mind, don't spend your time searching for the happy moment. You are that moment!

CHAPTER 10

It Is Better to Be Alone than in Bad Company

The Key to Being Alone Is Locked Inside

When from our better selves we have too long
Been parted by the hurrying world, and droop,
Sick of its business, of its pleasures tired,
How gracious, how benign, is Solitude.
—From *The Prelude* by William Wordsworth

Not that long ago, the lonely Maytag repairman was a big hit in television commercials. He appeared lonely because his services were rarely required due to the quality of the Maytag appliances he was trained to service. In one commercial, the Maytag man registered at a hotel and signed his company name at the desk. The receptionist said something like, "We'll try to make sure you're not lonely here."

In real life the receptionist would be fooling herself. No one can ever ensure that the Maytag man won't be lonely except the Maytag man himself. Many people are lonely in

> A man who finds no satisfaction in himself, seeks for it in vain elsewhere.
> —François, Duc de La Rochefoucauld

the company of others. Moreover, just because people spend substantial time alone doesn't mean that they are lonely.

Aloneness is not synonymous with loneliness. There are two sides to being alone. The painful side is loneliness, which leads to symptoms associated with boredom, such as anxiousness and unhappiness. These can further lead to ailments such as headaches, excessive sleeping, insomnia, and depression. At the extreme, people commit suicide.

The other side to being alone is the pleasant side—solitude. Solitude is an opportunity to indulge in many delightful activities that can only be enjoyed alone. Although loneliness can mean dejection and sadness, solitude can mean contentment and even ecstasy. Sadly, most people never discover the pleasant side to being alone. Indeed, some people run themselves off their mental rails if they are forced to be alone for more than ten minutes.

People who can't handle being alone for even the shortest period flip on the television or tune in to a radio talk show the moment they enter their homes. Elvis Presley, like many lonely people, hated being alone and turned on a television in any deserted room he entered. As previously mentioned, watching a great deal of television is a poor choice for leading a fulfilling life of leisure.

> City Life: Millions of people being lonesome together.
> —Henry David Thoreau

Most people use aloneness as an excuse for not being able to do anything enjoyable in their spare time. For example, a friend of mine was enthusiastic about cycling one summer. He bought an expensive new bicycle and then used it only once in the first year. He quit cycling because he had no one to accompany him.

I, on the other hand, often prefer to go cycling or jogging by myself, even when friends want to accompany me. I have to convince my friends that I don't find their company boring. Indeed, I like being around people. There are times, however, when I prefer the pleasure of my own company.

Although some people may view my behavior as odd, I realize that I am in good company when I am alone—in more ways than one. Through the ages many accomplished individuals have sung the praises of solitude. "I find it wholesome to be alone the greater part of the time," declared Henry David Thoreau. "To be in company, even with the best, is soon wearisome and dissipating. I love to be alone. I never found the companion that was so companionable as solitude."

Unfortunately, being alone is deemed antisocial behavior by society. Thus, most people learn early in life to spend all their leisure time with others. They join clubs, teams, and any other organizations that will ensure they are never alone. As is to be expected, if they wind up alone, they are totally lost. They will watch boring television programs or listen to radio deejays engage in idle chatter rather than deal with periods of silence. Some people even remain in terribly dysfunctional marriages rather than risk being alone.

Psychologists say loneliness has become a serious problem in North America, especially in big cities. Surveys indicate one quarter of the population suffer from chronic loneliness. A recent study cited in *Psychology Today* magazine found that over 50 percent of people in the United States suffer from loneliness, either sometimes or often. This means that over 100 million Americans experience loneliness.

People commonly attribute their loneliness to these factors:

- Not having enough friends
- Not being married
- Not having a relationship
- Living in a new city
- Living in a big city
- Having superficial friends

Their loneliness is even more tragic, given that no item in the above list ultimately causes loneliness. These may be contributing factors, but they don't cause loneliness. People are lonely simply because they allow themselves to get lonely. They become lonely because they are bored with themselves.

To overcome loneliness, we must learn how to spend our time alone creatively. The majority of us flee to society—as dull as society is—searching for some excitement to escape the greater dullness inside ourselves. We also flee to society because we fear being alone. Yet many of us can be lonelier in a crowd than we are by ourselves.

The inability to be alone reflects some basic inner insecurity. Some of the loneliest people in the world are those who are always around other people. Many lonely people are extremely charming and self-composed in the company of others. The minute they are by themselves, however, they are vulnerable to loneliness.

If this is loneliness, I want more of it.

Most people fail to look inside themselves for the source of their loneliness. Some take drugs or alcohol to keep the pace moving fast. Others—so they don't have to think—turn on the television or play the stereo to ensure there is always some sound when they are alone.

If you can only make it with people, and not alone, you can't make it.
—Clark E. Moustakas

The Sufi religious sect has a parable that illustrates the folly of people looking to the external world to solve a problem when they should be looking within.

A man named Mullah is on the street outside his house, on his hands and knees, looking for something. A friend happens to come by and says, "Mullah, what are you searching for?" Mullah says, "I lost my keys." The friend says, "I'll help you look for them." After some time, the friend finds looking for the keys a little tiresome and says to Mullah, "Mullah, do you have any idea where you lost the keys?" Mullah replies, "Yes, I lost the keys in the house." The bewildered friend then asks, "Why in the world are we looking for the keys outside?" Mullah answers, "Because there is a lot more light out here."

This parable is funny, but it also has a serious side. To handle loneliness, most of us look to the external world, where there is more light. Just as Mullah won't find his keys outside his house, we won't overcome loneliness by searching in the external world, regardless of how much light there is out there. After all, the key to handling loneliness is locked inside ourselves, where, for some of us, there is not as much light.

In Yourself Is the Universe

Can you enjoy being alone? If you can't, it's probably a sign that you aren't able to discover quality in your own character. Put another way, you have low self-esteem, a sense of feeling unworthy and undeserving of your own company. Not liking yourself can be a giant barrier to enjoying solitary leisure time. Incidentally, if you don't like yourself, why would you expect anyone else to like you?

In life there is no substitute for happiness, and there can be little happiness without self-esteem. Esteem from others and self-esteem are two different things. Self-esteem cannot be achieved through other people or through the environment; it is something that only you can give yourself.

How much you like yourself is reflected by how much effort you put into trying to get others to like you. If you are constantly afraid someone may not like you or may get upset with you, you undoubtedly have low self-esteem. Another sure sign of low self-esteem is your fear of what others will think of you if they find out that you spend a lot of time alone in leisure activities.

If you lack sufficient self-esteem, you must develop it. You will have sufficient self-esteem when you like yourself no matter what others think about you. You will get to keep your own scorecard based on your own standards, rather than on someone else's standards.

Your goal should be self-actualization, a state that will empower you to enjoy yourself with others and while alone. According to the well-known humanist psychologist Abraham Maslow, self-actualized people, who are at the highest level of self-development, don't flee from aloneness; they seek it. Indeed, these people are at their best and most effective when alone, whether at work or play.

Contrary to popular belief, self-actualized individuals who spend a lot of time by themselves aren't loners. Loners don't get along with anyone; they are neurotic, secretive, and poorly adjusted. Self-actualized individuals, in contrast, are psychologically healthy individuals who get along with virtually everyone. Maslow found that these psychologically healthy individuals are highly independent, yet at the same time they enjoy people.

Paradoxically, self-actualized individuals act like loners, but not only do they like to be with people, they can be the most sociable people around. Indeed, they are the most individualistic members of society and, at the same time, the most social, friendly, and loving. They get along with others, and, even more important, they get along with themselves.

With some internal development, you too can become self-actualized so that you have the ability to happily work alone and play alone. You must love yourself and the world before you can serve the world. Once you become self-actualized, you will learn how to accomplish, to achieve, and to triumph when alone. You won't always need other people to be fully involved in life. Above all, you will truly get to know yourself—and in yourself is the universe.

Don't Just Walk Away from Negative People: Run!

As a highly evolved human being, you will want to avoid being around certain people, even if the alternative is being alone. While you are trying to light the fire in your life, learn to ignore people who will try to put it out for you. Boring people may douse your fire somewhat, but negative people are even more dangerous to your happiness and well-being.

I was going to buy a copy of The Power of Positive Thinking, and then I thought: What the damn good would that do?
—*Ronnie Shakes*

Negative people are particularly noted for their lack of humor. They have the delightful view that life is a rip-off and that nothing is so bad that it can't get worse. As is to be expected, these people will seek your support for their notion that the world is a lousy place. Nothing irks negative people more than individuals who are positive and have high self-esteem. Negative people will do anything in their power to bring positive people down to a depressing level.

You must spot and avoid people who are likely to drain your energy. If you have friends or acquaintances who are constantly depressed and complaining about life, they will sap a lot of your positive energy. Don't spend a great deal of time with a person who has a negative attitude, unless his or her state of mind is temporary, due to some tragic event.

Life is much easier if you don't carry excess baggage, and negative people are excess baggage. On an airline, excess baggage will cost you money. Negative people will cost you much more than money, however. The price will be your time, energy, and happiness. Negative people can even cost you your sanity in the end. At best, you won't be as happy with them as you could be by yourself.

It's a mistake to try to change negative people—to expect their imminent transformation into more positive individuals. Richard Bach wrote in *One*, "No one can solve problems for someone whose problem is that they don't want problems solved." Generally speaking, negative people don't want to change; if they do change, it is only after a lengthy period—time you can't afford to lose. Instead of expending your energy trying to change someone else, use it to change *yourself* for the better.

Perhaps you are a Good Samaritan who likes to take on one or two neurotics as a personal project. I must warn you about the futility of the venture. Unless you can get these people to have personality transplants, all your efforts will be in vain. To put negative people in the proper perspective, here is an old tale about a scorpion and a frog:

A scorpion, wanting to get across a pond, spots a friendly frog. The scorpion says to the frog, "How about a lift to the other side of the pond? I can't swim and I would appreciate your helping me out." The frog says, "No way. I know what scorpions are like. If I let you onto my back, you'll probably sting me halfway across the pond where I could not swim to shore after being stung. I don't want to drown."

The scorpion replies, "Don't be silly. If I am on your back, I am dependent on you to get across the pond. If I sting you, I will drown too. Why would I want to do that?" The frog thinks about this and relents. "I guess you're right. Hop on."

The scorpion hops onto the frog's back, and they take off for the other side of the pond. The scorpion resists stinging the frog until they are about halfway across. Then the scorpion—who, like most of us, can resist everything but temptation—gives the frog a big whopper of a sting.

As they both start to go under, the frog says, "Why in the world did you do that? Now both of us are going to die." The scorpion's answer is one you may have heard before from human scorpions: "I couldn't resist. It's my nature to be that way."

Negative people are like the scorpion in this fable. Even if their happiness and survival are at stake, they won't change. Although they *could* change, these people go on defending their point of view at all costs while looking for new converts. Indeed, misery doesn't only love company; it demands it.

In short, it is futile to spend your time trying to make an unhappy person happy. Near as I can tell, you'd have to be a magician to pull it off. There is only one way to effectively deal with negative people: eliminate them from your life.

I agree wholeheartedly with George Washington: "It is better to be alone than in bad company." You must avoid negative people for the sake of your own happiness. When you find yourself in their company, don't walk away: run!

Alone in Your Tree

Being alone forces you to confront yourself. You will discover that being alone allows you to experience the world and yourself in a way not available when you are with other people. You get to fly solo rather than with someone else—and in the process, you reach even greater heights.

> The great misfortune—to be incapable of solitude.
> —Jean de la Bruyère

There are two ways to react when you feel lonely while alone. One response is sad passivity. This includes crying, moping, excess eating, sleeping, and feeling sorry for yourself. This reaction is often the result of low self-esteem and a lack of defined goals for handling aloneness.

Other unhealthy ways to handle loneliness are getting stoned, boozing, gambling, and shopping. In the short term, these seem to help alleviate loneliness. In the long run, however, they don't enhance social skills, help form close relationships, or develop high self-esteem.

> *Once in a while you have to take a break and visit yourself.*
> —Audrey Giorgi

The other response to loneliness is creative action based on a well-defined plan. The plan can include activities such as reading, writing letters, studying, listening to music, working on a hobby, or playing a musical instrument. Acting according to your plan will enhance your identity and help develop a sense of security for when you find yourself alone again.

Exercise 10-1. Being Alone in Your Tree

Aloneness is an opportunity to do the things that are difficult to do around other people. Go back to your Get-a-Life Tree and add a primary branch for activities you can do alone. Now expand your tree by adding as many activities on secondary branches as you possibly can.

Here are just a few of the many things you can pursue without having someone by your side:

- ➤ Meditate.
- ➤ Read books and magazines you haven't been able to read before.
- ➤ Visit people you may not visit when you are with another person.
- ➤ Do something artistic or creative.
- ➤ Volunteer for a charity.
- ➤ Find time to dream your dreams.
- ➤ Discover a new hobby.
- ➤ Watch people.
- ➤ Go to coffee places to meet people.
- ➤ Cycle, jog, or swim.
- ➤ Design a new tool or object.
- ➤ Fix your car.

➤ Remodel your house.

➤ Go for a walk in the park.

➤ Walk in the rain.

➤ Take a nap.

➤ Write letters.

➤ Listen to music.

➤ Work on a hobby.

➤ Take up gardening.

Solitary activities will develop your individuality and create quality in your leisure. There is substance to being alone because it makes demands on your capacity to rely on yourself. You must take more responsibility for yourself when you are alone than when you are with your spouse, family, or friends. Taking responsibility means you are the sole author of your experiences, regardless of what solitary activity you indulge in.

Give Solitude a Chance

Many individuals haven't learned how to handle being alone simply because they don't give solitude a chance. To deal with aloneness, these individuals immediately turn on the television or spontaneously decide to go shopping for something that they don't need or can't afford. Because they don't give solitude a chance, they never get to appreciate it.

After having been with people for any length of time, we all get addicted to having someone around us, particularly when we are with quality people. Richard Bach, in his book *Illusions,* related how it always took some effort and adjustment to return to being by himself after having been around people for some time. "Lonely again," wrote Bach. "A person gets used to being alone, but break it just for a day and you have to get used to it again."

Writing books forces me to get used to being alone. For the first fifteen minutes to half hour, I

Great! All the other leaves are gone. Now I can enjoy some solitude.

often have the urge to make phone calls or to tune in to a radio talk show that has absolutely no relationship to my projects. After I confront the reality that I am alone, I settle into writing and actually enjoy being alone.

When I am alone with all my conveniences—such as the telephone, radio, books, computer, magazines, and various forms of transportation—I may feel just a little lonely for a short period of time. But I remember that highly evolved individuals have experienced long periods of solitary confinement without feeling their lives were terrible or meaningless. Recollecting the true story of Sidney Rittenberg is enough to put my being alone in proper perspective.

Sidney Rittenberg, originally from Charleston, South Carolina, went to China with the military in the mid-1940s and stayed to embrace the cause of the communist revolution. Although Rittenberg lived alongside the revolutionaries and was invited into their inner circles of power, he was later accused of being an American spy. First arrested in January 1949 and released six years later, Rittenberg was arrested again in February 1968 and released in 1978. Both times he was exonerated.

> If you are afraid of loneliness, do not marry.
> —Anton Pavlovich Chekhov

Interestingly, Rittenberg spent his two prison terms in solitary confinement and claims that he wasn't lonely. For years, the guards wouldn't even allow Rittenberg to talk to himself; he also wasn't allowed to have a pen and paper to write letters. Rittenberg said that he kept reminding himself he could be in downtown New York, among 10,000 people, and be lonelier than he was in solitary confinement all those years. If Rittenberg can spend eleven years in solitary confinement without any conveniences and come out of it well-balanced, certainly all of us can deal with being alone for at least a few hours a day.

If Sidney Rittenberg could make the choice to be happy in his own company, certainly you can do the same. When you find yourself alone, don't try to escape at the first sign of anxiety or fear. You don't have to feel abandoned or disconnected. Rather than thinking of yourself as being without someone, realize that you are in the company of someone really important—yourself. This is an opportunity to pursue the rewards that only dynamic solitude has to offer.

Being Alone Today Makes for a Happier Tomorrow

It is a good thing, every so often, to separate yourself from people, newspapers, radio, and television for at least a day or two. Even if you don't have to spend much time alone at this stage in your life, it is good practice. If you learn to be alone now, you will be better prepared for solitude in the future when you are forced into it.

Changes occur in our lives that alter the friendships and the social structures we are used to. Retirement from work, moving to another city, or the death of someone close to us can force us to spend more time alone. Handling being alone prepares us for the times when we may not have as many people around.

Living single and learning how to be happy alone early in life can be advantageous for handling loneliness in later years. Vancouver social workers Gloria Levi and Beryl Petty found that never-married individuals handle old age much better than individuals who are on their own after having lost their spouse through death or divorce. Seniors who have lived alone all their lives don't experience much loneliness. Because they have lived alone a long time, these seniors have found ways to attain satisfaction in their lives without a marriage partner.

Often older people, especially men, tend to die within a year or two after losing a spouse, unless they find someone else to marry. Older men tend to be ex-workaholics who relied on their wives for support. With the job long gone, and now the wife, these men have a difficult time coping with life in general. Many older women also have a hard time coping as widows, because they relied on their husbands for managing finances, looking after the home maintenance, and making key decisions.

> Solitude makes us tougher towards ourselves and tenderer towards others: in both ways it improves our character.
>
> —Friedrich Nietzsche

On the other hand, according to Levi and Petty, some married men and women who lose a spouse actually are very excited about being alone, once they get over the sadness and grief. These individuals discover their creativity, which they channel into activities such as writing and painting. These new singles also experience freedom and independence that they didn't have in their marriages, and they enjoy life like never before.

An Artistic Day to Celebrate Aloneness

One way to appreciate solitude is to get in touch with the artist or creator within yourself once a week on a planned Artistic or Creator's Day, or whatever you want to call it. This is a special outing during which you celebrate your imagination and your unique interests. It doesn't matter whether you think you have artistic talent or not. This weekly routine of taking time for yourself will trigger creative talents that you haven't used for some time or didn't know you had.

On this day, once a week, for the next three or four months, you get to be alone to pursue something new that you have always wanted to pursue, or have previously enjoyed doing but have since set aside. It's important that you be alone when you participate in this activity. You don't want to be concerned about criticism from others. This is also a time to enjoy being alone.

If you haven't been using the God-given creative ability you used as a child, rediscovering your creativity will do wonders for fulfillment. Writing is one way to express your creativity. Write a novel or keep a daily journal in which you write your life story. If writing isn't for you, then try woodcarving or restoring an old car.

An artistic pursuit is an activity that speaks directly and profoundly to your creative soul. Your artistic pursuit—whether it's painting pictures, writing poetry, or making pottery—will rekindle a part of you that has been suppressed for years by the structure of a job and the routine of daily life.

> When all is said and done, monotony may after all be the best condition for creation.
>
> —Margaret Sackville

The activity can be something truly artistic, such as painting, sculpturing, or writing. It can also be an activity, such as taking a series of photos, which is considered less artistic by some elitists. Start by listing fifteen artistic activities that you like doing or have always wanted to pursue. Here are a few examples:

- ➤ Write a book.
- ➤ Paint a series of pictures.
- ➤ Critique ten movies.
- ➤ Explore all the interesting sights in your city.
- ➤ Write a number of songs.
- ➤ Photograph all the species of birds in your area.
- ➤ Visit a variety of restaurants to discover the diversity of available meals in your city.
- ➤ Attend and critique symphony, opera, and live theater performances.
- ➤ Learn to play a musical instrument.

From your list, choose one interest to pursue with focus, purpose, and concentration. You must stick to this activity for at least twelve weeks. For twelve weeks or more, you get to be the creative artist. You will discover why solitude is a great inspiration to most creative artists. Most painters, sculptors, poets, writers, and composers spend most of their time alone because they can be much more creative and get more work done. Moreover, solitude is an opportunity for reflection and renewal.

It's important to celebrate the creative process and not the outcome. For example, if you have chosen to paint a landscape, it doesn't matter if you end up selling it through an art gallery. The process of painting the landscape is important because you are actually painting it, instead of just thinking about it, the way you have for years.

Your Artistic or Creator's Day will help you connect yourself with your creativity, which you have always had, but suppressed. You will discover you are much more creative than you thought you were. Indeed, when you eventually finish your project, you will experience a great deal of satisfaction and self-confidence.

Conversation enriches the understanding, but solitude is the school of genius.

—Edward Gibbon

Upon completion, you must also celebrate the outcome. If you have painted a landscape, so what if some people think it looks like the bottom of Lake Superior? You will have satisfied your deep-seated desire to produce something artistic. Above all, taking the time to do something imaginative by yourself will have helped you to develop more self-confidence in your artistic ability and the courage to spend more time alone.

For Happiness and Longevity, Try Eccentricity

Alan Fairweather of Scotland eats only potatoes, either baked, boiled, or fried. On rare occasions he may break this rule and eat a chocolate bar to add variety to his life. Fairweather not only chooses potatoes as the mainstay in his diet—he makes potatoes his life. He works as a potato inspector for the Agricultural Ministry in Scotland. Needless to say, Fairweather loves potatoes.

You are probably thinking: "Fairweather is an eccentric." You are absolutely right. Whatever else you are thinking, don't feel sorry for Fairweather and others like him. Fairweather is a "true eccentric" according to psychologist Dr. David Weeks and writer Jamie James, co-authors of the book *Eccentrics*.

Eccentrics like potato-lover Fairweather spend a great deal of time alone. They are not unhappy people, however. Surprisingly, Weeks and James found that eccentrics are much happier than the rest of the population. Moreover, they are healthier and tend to live much longer.

Contrary to popular belief that people like Fairweather are crazy, Weeks and James concluded that eccentrics are much more intelligent than the general population. True eccentrics are nonconforming, highly creative, curious, idealistic, intelligent, opinionated, and obsessed with some hobby. Weeks and James studied over 900 eccentrics and found that the majority of these men and women live alone because others find them too peculiar to live with. Nonetheless, spending time alone is not a problem for true eccentrics; they thrive on it.

Eccentrics like Fairweather give themselves the freedom to be themselves, a luxury that most people in society haven't learned how to exploit. Eccentrics are free to pursue hobbies and lifestyles that are their passions. Freed from the need to conform, eccentrics aren't bothered by what others think of them.

> Knowing others is wisdom.
> Knowing yourself is
> Enlightenment.
>
> —Lao-tzu

Indeed, by Abraham Maslow's standards, eccentrics have many of the same traits as self-actualized people. Their most important traits—high self-esteem, self-confidence, and a sense of freedom—help them achieve happiness and longevity.

So, for happiness and longevity, try eccentricity. Your self-development and movement toward self-actualization will be wondrous, mysterious, and fascinating. Especially when you start spending substantial time alone, you will find a spiritual side to leisure, which will help you to reflect, to meditate, and to grow.

Above all, don't just enjoy solitude; seek it. Love yourself while getting to know yourself better. Within yourself is the paradise you have been looking for. Here you will find all the happiness you will ever need.

CHAPTER 11

Financial Independence on Less than Twenty Dollars a Day

Put Money in Its Place

Mere wealth can't bring us happiness;
Mere wealth can't make us glad;
But we'll always take a chance, I guess,
At being rich, and sad.
—C. C. Colton

This chapter is about money and the role it plays, not only in our enjoyment of leisure time, but also in our enjoyment of life as a whole. Money plays a role in our happiness, but not as big a role as the majority in our society believes.

There are two sides to money—the good and the bad. "The universal regard for money is the one hopeful fact in our civilization," declared George Bernard Shaw. "Money is the most important thing in the world. It represents health, strength, honor, generosity, and beauty. . . . Not the least of its virtues is that it destroys basic people as certainly as it fortifies and dignifies noble people."

When and where money is involved, common sense often flies out the window. Psychologists say that most of us have more hang-ups about money than we do about sex. Considering all the problems we have with money, it would be better if we could do away with money.

> Too many people are thinking of security instead of opportunity. They seem more afraid of life than death.
> —James F. Byrnes

Alas, we all have to play the money game to some extent. Food, housing, education, transportation, health care, and clothing all require money. It follows that most of us have to expend time, energy, and effort to make a living. This interferes with our enjoyment of the many enjoyable things that life has to offer.

In the western world, money shouldn't be the big problem most people make it out to be. The money game is actually quite easy to play if you know the secret that was passed on to me some time ago. The secret is about two powerful ways of handling money. If you don't know the secret, I will share it with you later in this chapter.

Individuals who are able to satisfy their basic needs in life can alleviate their financial problems by putting the concept of money in its

> My riches consist not in the extent of my possessions but in the fewness of my wants.
> —J. Brotherton

place. Our socioeconomic problems have more to do with values and expectations than with problems with the economy. Most of us can already meet our genuine material needs. We don't have the time to enjoy what we have, and we want more. To be sure, if we presently don't have time to enjoy what we already have, we will have difficulty in finding the time to enjoy more things. Yet we constantly yearn for the new that we don't have.

The following letter was sent to me by Lisa Mallet (her name has been changed due to the personal aspects of the letter). The last part of the letter relates to money and how it can affect people.

Dear Mr. Zelinski,

I just finished reading your book *The Joy of Not Working*. It was the most helpful item I've read in a long time. I stumbled on your book by accident. My husband and I were listening to "Cross Country Checkup" on CBC radio. The topic was "Are you working too hard?"

Well, I haven't been working for two years. Your book helped me deal with some of the issues and emotions of being unemployed. I was feeling guilty about quitting my last job. But, looking at the situation now, where I worked was the office from hell that you described in your book. Plus, I was getting migraine headaches twice a week. And over the last two years, this particular company has laid off everyone I worked with. Yet, I was feeling guilty because I quit. And I was worried that I may never find work again.

> Few rich men own their property. Their property owns them.
>
> —Robert G. Ingersoll

I don't know what the future will bring, but I certainly have changed my attitude toward work. I'm not sure, just yet, what I will do to generate an income, but I certainly am enjoying my leisure time. And when people want to know what I'm doing, I tell them I'm enjoying the moment, rather than doing nothing. My husband and I are swimming every day, plus I took a pottery class (using a wheel)—it was great fun, and I plan on doing more—a great hobby.

The kicker is, I really don't have to work. I am the beneficiary of a trust fund. It doesn't generate a whole lot of income, but it certainly pays the rent and buys the groceries. My husband is retired and collecting a pension. I have always had a fear of not having enough money for retirement. But, if I'm careful, I can certainly make it. Both my husband and I have lowered our cost of living and are living within our means. And it beats working in an awful environment. I have also seen what a lot of money can do to people. There is a lot of money floating around in my family, and all of them, except my mother, are very manipulative, back-stabbing people.

Thanks again for the book. It certainly helped me and opened my eyes to a lot of the baggage I was carrying around. Take care.

Sincerely,

Lisa Mallet

Sadly, some people who have excessive designs on bettering their financial position allow themselves to be manipulated, humiliated, and degraded in their pursuit of money. Moreover, unrealistic expectations for what money can do for them lead them to experience the negative emotions of envy, deprivation, dejection, and disillusionment. Still worse, the pursuit of wealth eventually costs many people their lives. They forget how to relax, how to laugh, and how to enjoy themselves—even if they do acquire wealth.

> If I keep my good character, I shall be rich enough.
>
> —Platonicus

Our chase after money and material goods is a misdirected effort to make up for the spiritual and emotional fulfillment that is missing in our lives. This chase undermines some of the precious things that we already have, such as our relationships with others. The problem is, we judge ourselves by what we can show for our money. By working harder to accumulate more consumer goods, we end up with less time for the things in life that can make us happy and give us peace of mind.

> I have the greatest of riches:
> That of not desiring them.
> —Eleonora Duse

When Enough Is Never Enough

Not long ago, the *Wall Street Journal* commissioned the Roper Organization to see how U.S. citizens defined the American Dream, and whether the Dream was attainable. At one time, the Dream represented liberty. Now, to most people, the Dream signifies prosperity or being well-off. People feel free only insofar as they have access to lots of money.

Most of us would guess that a much higher percentage of affluent people than of those who weren't well-off would say that they were living the American Dream. Surprisingly, this wasn't so. Only 6 percent of those earning $50,000 or more a year said they had attained the Dream, compared with 5 percent of people earning $15,000 a year or less. Those with incomes of $15,000 a year or less felt that the American Dream could be attained with a median income of $50,000 a year, while those with incomes of $50,000 or more felt that it would take at least $100,000.

> To be handed a lot of money is to be handed a glass sword, blade first. Best handle it very carefully, sir, very slowly while you puzzle what it's for.
> —Richard Bach

Contrary to popular belief, economic growth won't bring more happiness to most middle-class North Americans. Most financial problems of the middle-class are really psychological problems in disguise. The well-being of North Americans is suffering both emotionally and physically because they lack rich human relations and don't take time to enjoy constructive leisure activities.

In Canada and the United States, the poverty line is now drawn at a level that would be considered middle-class or upper-class in many Third World countries. At one time, owning one black-and-white TV set was a luxury for the North American middle class. Then, a color set was a luxury. Now, a color set is considered a necessity; indeed, practically all families below the poverty line own one. If you own two color sets today, it's no big deal, considering that over 50 percent of North American households own two or more.

Americans reported the highest level of satisfaction with their lives in 1955. Ever! The level of satisfaction today is significantly lower, despite the fact that the number of American households that own dishwashers has gone up sevenfold and the percentage of households that own two or more cars has tripled. Today, the average North American owns and consumes more than twice as much as the average North American did in the 1950s. Nevertheless, the average North American today probably complains at least twice as much as the average North American did in the 1950s.

It follows that the problem is greed. Indeed, many people want to have it all: a lot of money, a mansion in a trendy area, two or three cars, and increasingly exotic vacations in the Caribbean. While we are at it, let's not forget a vacation home that has three times as many bathrooms as needed, the latest computer with 450 horsepower and backup lights, and new designer clothing for the most insignificant of occasions. This have-it-all mentality has led to a lower degree of satisfaction, even though people today have more than people of any other generation.

The have-it-all mentality is a powerful and insidious force in western society today. Advertisers have convinced many people that not only are they entitled to aspire to every imaginable luxury, but they deserve it as well. Most people's expecta- *The only thing wealth does for* tions are so high, in fact, that even God would *some people is to make them* have a hard time providing them with everything *worry about losing it.* they would like.

—*Antoine de Rivarol*

Ultimately, the have-it-all mentality won't bring more happiness and satisfaction. How can it? In the quest to have it all, people work far too much to enjoy the things that they do acquire. Sadly, they never stop to figure out that one of the greatest time wasters—and life wasters—is their insatiable desire.

Unfortunately, we have allowed ourselves to be programmed to believe that the best material comforts and long-term financial security are necessary for happiness. In western societies, most of us are protected from extreme poverty, hunger, disease, and natural catastrophes to a degree that people in previous generations couldn't have imagined. Moreover, most people in Third World countries would be happy to have a tenth of what we have. Yet we complain about how horrible things are if the economy goes into a slight downturn and a few *Poor and content is* of us are temporarily unemployed. *rich and rich enough.*

—*William Shakespeare*

Conspicuous consumption isn't something that comes naturally to human beings. The drive for constantly increasing ownership of material goods is programmed behavior that showed up with capitalism, the industrial revolution, and the work ethic.

Television also plays a role here. Many of the messages television commercials bombard us with can be detrimental to our well-being. We are led to believe that we will be losers or failures if we don't acquire the latest gadgets and trinkets. We are told what sort of people we should be, how we should dress, which gadgets we should own, the type of car we should drive, and the size of house we should live in. Commercials promise us that everything—including self-esteem, happiness, and power—will be ours if we just purchase their products. As a matter of course, some of us feel inadequate because we can't live up to these images of success.

All told, we would be better off if we didn't see these advertisements. Underarms that smell like wild roses and automatic climate controls in automobiles certainly aren't the keys to happiness. Moreover, advertisements keep us in constant want. The next purchase is supposed to make us happy, but how could it? After all, we wouldn't purchase anything else if we had attained the happiness we are supposed to experience with the first one. Satisfaction from any purchase is always short-lived, if experienced at all. So we yearn for more. Enough is never enough.

The American writer Maurice Sendak once remarked that there must be more to life than having it all. Indeed, Sendak was right. If more of us contemplated how much is enough in our lives, a lot more people in this world would be happy and satisfied. In our quest to have it all, we end up experiencing less peace, happiness, and satisfaction than we would if we learned how to be satisfied with much less.

Just because 20 percent of us in North America have 80 percent of the money doesn't mean the rest of you have to be so grumpy about it.

How More Money Can Add to Our Problems

A few years ago the bishop of Liverpool called for the government of England to review the concept of lotteries. The bishop suggested that, if nothing else, the prizes should be smaller. The bishop's request was made after a man in Liverpool committed suicide when he thought he had missed out on a lottery win worth the equivalent of about US $13 million.

Sadly, Timothy O'Brien, a fifty-one-year-old father of two children, shot himself after he failed to renew his weekly bet in a lottery on which he had bet the same numbers for over a year. O'Brien figured he had missed out on the good life after these same numbers were apparently drawn the week he missed placing his bet.

To be without some of the things you want is an indispensable part of happiness.
—Bertrand Russell

Timothy O'Brien didn't realize that his life might not have changed for the better had he won. Many lottery winners wind up worse off after the big win because of the unexpected problems that accompany having a great deal of money. And the big win certainly wouldn't have made O'Brien happy in light of his being the type of individual to commit suicide because of what might have been. If anything, O'Brien would likely have had many more problems had he won. Ironically, at O'Brien's inquest it was discovered that he actually would have won only about US$100 had he bought a ticket with his regular numbers.

Because of the false expectations that we place on being rich, the prospect of acquiring a great deal of money has disoriented many people like Timothy O'Brien. People often make declarations like these:

➤ If I had a lot of money, then I would be happy.
➤ If I had a lot of money, then I could enjoy my leisure time.
➤ If I had a lot of money, then I would feel good about myself.
➤ If I had a lot of money, more people would like me, and then I could find a marriage partner.

If you believe any of the above, you put way too much trust in money. To you, having a lot of money means security. If you believe money is synonymous with security, however, you won't be happy with the modest amount of money that many genuinely secure people are content with. With a modest amount, you will be afraid that you don't have enough to take care of yourself in the future. If you acquire a lot of money, you will be afraid of losing it. Ultimately, money won't make you feel secure or happy.

Whether he admits it or not, a man has been brought up to look at money as a sign of his virility, a symbol of his power, a bigger phallic symbol than a Porsche.
—Victoria Billings

Various studies conducted by researcher Ed Diener, a University of Illinois psychologist, confirm that more money than is needed for basic necessities can't buy happiness or solve all the personal problems people think money can solve. "As you start meeting basic needs, increases in income become less and less important," says Diener.

People who receive a pay increase may be happier for a short time, but once they get used to the increase, they set their sights on more and more money so they can fulfill their new expectations. They want bigger houses, fancier cars, and more exotic vacations. These don't provide long-term happiness.

Surprisingly, Diener found that most people actually wind up with more problems when they acquire more money than they need for basic needs and desires. Here are some of them:

➤ Relationships with friends and acquaintances suffer.

➤ Individuals may be alienated from their peer group.

➤ Monitoring finances becomes more troublesome and time-consuming.

➤ Looking after possessions requires more time and energy.

➤ Fear of theft of property and money becomes more acute.

➤ The fear of losing money in investments increases.

➤ Life becomes more complicated in general.

Many affluent individuals have all the material comforts they desire, yet lead lives of quiet desperation. Some people are wealthy in material goods, but poor in spirit. Other rich people don't know how to spend and enjoy their money. Still others don't know how to share their resources with others who are less fortunate.

A million dollars doesn't always bring happiness. A man with ten million dollars is no happier than a man with nine million dollars.

—Unknown wise person

Ed Diener's conclusions from his many years of research into the relationship between money and happiness shouldn't be a big surprise to us. After all, many wise people over the ages have warned us that money won't solve our problems or bring us happiness. Yet most of us ignore this wisdom and strive for material wealth regardless of the required sacrifices. Virtually everyone will agree at some level that money doesn't buy happiness, but deep down they haven't accepted it. Regardless of how old you are, you will show wisdom well beyond your age when you truly accept that money can't buy contentment and peace of mind.

When It Comes to Security, Your Creativity Beats Money Ten Times Out of Ten

To working and nonworking people alike, money is a necessary commodity for survival. Money is also a means for enhancing the ways in which they enjoy leisure time. Unfortunately, many people look at money as an end rather than a means, which leads to much disappointment and dissatisfaction.

Exercise 11-1. How Secure Are You?

Honestly answer this question: how much money would it take before you could say that you are secure?

We have been conditioned to believe that we should be accumulating material wealth as security for our retirement and for the unexpected events in our lives. Accountants, stockbrokers, financial planners, bankers, and retirement consultants have convinced most of us that building an impressive portfolio of real estate, stocks, bonds, and T-bills will make us secure. Yet you will be severely disappointed if you look to money for true security. Just as you can't buy love and friends and family, you can't buy true security.

I like money for its intrinsic value, but I always make such a pig of myself with it.

Security, as traditionally defined, isn't nearly as big a contributor to emotional comfort as most people believe. "No one from the beginning of time has had security," declared Eleanor Roosevelt. What Roosevelt meant is that security based on materialistic and monetary pursuits is tenuous at best. The superrich can be killed in car accidents and terrorist attacks just as easily as the poor. Their health can fail at a much earlier age than that of someone with less money. And most rich people worry about losing their money in the event of a monetary collapse. Weird, isn't it? On one hand we want and strive for security; on the other hand there may not be anything that even closely resembles security.

When a man says money can do anything, that settles it. He doesn't have any.

—Ed Howe

Security based on external possessions is, in fact, one of life's greatest illusions. Paradoxically, people pursuing security are among the most insecure, and people who least care about security are the most secure. Emotionally insecure people seek to offset their unpleasant feelings by accumulating great amounts of money as security against attacks on their egos. Clearly, people striving for security are by their very nature insecure. They depend on external things—such as money, spouses, houses, cars, and prestige—for security. If they lose these things, they lose themselves, because they lose their identities.

> Your real security is yourself. You know you can do it, and they can't ever take that away from you.
>
> —Mae West

To some, security is a steady job with normal work hours, unambiguous activities, strictly defined responsibility, and a foreseeable future. These people need a steady paycheck and will settle for a regular income with modest increases in pay. They don't realize that holding on to a job does not bring true security. Jobs in modern times aren't as secure as they were just a few years ago. A job may be security for paying bills today, but when security-minded people lose their jobs, they lose their security.

It's no wonder that Tennessee Williams declared, "Security is a kind of death." The security-minded individual demonstrates, better than anyone else, that the preoccupation with security is incompatible with living a relaxed and prosperous life. Paradoxically, in order to feel more secure in this ever-changing world, people must become less concerned with security, as defined in the modern-day sense.

You may be surprised to learn that the present-day concept of security is far different from the original meaning of the word. If anyone in this world has any security, as originally defined, that security isn't based on money and material possessions. The word "security" comes from the Latin word *securus*, which means "without care." In this regard, true security is an internal state of being, not determined by how much money an individual is able to acquire.

Clearly, to be obsessed with security, as we define it today, is to avoid living in the truest sense. You can't have the space for prosperity and success when you are obsessed with security. It is not possible to obtain unwavering security—physical, emotional, or economic—by having money. Keep in mind that security, like success, can be defined in many ways. If you focus less on how much your financial assets are worth, and more on what a creative and well-balanced individual you can be, security will take on a new meaning.

"Your security is not your job, or your bank account, or your investments, or your spouse or your parents," writes metaphysical author Louise Hays. "Your security is your ability to connect with the cosmic power that creates all things." When it comes to security, your creativity beats money ten times out of ten. Your best security is your self-confidence to handle or overcome all the normal problems and unexpected situations that occur in everyday life. In short, knowing that you have the creative ability to always earn a living, and live happily when you don't have a job, is your best security.

If Money Makes People Happy, Then Why ...?

Although most people don't know what exactly they want from life, they are absolutely sure that money in large amounts will provide it for them. But most people don't tell the truth about money. Money is more often misused and abused than used intelligently. People make many assumptions about money, most of which are absurd. One such assumption is that money will guarantee their happiness.

Let's put money and its relationship to happiness in proper perspective. Money is an important element for our survival, but how much money we need to be happy is another matter altogether. Hotshot motivational speakers tell seminar participants that millionaires are winners. This implies that the rest of us are losers. Yet most people of modest means are winners compared to millionaires who make the news because of their unethical and corrupt behavior. How happy can these millionaires be if they have to resort to unethical or corrupt behavior when they are already richer than 99.9 percent of humanity?

Although money represents power, status, and safety in our society, there is nothing in its inherent nature to make us happy. To give yourself a sense of the inherent nature of money, try the following exercise:

Exercise 11-2. Will Money Love You?

Take out the money you have on you or around you at this time. Touch it and feel its warmth. Notice that it is fairly cold. It won't keep you warm at night. Talk to your money and see what happens. It won't respond. And no matter how much you love it, money won't love you in return.

> Having lots of money doesn't change anything. It just amplifies it. Jerks become bigger jerks, and nice guys become nicer.
>
> —Ben Narasin

Clearly, making money for money's sake is not a purpose worthy of great people. The degree to which money can enhance our lives depends more on how we intelligently use the money we have than on how much we have. Michael Phillips, a former bank vice-president, thinks there are too many people whose identities are tied to money. In his book *The Seven Laws of Money*, Phillips discusses seven interesting money concepts:

> ➤ Money creates and maintains its own rules.
> ➤ Money will appear when you are doing the right thing in your life.
> ➤ Money is a dream—in fact, it can be a fantasy as deceptive as the Pied Piper.
> ➤ Money often is a nightmare.
> ➤ You can never truly give money away as a gift.
> ➤ You can never truly receive money as a gift.
> ➤ There are many fascinating worlds (cultures) without money.

Here are six more little-known money concepts that you should pay heed to:

> ➤ If money becomes your primary focus in life, then money is all that you will get.
> ➤ The person with no money may be poor, however, not as poor as the person who has nothing but money.
> ➤ Abundance isn't a matter of acquiring how much money you desire; it's a matter of being happy with how much you presently have.
> ➤ It's better to be out of money than out of new creative ideas on how to make money.
> ➤ Spending a lot of money will get you trapped into thinking you are having a good time when all you are doing is spending a lot of money.
> ➤ Above all, the value of money lies in the creative and spiritual uses to which it can be put and not in how many possessions it can buy.

To be sure, there are many uses for money. No one can challenge the important roles money plays in society and business. If we pay attention, however, there is much evidence that money is not synonymous with happiness.

I wonder: If money makes people happy, then . . .

> ➤ Why did one study by University of Illinois psychologist Ed Diener show that one third of the wealthiest Americans are actually not as happy as the average American?
> ➤ Why did a recent survey indicate that a higher percentage of the people making over $75,000 a year are dissatisfied

with their salaries than are people making less than $75,000 a year?

➤ Why did Ivan Boesky, who illegally accumulated over $100 million through insider trading on Wall Street, not stop his illegal actions after accumulating $2 million or $5 million, but instead continue accumulating more millions until he got caught?

➤ Why did members of a family I know (even though their financial net worth is in the top 1 percent for North American families) tell me how much happier they would be if they were to win a major lottery?

➤ Why did a group of major lottery winners in New York form a self-help group to deal with post-lottery depression syndrome—a case of serious depression they had never experienced before winning their large sums of money?

➤ Why do so many well-paid baseball, football, and hockey players have drug and alcohol problems?

➤ Why do doctors, one of the wealthiest groups of professionals, have one of the highest divorce, suicide, and alcoholism rates of all professionals?

➤ Why do the poor give more to charities than the rich?

➤ Why do people who achieve success early in life have shorter life spans than those who achieve greatness in their golden years?

➤ Why do so many rich people get in trouble with the law?

➤ Why do so many wealthy people go to see psychiatrists and therapists?

Benjamin Franklin expressed as well as anyone could the folly of trying to achieve happiness through money. "Money never made a man happy yet nor will it," he observed. "There is nothing in its nature to produce happiness. The more a man has, the more he wants. Instead of its filling a vacuum, it makes one."

> Let us all be happy and live within our means, even if we have to borrow to do it.
> —Artemus Ward

Exercise 11-3. Which Is Easier to Come By?

Most people aspire to being rich and happy. On that note, which is easier to acquire: a lot of money or happiness? (The answer is at the end of this chapter, on page 188.)

Here is my theory on how much happier and more emotionally "well-off" we will be with substantially more money. After we have satisfied our basic needs, money will make us neither happy nor unhappy. If we are happy and handle problems well when we are making $25,000 a year, then we will be happy and handle problems well when we have more money. On the other hand, if we are unhappy, are neurotic, and don't handle problems well on $25,000 a year, we will behave much the same even if we win a $10 million lottery. We will still be neurotics who can't handle problems—living with more comfort and style, and still unhappy. Indeed, we may even be less happy, because we will no longer be able to attribute our unhappiness to lack of enough money.

Financial Independence on $6,000 a Year

Achieving true financial independence may be easier than you think. It may come as a surprise to you that it's possible to achieve financial independence without having to increase your income or financial assets. Moreover, it's even possible to achieve financial independence by reducing your income and financial assets. The key to achieving financial independence is to first properly define what it is, and then do whatever it takes to attain it.

> Taking it all in, I find it is more trouble to watch after money than to get it.
> —Michel de Montaigne

Exercise 11-4. True Financial Independence

Which item from the list below is essential in order for you to achieve financial independence?

- ➤ Winning a million-dollar lottery
- ➤ Having a good company pension complemented by a government pension
- ➤ Having inherited a bundle from wealthy relatives
- ➤ Being married to a multimillionaire
- ➤ Making the right investments

Contrary to popular belief, none of the above factors can guarantee financial independence. The late Joseph Dominguez, co-author of the financial bestseller *Your Money or Your Life*, became financially independent at the age of twenty-nine. Dominguez felt that true financial independence could be achieved at an early age by many more

Americans. True financial independence shouldn't be confused with being a millionaire, however.

Before he retired, Dominguez was a stockbroker on Wall Street. He was appalled to see many people living at high socioecomomic levels who were unhappy. Eventually Dominquez decided that he didn't want to work in this environment, so he designed a personal financial program based on a simplified lifestyle. He was able to save a modest amount of funds that he invested in U.S. Treasury bonds. After Dominguez retired, his lifestyle was comfortable, but only cost $6,000 a year. Because his needs were few, he was able to donate all the money he made from his public seminars and his bestselling book to nonprofit organizations.

My friend Mij Relge, first mentioned in chapter 9, is not only constantly mastering the moment, he's also financially independent on an income of only $500 a month—an income many people consider well below the poverty line. Jim is financially independent because he earns $500 a month and spends less than $500 a month.

> Money doesn't buy happiness, but it pays for the illusion that it does.
>
> —Unknown wise person

Financial independence requires nothing more than having more money come in than goes out. If you are making $500 a month and spending $499, you are financially independent. On the other hand, if you are earning $200,000 a year and spending $250,000, you are not financially independent. In the same vein, if you win a million-dollar lottery, and you blow the proceeds in a year or two, you will no longer be financially independent.

No doubt financial independence may help you sleep better, as it has done for my friend Mij. Financial independence, however, does not depend only on how much you earn or how much you have in the bank. The choices you make in all areas of your life—such as where you choose to live—will determine whether you achieve financial independence. Mij lives in an older Airstream trailer parked on a friend's piece of land. And he is one of the most well-balanced and happiest individuals that I know. All of his friends—two of whom are millionaires— share my sentiments about Mij.

The extent to which you choose well in all areas of your life will determine whether you attain financial independence. If you are having trouble making ends meet and not saving any money from your regular income, I suggest that you read *Your Money or Your Life* by Joseph Dominguez and Vicki Robin. Thousands of readers have achieved financial independence by following their advice. Above all, you must have less money go out than comes in. Your expectations for the good life, the influences of your spouse and children, your self-esteem, any envy you feel, and your need for perfection will all play a role in how much money you spend and whether you can attain financial independence on the money you earn.

It's Never Too Early to Retire

Results from a recent survey indicated that, in order of importance, the biggest concerns for people just before retirement were finances, health, and having a spouse or friends to share retirement. Interestingly, shortly after these people retired, health was considered the top priority, and finances moved to third place. Apparently these retirees' concept of financial independence changed once they retired. Although their expected income remained the same, they realized that they could maintain financial independence, simply because they could get by with much less than they first imagined.

Retirement can be a great joy if you can figure out how to spend time without spending money.

—Unknown wise person

Indeed, more people could retire early if they put financial independence into proper perspective. Most financial advisors paint a picture of a penniless and destitute retirement for those with less than a million or two in their retirement portfolios. Unfortunately, they emphasize higher earnings instead of lower spending as the key to having sufficient money to retire.

In his letter to me, Dennis Anstett of Calgary, Alberta, shared how he and his wife were able to retire early.

> Dear Sir:
>
> After just reading *The Joy of Not Working*, I felt compelled to drop you a line. Reading and highlighting all the common sense were wonderful. Congratulations. The material will help many people get past all the hype that more is better.
>
> My in-laws "retired" in their mid-forties. That was twenty years ago. They were ahead of their time. They now say they have twenty years' seniority, in the leisure business. Only government and big business frown on this mentality. Tough.
>
> I lost my nineteen-year career due to downsizing. It was the worst of times that turned into the best of times. After the transition, which took about a year, my wife and I decided to say good-bye forever to the corporate world. Never again would some entity ever take control of our lives and happiness.

We just decided we had enough "stuff." And we also had enough of the rat (human) race. We now enjoy a simple, relaxed lifestyle on about $30,000 a year. There is no life like it.

No one ever said you have to wait until sixty-five to use your Registered Retirement Savings Plan and "retire." My wife and family have been saying for some time that we're not going to be the richest people in the cemetery. We are, however, very rich. We have time—I call it the most expensive commodity of them all. It's comforting to know that many other people feel and think the same way. Mainstream society has got it all wrong.

Sincerely,

Dennis Anstett

Most North Americans have been conditioned to believe leisure is something that only money can provide. Much of what Madison Avenue wants us to do in our spare time is based on conspicuous consumption; it requires that we own a financial gravy train that doesn't lose any locomotion. Creating more spare time is encouraged only for the purpose of buying more "stuff."

> Money is what you'd get on beautifully without if only other people weren't so crazy about it.
> —Margaret Case Harriman

Yet the things that matter most don't require much money. In fact, some of the best things in life are free! Leisure goals don't have to be hard on the pocketbook or on the environment. Keep in mind that the most environmentally friendly activities are ones that cost us the least money. Watching sunsets, going for walks, meditating, having interesting conversations, wading through streams, and exercising in the park are activities that cost us virtually nothing and help preserve the environment. These inexpensive activities are also enjoyable enough to suit royalty.

Enjoyable leisure is not what advertisers are trying to sell us. Vacations, for example, don't require much money. You don't have to get away to have a get-away vacation. Before venturing across the world in search of greener grass, check out the wonder of the world in your own backyard. Sometimes the grass is greener on our side of the fence. I am not saying you shouldn't see the world. What I am saying is that it isn't necessary to travel to exotic locales to enjoy yourself.

> Jesus, please teach me to appreciate what I have before time forces me to appreciate what I had.
> —Susan L. Lenzkes

If you are looking forward to retirement, you must determine what sort of lifestyle will make you happy and how much money you will need to support it. You must then take steps to ensure that you will have enough money to support this lifestyle. Of course, the less lavish the lifestyle, the easier it is to attain financial independence and retire at an early age.

Jason Hanson of Saskatoon, Saskatchewan, wrote to me about how *The Joy of Not Working* influenced him to achieve financial independence and retire early by the age of—get this—twenty-seven. Here is how he did it:

Hi, Ernie,

Well, it's taken me almost ten years to write you. How's that for mastering the moment?

To be honest, I feel a little silly for having waited/procrastinated this long to let you know what an incredible influence you and *The Joy of Not Working* have been on my life. It inspired me to take many of the paths I've taken in my life, and while it hasn't always been easy, I've never regretted a single one. Since I believe in giving credit when it is due, I should have thanked you a long time ago.

When I got your book, I was already looking for a way out of the rat race, and I was only twenty years old! I had been a home-schooler and had therefore developed an early and serious taste for freedom, freedom from schedules, deadlines, and all work-load pressures in general.

Unfortunately, as soon as I entered the workforce, I could feel that freedom inexorably sliding away from me (and at Domino's Pizza, no less!). Then along came *The Joy of Not Working*. It made me see the world in a new light. Fools, they all were, those little worker drones, scuttling about like ants serving their queen. But I could, no, would escape with your book as my guide.

To make a long story fit on this page, I didn't escape until April of '98. I had managed to buy a house and rent out the basement, as well as save some money, so I was close to the life of Riley and his $6,000 a year. What really cinched it, though, was the passing away of my father. He left some life insurance money, and I decided then that it was time to escape the system that I felt had certainly led him to an early demise.

Today, I am to my friends an Earthwalker. (In the movie *Pulp Fiction*, an Earthwalker is one who walks the earth helping people, or a bum.) I have managed to cast off the notions of a career, of indebtedness to material accumulation, and of "working for the man." I spend my time reading, thinking, and playing—and have dreams of someday becoming a good enough writer to actually finish a novel. I volunteer for environmental groups, trying to make the world a better place, design graphics on my computer, spend time with friends, cycle, jog, and listen to music.

And so on, and so on. In short, I am, in my own judgment, really living. And I just wanted to thank you for helping me to get to this point.

Cheers,

Jason

Retirement planners tell us that we need large portfolios to be happy, but they should pay more attention to genuine, interesting individuals such as Jason Hanson and Dennis Anstett and his wife. These experts would learn a lot about what truly contributes to a happy retirement. A success-ful retirement encompasses not only adequate financial resources, but also all other aspects of life—purpose, family, friends, interesting leisure activities, creative pursuits, and mental, physical, and spiritual health.

> When one has had to work so hard to get money, why should he impose on himself the hardship of trying to save it?
> —Don Herold

Of course, if you are a shallow person who believes that you need the latest SUV, a large house, and the latest fashions to overcome low self-esteem and be happy, you will require a great deal of money for your retirement years. Just be clear, however, that you won't attain true hap-piness, or peace of mind, this way—just as you haven't all your working years. You will continue to fool yourself on the surface, knowing deep down that there is an emotional and spiritual void within you that can never be filled, regardless of how much money you acquire.

All things considered, it's up to you, and not anyone else, to decide when you are financially ready to retire. In the event that you don't like working, and would like to retire as early as pos-sible, heed the words of Robert Benchley, who put it much more eloquently than I ever could: "The thing to do is to make so much money that you don't have to work after the age of twenty-seven. In case this is

> You'd be surprised how much it costs to look this cheap.
> —Dolly Parton

impractical, stop working at the earliest moment, even if it is a quarter past eleven in the morning of the day when you find you have enough money."

If You Believe That Happiness Can Be Bought, Why Don't You Try Selling Some of Yours?

Obviously, it's a lot easier to avoid trouble than to get out of trouble. Yet many of us go to great extremes to invite trouble into our lives. Mishandling money is one of our favorite ways to get ourselves into deep water. We seem to easily forget that each spending choice we make determines how much we are enhancing our present-day prosperity, and the amount of wealth we will have attained in the future.

Money, unfortunately, brings out the eccentricity, and even the insanity, of which each and every one of us is capable. A quirk or peculiarity in our spending habits here and there is normal; harboring several of them, however, can have serious consequences for our personal and financial well-being.

Ninety percent of my money I intend to spend on wild women, booze, and good times and the other ten percent I will spend foolishly.

—Tug McGraw

Perhaps your spending habits make your respectable income no match for your expenses. Indeed, you may not even know your true ability and capacity to spend money. Your philosophy is that life is too short to waste time on insignificant things such as finding a better deal or paying off your credit cards. Your spending feats still haven't gotten you into the *Guinness Book of World Records*, but only because you haven't sent in your name and credit-card statements.

A devil-may-care approach to life in general is somewhat healthy, but taking the same approach to your money will eventually get you into serious trouble. Clearly, living with the worry of losing your job, and not having any funds to cover the lease on your flashy new car, your $2,000 mortgage payment, and your fitness club membership, isn't the relaxed way to prosperity and financial independence. How can you be relaxed when you are in debt up to your ears? Sooner or later, you will have to come to grips with reality and realize that you can't spend yourself to self-respect, happiness, and prosperity.

I owe, I owe, and off to work I go.

—Unknown wise person

It's time to reveal the second of those two powerful, equally effective secrets to handling money. The first, which I've already discussed, is to spend less than you earn. If you have tried this and it hasn't worked, the second one is definitely for you. The second powerful way is to earn more than you spend. That's all there is to the money game. Follow only one of these powerful principles, and you have handled money successfully.

If you never have enough money, regardless of how much you make, you are probably squandering money on things that you don't need. Finding out why you are a spendthrift living on the edge is important. You must spend some time learning how to handle money. It's actually quite easy once you realize that cutting back on your lifestyle and expenses won't leave you feeling deprived. You will be amazed by how little you actually need. If you need less money in your life, you won't have to work as much and as hard for it, and you can still experience a full, relaxed, satisfying, and happy life.

Miguel de Cervantes advised, "Make it thy business to know thyself, which is the most difficult lesson in the world." The more you know and accept yourself, the less you have to try to impress others. Knowing yourself and what drives you to spend your money—whether it's for cars, homes, fashions, or cool stuff—is essential for having total control of your finances. It can be the difference between having a nice nest egg for retirement and not having anything.

On the other extreme from squanderers who misspend are the misers who can't spend. Misers can't enjoy their money regardless of how much they acquire. If you are one of these people, you are suffering from a disease. The cure is to realize that there is only one purpose for money—to spend it—and start spending.

> Having money is rather like being a blond. It is more fun but not vital.
> —Mary Quant

What is the point of having much more money than you need if you haven't learned how to enjoy it? Celebrating your prosperity is essential for getting fulfillment from your money. If you have never been to a restaurant that doesn't have self-service trays, now is the time to dream up some creative and fun ways to spend more money. If you can't come up with any, give me a call. I'll have no problem helping you spend your excess cash. No amount will be too big for me!

Money can be a vehicle for enjoying life to the fullest, provided you take the time and effort to get a good grasp of what money can and can't do for you. Riches will enhance your life if you have a healthy attitude toward money; they can poison it if you don't. Put another way, understanding what money can do for you can help you get what you want from life. In the same vein, knowing what money *can't* do for you can save you a lot of disappointment, dissatisfaction, disillusionment, ulcers, and nervous twitching.

Discontent may be robbing you of a really good life. You may already have a good life yet fail to appreciate it. More money will likely not add to your happiness if your basic needs for food, water, shelter, good health, and clothing—along with a few luxuries here and there—are being met. "Now is not the time to think of what you do not have," advised Ernest Hemingway. "Think of what you can do with what there is." Indeed, the way to be happy is to express gratitude for what you have.

> If I had known what it would be like to have it all, I might have been willing to settle for less.
> —Lily Tomlin

Money touches every area of our lives to some degree. The amount of money we have at our disposal can affect the quality of our relationships, friendships, housing, leisure, and health. If we use our imaginations, we can think of an unlimited number of ways in which we can use money to add comfort and pleasure to our lives.

Yet, for all its wondrous potential, money can be terribly disappointing. This directly contradicts a basic axiom that guides nearly all human behavior—the axiom that the more money we have, the happier we will be.

Your mind may be your greatest asset, but remember, it can play tricks on you as well. The most common trick it plays is making you believe that you need all the things that you buy. If you allow it to keep playing that nasty trick, it can cost you your money, your health, your individuality, your self-esteem, and your sanity. Indeed, it can cost you a happy and satisfying life.

> That man is the richest whose pleasures are the cheapest.
> —Henry David Thoreau

It's important that you see wealth as a means to an end instead of a measurement of your worth as an individual.

Working hard just for the sake of making a lot of money is an act of desperation. Ironically, the less you evaluate your self-worth based on money, the more freedom you give yourself to be creative, and the more wealth you are capable of generating in the long term.

Money, in fact, reflects your creative energy. Creatively working at an enjoyable job with a higher purpose will bring you abundance. The more willing you are to risk and follow your inner calling in life, the more money you will attract in the long term. Moreover, you will need less money to be happy because your self-fulfillment will come from pursuing something you enjoy. Earning a lot of money from your work will be a bonus. Although you can do without this bonus, you can also celebrate and enjoy it when it comes.

Above all, never lose sight of your true wealth: the ability to think, creatively and spiritually. It is better to have a million dollars' worth of thinking ability than a million dollars. The million dollars, can be spent or lost easily. Your million dollars' worth of creativity and spirituality is always there when you need it.

One final note: perhaps this chapter didn't sway you away from your strong beliefs that lots of money, more than anything else, can guarantee happiness. Since you believe that happiness can be bought, why don't you try selling some of yours?

Answer to exercise 11-3: Money, it appears, is easier to come by than happiness. This is based on someone's observation that there are no happy neurotics, but there are many rich ones.

CHAPTER 12

The End Has Just Begun

There Is Life after Retirement

A retired man went to a doctor for a general check-up. The doctor told the retiree that everything was fine and that, in fact, he was "in real good shape for a man of ninety-three."

"That's good to know, because I'm getting married in two weeks," said the retiree.

"Getting married! That's wonderful! Who's the lucky bride?" asked the doctor.

The retiree replied, "She's a twenty-seven-year-old bar maid I met at the local pub."

"Only twenty-seven!" The doctor paused before he advised, "Then you will need some Viagra."

The man replied, "No way, I never take drugs of any type. It's against my principles."

The doctor took some more time before he responded with: "You are in good shape, but nevertheless you are ninety-three. May I suggest that you and your wife take in a boarder?"

> Here is a test to find whether your mission on earth is finished: If you're alive, it isn't.
>
> —Richard Bach

"Why a boarder?" asked the retiree.

"Well, you know, at your age," winked the doctor, "you may not be able to do all the things a young woman would like a husband to do around the house. A boarder will be able to help."

The retiree shrugged and said, "I guess you are right," as he walked out of the office.

A year later, the retiree, now ninety-four, came back to the doctor for another checkup. "How's married life?" asked the doctor.

"Amazing, it couldn't be better. I should have remarried years ago."

"How's your wife?" asked the doctor.

"She's doing fine," announced the retiree, "and she's pregnant."

"Pregnant!" exclaimed the doctor. "I take it that you took in a boarder who has fit in quite well?"

"'Yes, and she's pregnant too," grinned the retiree.

The moral of this story is: there is life after retirement, despite the preconceived notions that many of us—even doctors—have about retirement and how limiting it can be, particularly as people grow older.

When I grow up I want to be a little boy.

—Joseph Heller

Beliefs about retirement and old age can become self-fulfilling prophecies. We are likely to come up with excuses for not pursuing activities that we can, in fact, pursue well into our seventies, eighties, nineties, and beyond. Taking a new approach to life, rather than retreating from it, is the key to enjoying retirement. Regardless of how old we are, we should always seek new opportunities for personal growth, achievement, and satisfaction.

Many people aren't prepared for retirement because they aren't aware of the commitment that is required for getting satisfaction and fulfillment from leisure time. In her letter, Lynn Bolstad of Toronto relates how she was unprepared for the Life of Riley.

Dear Ernie,

After reading *The Joy of Not Working* I feel I can call you Ernie.

Six months ago I accepted an early retirement package (under fifty-five) from the company where I had worked for thirty-seven years. Nothing prepared me for the reactions I experienced after leaving: loss of who I was, fear of the future, and a feeling of helplessness after being structured all those years.

So, I decided to give myself some time to sort out what I would do. I spent seven weeks at the beach just walking, reading, and enjoying life. It was the best medicine. I was always involved with not-for-profit organizations through my job. So I am spending more time with these organizations, and I signed up with a seniors' organization. Lo and behold, I have been asked to do part-time contract work for a nonprofit group (this is scary but fun).

Your book has helped me tremendously in setting some goals for my new life. I will read it again and again, as I am sure there will be times when my confidence slips. I also plan to give copies of the book to friends as gifts.

Well, I'm off to go skating with a friend this afternoon. There is really joy in not working.

Sincerely,

Lynn Bolstad

According to a 2002 survey conducted by AIG SunAmerica, the people most likely to enjoy retirement are those who have planned for it. This is borne out by the fact that 78 percent of people who prepare for retirement both financially and psychologically view it as "a whole new life" or a "continuation of life as it was."

If you are not presently retired, it's important to spend many preretirement days thinking about what you want to do when you walk out of your workplace for the last time. As seventy-one-year-old Florida retiree Howard Salzmann stated, "If you didn't learn how to live before you reach sixty-five, it's very difficult to teach you how to live afterwards."

Planning for a meaningful life in retirement should start as early as possible. If you are still in the workplace and contemplating retirement, you should be thinking long and hard about what you will do with your time and the challenges you may face when you no longer have the routine, structure, and purpose of working life to rely on.

As part of his research for his book *Breaking the Watch,* Joel Savishinsky followed a group of retirees in Shelby, New York, for about six years. He discovered that retirees must know themselves, have passions in which to indulge, and be prepared for the unexpected. "They realized there was a lot more to retirement than putting together a portfolio," states Savishinsky. "It was more about putting together a life."

Work is what you do so that some time you won't have to do it anymore.

—Alfred Polgar

When happy and successful retirees are asked what advice they would offer to a person just entering retirement, most will respond with a variation of: spend as much—or considerably more—time thinking about how you will utilize your days and months as you do contemplating your finances. As one retiree told a newspaper reporter, "Retirement could well represent 25 percent or more of your whole life. Why leave it to chance?"

Although virtually everyone needs a modest amount of money for essentials and a few luxuries from time to time, people who spend all their time and energy on building a huge nest egg often forget how to live happily during their working lives. They compromise their health, they neglect their friends, and they don't develop interests outside of work. Once they retire, they realize that no amount of money can buy excellent health, great friends, or the ability to enjoy leisure activities. Sadly, they wind up even less happy in retirement than they were in their working lives.

> The best time to start thinking about your retirement is before your boss does.
>
> —Unknown wise person

We all know that we have to prepare financially. But we have to prepare psychologically and socially as well. Ironically, too much emphasis on saving for retirement can make you forget what it takes to enjoy retirement. In my view, living according to the following principles will best prepare you for retirement.

- ➤ Establish a good work/life balance many years before you retire and zealously maintain it.
- ➤ If you work at a regular job, refrain from working on weekends.
- ➤ Do as much as you can to maintain optimum health while you are working.
- ➤ Be open to learning new things at work and in your personal life.
- ➤ Read Barbara Sher's *It's Only Too Late If You Don't Start Now: How to Create Your Second Life at Any Age.*
- ➤ Have a major life purpose other than your work.
- ➤ Develop close friendships outside of your workplace.
- ➤ Maintain—that is, don't neglect—your true friendships so that they are still thriving when you retire.
- ➤ Learn how to handle freedom—one good way is to become self-employed for at least a year or two before retirement.
- ➤ Accept that money may buy style and comfort, but it won't buy you happiness.
- ➤ Spend a lot of time alone while learning how to enjoy solitude.
- ➤ Indulge in regular strenuous exercise so that you will be physically fit and able to enjoy retirement activities.
- ➤ Take all your paid vacation time so that you learn how to be more leisurely.
- ➤ Travel a lot—people who don't get to enjoy travel before retirement seldom develop a liking for it after retirement.
- ➤ Don't tie your identity to your job.

➤ Find many ways to connect with the world.

➤ Regularly take a day off work and ensure that you loaf it all away to experience what it's like to be a member of the leisure class.

➤ Take a preretirement course that deals with the personal issues as well as the financial issues.

➤ Above all, don't put off being happy until you retire: the ability to be happy *before* you retire—regardless of your financial circumstances—is the key to having a happy retirement.

Prescription for Lifelong Happiness

Following is my prescription for lifelong happiness, first introduced in *The Lazy Person's Guide to Happiness*. This prescription is based not solely on my opinions, but also on what the wise people of the world have said over the ages.

> Purpose enough for satisfaction
>
> Work enough for sustenance
>
> Sanity enough to know when to play and rest
>
> Wealth enough for basic needs
>
> Affection enough to like many and love a few
>
> Self-respect enough to love yourself
>
> Charity enough to give to others in need
>
> Courage enough to face difficulties
>
> Creativity enough to solve problems
>
> Humor enough to laugh at will
>
> Hope enough to expect an interesting tomorrow
>
> Health enough to enjoy life for all it's worth
>
> Gratitude enough to appreciate what you have

Retirement can be the best time of your life if you learn to be happy each and every day. This is what Abraham Lincoln had to say about happiness in general: "Do not worry; eat three square meals a day; say your prayers; be courteous to your creditors; keep your digestion good; exercise; go slow and easy. Maybe there are other things your special case requires to make you happy; but my friend, these I reckon will give you a good life."

Don't Let How Old You Are Dictate When You Enter Old Age

Retirement is often associated with old age, even though it shouldn't be. The fact is, however, if you are retired long enough, sooner or later some people will think of you as an older person. Whether *you* perceive yourself as having entered old age will depend upon your attitude more than anything else.

"He who is of a calm and happy nature will hardly feel the pressure of age," Plato told us, "but to him who is of an opposite disposition, youth and age are equally a burden." After all these years, experts are still trying to prove Plato right. In a study reported in the August 2002 issue of the *Journal of Personality and Social Psychology*, researchers claim that elderly people can actually think themselves into the grave a lot faster than they would like to get there. Indeed, people with negative views about aging shorten their lives by 7.6 years compared to their counterparts who have a more positive view of life.

> For the ignorant, old age is as winter; for the learned, it is a harvest.
> —Jewish proverb

A positive view about aging can actually have a greater effect in this regard than good physical health. The researchers, led by psychologist Becca Levy of Yale University, reported that "The effect of more positive self-perceptions of aging on survival is greater than the physiological measures of low systolic blood pressure and cholesterol, each of which is associated with a longer lifespan of four years or less."

"Our study carries two messages," concluded the researchers. "The discouraging one is that negative self-perceptions can diminish life expectancy. The encouraging one is that positive self-perceptions can prolong life expectancy."

The lesson here is that you shouldn't waste too much time and energy worrying about getting older. "Never think oldish thoughts," stated James A. Farley. "It's oldish thoughts that make a person old." If you talk to active elderly people with a joie de vivre, you will learn that they are young at heart and don't perceive themselves as old. Sure, they realize that they are physically limited to some degree, but psychologically they don't see age as having much to do with their true selves. This applies whether they are in their sixties or their nineties.

> How old would you be if you didn't know how old you were?
> —Satchel Paige

Many upbeat retirees feel extremely uncomfortable when in the presence of people their age, primarily because most people their age think and act old. Elderly people who are active and happy don't want to waste their retirement years listening to other people of their age complain about the problems of being old. Like these active and happy retirees, you shouldn't let how old you are dictate when you enter old age. Above all, the secret to happiness in your later years is to forget how old you are—and the older you get, the more important this becomes.

The Best Is Yet to Be

Thinking young can help you to stay busily and happily involved in your later years. "The most successful old-old people are those who have an important connection, a hobby, or something that gives them a zest for life," states Kevan H. Namazi, gerontologist at the University of Texas's Southwestern Medical Center in Dallas. Being productive well into your later years will enhance your self-esteem and contribute to intellectual stimulation and social interaction. Moreover, you will enrich the lives of others while enriching your own at the same time.

> Grow old along with me!
> The best is yet to be . . .
> —Robert Browning

Here are a few examples of individuals who kept themselves active and creatively alive in their later years.

> ➤ Mary Baker Eddy was eighty-seven when she followed her personal mission—creating a new newspaper with a religious influence. She called it the *Christian Science Monitor.*

> ➤ Albert Ellis developed what is now called rational emotive behavior therapy (REBT) in the mid-1950s. In 2001, at the age of eighty-seven, Ellis was still lecturing, writing, and seeing seventy or more clients per week, applying REBT to help them get over behavioral and emotional problems by replacing irrational thoughts with rational ones.

> ➤ At ninety-four, Bertrand Russell was actively promoting international world peace.

> ➤ At ninety, Picasso was known for his artistic production, still creating stunning drawings and engravings.

> ➤ Luella Tyra was ninety-two in 1984, when she competed in five categories at the U.S. Swimming Nationals in Mission Viejo, California.

> ➤ Lloyd Lambert was an active skier at eighty-seven and operating a seventy-plus Ski Club that had 3,286 members, including a ninety-seven-year-old.

➤ In her eighties, Maggie Kuhn was still active in promoting the goals of the Grey Panthers, a seniors group that she helped found when she was sixty-five.

➤ At ninety-three, George Bernard Shaw wrote *Farfetched Fables.*

➤ Ben Franklin was over eighty when he assisted in drafting the U.S. Constitution.

➤ Mildred Wirt Benson (the author who began the Nancy Drew series) wrote a column for the *Toledo Blade* until her death at ninety-seven.

➤ Between age seventy-five and eighty, Henri Matisse created six major illustrated books that contained hundreds of paintings. He also designed the Chapelle du Rosaire, including the stained-glass windows and murals.

➤ Buckminster Fuller actively promoted his vision for a new world while in his eighties.

➤ When he was ninety, Artur Rubinstein, the Polish-born American pianist particularly known for his interpretations of the works of Chopin, gave a sensational performance at Carnegie Hall.

➤ Mary Baker Eddy was still head of the Christian Science Church at age eighty-nine.

➤ Not only did he write great poetry from the time he was seventy-one until his death at eighty-nine, Michelangelo was also chief architect of St. Peter's Cathedral in Rome, supervising the construction of the body of the church.

➤ *The Kosmos* was written by Alexander von Humboldt from the time he was seventy-six until he turned ninety.

➤ Writer, actor, director, and producer George Abbott had his first hit (simply called *Broadway*) on Broadway when he was thirty-nine. At seventy-five, he produced *A Funny Thing Happened on the Way to the Forum.* When he turned one hundred, Abbott brought *Broadway* back to Broadway.

Learn as if you were going to live forever. Live as if you were going to die tomorrow.

—Unknown wise person

These people appear to be somewhat remarkable— and of course, each of them is in her or his own way. Nevertheless, they are not unusual. Hundreds of thousands of people in their seventies, eighties, and nineties have an incredible zest for life and show great vigor, enthusiasm, and physical ability in living.

Life Begins at Your Leisure

My wish is that this book will inspire you to experience a few things in life with as much enjoyment and fulfillment as I have experienced from writing the book. I trust that the process of enhancing your leisure time has already begun for you; just having read this book is a significant accomplishment in itself.

Now you must do something with what you have learned. Activity and inner mobility will go a long way. You have to love the world to be of service to it. Always try to seek growth, not perfection.

Keep in mind that attitude is an important element. By shaping your own attitude, you make life what it is. No one but you gets to make your own bed. No one but you can ever put in the effort to make your life work. No one but you can generate the joy, the enthusiasm, or the motivation to live life to the fullest.

> The really efficient laborer will be found not to crowd his day with work, but will saunter to his task surrounded by a wide halo of ease and leisure.
>
> —Henry David Thoreau

Remember that conventional success invariably comes at a high price. Know what the price is before you seek it. Being unprepared will mean you have to pay the biggest part of the price after your success—not before.

Zen masters tell us that we become imprisoned by what we are most attached to—cars, houses, money, friends and lovers, and egos and identities. Let go of your attachment to these things, and you will be set free.

Above all, let go of your attachment to the idea that you should work hard. Clearly, hard work doesn't guarantee happiness. If hard work guaranteed happiness, over 90 percent of Americans would be happy. Yet the highest figure psychologists and psychiatrists will give for the number of happy Americans is 20 percent.

Contrary to popular belief, the most difficult way to make a living is to work hard for it. To repeat, hard work is the best thing ever invented for killing time—as well as killing you. The secret is to work as hard as

I'm getting pretty good at this. Maybe I should give other people sleeping lessons.

you have to for a comfortable living—and as little as you can get away with.

Since you could spend a third or more of your waking hours at work, it's important that you enjoy it. Happiness from our work comes only when it's of great benefit to others and ourselves. So, don't work just for the money. You are a slave if you do. Your work should enrich your mind and soul as much as your financial well-being.

You work best at what you most need to become. So, work to grow, not just to acquire. Whatever you want to be, don't bother with other things. For it's not what you become, but what you don't become, that will hurt most in the end.

It is all too easy to demand of life more than it has to give. Try to be everywhere at once, and you will get nowhere. Try to do everything, and you will do nothing. Try to be loved by everyone, and you will be loved by no one. So, follow your dreams, but know your limitations.

You are the creator of the context in which you view things. It is up to you to find a way to enjoy the activities you undertake. Your task is to fill up any idle time, so that anxiety, boredom, and depression have no place in your world. Let your interests be as wide as possible.

> Each day, and the living of it, has to be a conscious creation in which discipline and order are relieved with some play and pure foolishness.
>
> —May Sarton

When you have no zest for life, find a way to turn on your enthusiasm fast. Routine and the need for security can doom you to a life of indifference and boredom. Try to deliberately seek new pursuits, just to keep some freshness and excitement flowing. Invite new people and events into your daily life. Take more chances and risks. Learn to enjoy interesting people, interesting food, interesting places, interesting culture, and interesting books.

To conquer boredom, put your boredom at risk. Too much safety is dangerous. You can climb Mount Everest "because it's there." Or you can climb an imaginary mountain "because it isn't there." Which do you think will bring you more satisfaction and happiness?

Court the unexpected. Some of the most fascinating things in this world turn out to be things that we don't go looking for. Thus, allow more chance into your life. The more chance you allow, the more interesting your world will become.

I must also emphasize simplicity. Remember that the greatest pleasures don't necessarily come from spectacular events or incredible moments. You can experience intense pleasure from many basic things in life. Do something every day to make your life less complicated. Learn to identify the unimportant. You will find that life's a breeze when you work as hard at simplifying it as you now do at complicating it.

Gratitude for what you have will do wonders for your well-being. "Just think how happy you would be," an unknown wise person declared, "if you lost everything you have right now, and then got it back." When you regularly take the time to appreciate the things you have—your health, your home, your friends, your music collection, your knowledge, and your creative ability—you won't have time to be envious of others or unhappy with your position in life.

You only live once. But if you work it right, once is enough.

—Fred Allen

You don't have to seek happiness in your leisure time. Allow it to find you. Three gifts were given to you when you were born: the gift of love, the gift of laughter, and the gift of life. Use these gifts, and happiness will follow you wherever you go.

Always keep in mind that happiness is a mode of traveling and not the destination. Zen masters tell us that we corrupt the beauty of living by making happiness the goal. They say happiness is the practice of living in the moment; it's in everything we do.

Again, don't wait for retirement to be happy and really start living. Invariably, people who try this find out that they have waited much too long. As Henry David Thoreau warned us, "Oh, God, to reach the point of death and realize you have never lived at all."

Leisure is a treasure to cherish and cultivate at all stages in your life. Think about this quietly and carefully: on your deathbed, as you review your life, what may you regret not having done? Clearly, you won't wish you had worked longer and harder. Nor will you regret not having accumulated more possessions. Whatever it is that you'd really wish you had done, shouldn't you be doing it now?

Let business wait until tomorrow.

—Greek proverb

"So," in the words of Mark Twain, "throw off the bowlines. Sail away from the safe harbor. Catch the trade winds in your sails. Explore. Dream. Discover."

In my view—no doubt Mark Twain would have agreed—the most precious moments you will experience are those that come from the joy of not working. Your life begins at your leisure . . . bon voyage!

Additional Letters from Readers

Introduction to Letters

This new section includes some of the most interesting letters that I have received since the third edition of *The Joy of Not Working* was published in 1997. Since the book was first published, I have been particularly amazed by how it has affected people differently. Some readers indicated that they developed a better work/life balance after reading the book; others revealed that they quit their jobs; still others said that they were inspired to leave a boring job that they worked at just for the money and find a job that they really like.

I must admit with some embarrassment that a few of these readers are living *The Joy of Not Working* better than I am. Although I don't work hard or long hours, lately I haven't taken a one-year break, or longer, from work as some readers have. Undoubtedly, I have something to learn from them.

> Sometimes you wonder how you got on this mountain. But sometimes you wonder, "How will I get off?"
> —Joan Manley

I hope that these letters will inspire you to make your life a lot more interesting and enjoyable. Most people go to their graves regretting things they haven't done. The easiest way to become one of them is by joining society's chorus instead of singing your own songs. As you can see, most of the following individuals are singing their own songs, and they're much happier because of it.

Angst from a Reader in France

Michaël Roche of Isère, France, wrote to me in January 2002 after reading the French edition of *The Joy of Not Working*.

Dear Ernie,

Your book *The Joy of Not Working* is a little gem. I found it by accident in a bookshop, and I must confess it was a happy accident.

I am a twenty-two-year-old student, and my impending entrance into the world of work is a real angst. For many years, I have known that I am not made for working. Spending forty hours a week in an office forty years of a life is a waste of time. It is an opinion which is difficult to accept; the look of others is merciless. Free time is not a problem for me. I have a lot of desires, and I know many interesting and fascinating activities, but a life devoted to work cannot allow me to have enough leisure time. I do not refuse to work, however. I just refuse a certain lifestyle some people (my family, my friends, my teachers, my neighbors, my potential bosses, etc.) try to impose on me. About this point, your book is comforting. I am not the only human being who thinks these things. What a relief!

> We work to become, not to acquire.
>
> —Elbert Hubbard

In the next few months, I will have to make a decision about the rest of my life. If I decide to follow MY way, there will be cries and incomprehension. But thanks to you, I know that if I follow the way of easiness I risk to spend the rest of my life in satisfying the wish of someone else. This way is the synonym of renunciation, resignation, compromise, frustration, regrets, and remorse. Unfortunately, it is the easiest way to follow; society has drawn it for me.

I will need a lot of courage, and your book is a precious help for that. Thanks for being alive, Mr. Zelinski, and thanks for your great book.

All apologies for my English.

Michaël Roche

Putting the Get-a-Life Tree Activities to Good Use

Duval C. Sherman of Los Angeles, California, wrote to me in May 1999. As you can see from his letter, he found the Activities for Your Get-a-Life Tree (known as a Leisure Tree in previous editions; see pages 114 to 119) useful for planning what he will do in his retirement.

Dear Ernie,

I recently finished reading your fine book, *The Joy of Not Working,* and I am surprised that it has not sold over one million copies.

I retired from my very stressful job as a bus operator in Los Angeles, Calif. on October 29, 1997, at the ripe "old age" of forty-six. My former coworkers' favorite refrains were, "What will you do?" and so on and so forth. That is when it dawned on me that these people had no life away from the job. How sad!

Now that I am no longer stressed out, and have had enough time to clear my mind, I feel much happier and healthier. Your Activities for Your Leisure Tree have been very helpful. I saw things on there that I may have never thought of. For the time being, I have chosen about seventy of them that I think should keep me pretty busy for quite some time, with more to be added later. In fact, Ernie, as I write this I am in the middle of trying one of the activities now, writing my autobiography.

I have ordered two more copies of your book to send to two cousins of mine. On has been a teacher for thirty-one years and is debating whether or not she should retire. I am hoping that your book, and my continued urging, kind of push-es her along in that direction so she will have the time to pursue some of the other things that she has told me she is interested in. My other cousin is an obstetrician with her own clinic who shows absolutely no sign of slowing down. I am just hoping that she will take a little time to "smell the flowers" and find the time to read your fine book.

Whenever you are able to take a little time away from your "leisure," would you please be kind enough to send me a reply?

Thanks.

Sincerely,

Duval C. Sherman

> When pleasure interferes with business, give up business.
> —*Unknown wise person*

From a Mother Who Decided
to Opt for Part-Time Work

Jennifer Andrew of Cary, North Carolina, wrote to me in July 2000.

Dear Ernie Zelinski,

Just got through about half of your book *The Joy of Not Working*. I had to write to you, even before reaching the end.

I recently started working a part-time schedule so I could spend more time with my two-year-old. In addition, so I could spend more time "living"! It was hard to negotiate, but I managed, and with benefits. So far, I love it, but I have to admit I have been a little bored. When I picked up your book at the library, I started to realize why. It is true that it takes a lot more creativity to set a schedule for yourself. However, it can be done! Spending time is too broad a goal. I realize we need more purpose, and I need activities that are just for me, not just me as a Mommy. Our first goal is going to be physical fitness. I plan to take both of us on as many walks, swims, and trips to the playground as we can handle. Also, to set more of a daily schedule for our activities.

More men are killed by overwork than the importance of the world justifies.

—Rudyard Kipling

There is so much pressure these days to work, and work hard. Especially now that the U.S. economy is booming. The unemployment is so low, that being fired does not worry most as much as it did, even when your book was first written. This is why I think it is even harder to take time out to "smell the roses." Raise a family, have a great career, save for retirement, etc. I discovered I could not do it all, at least not at the same time. I have officially taken myself out of the rat race! Yippee!

I truly believe that being too caught up with "trading up" (new car, bigger house, etc.) is just a sign of deep personal dissatisfaction and boredom. Your book made me realize I have let myself grow boring. I have never discovered what I was good at, what I enjoyed just for its own sake, not what would be the most profitable career. I plan to enroll in some classes at the local community college, join a church that sounds interesting, and get involved in community service. I also am going back to grad school, but I am not rushing it. At twenty-six, I know I have a while, and I want to enjoy every drop of life that I can.

I have been feeling many of these things for awhile, but never verbalized them before. I always wondered why the weekends got me down and lots of alone time made me anxious. Hope to hear from you, if you can take the time from your fun activities.

Sincerely,

Jennifer Andrew

From Someone Anonymous in South Africa

One of the most curious letters came from South Africa. It was in fact just a normal letter-size envelope with nothing inside. However, two quotes from the New Testament were written on the back of the envelope along with "From Anon" below the quotes.

To work is simple enough; but to rest, there is the difficulty.

—Ernest Hello

"It is vain that you rise so early and go late to rest, eating the bread of anxious toil, for he gives to his beloved sleep."

—Psalm 27 (126) : 2

"Blessed is one who fears the LORD who walks in his ways! You shall eat the fruit of the labor of your hands; you shall be happy, and it shall be well with you."

—Psalm 28 (127) : 1 + 2

From Anon

Dropping Out of College Means Dropping In to Life

Matt Moss of Delray Beach, Florida, wrote to me in December 2000.

Ernie,

I just finished reading your book and couldn't agree with you more. It's so nice to see it all right there in black and white. We all need to slow down and take a hard look at what's really important.

I am only twenty years old but feel as if I can relate EXACTLY to what made you do exactly that. I stopped going to college after two years of mechanical engineering classes and internships. It was a difficult decision for me to make because to so many people in my life I was just deemed a college dropout. I don't feel as if I dropped OUT of anything; I was dropping IN.

I have never been a happier person. I have learned so much more in the past year than I would have ever learned at school. I have traveled all over and had all kinds of adventures. I worked at a summer camp for kids and discovered how wonderful the innocence of a child's mind can be. It's hard to accept that half these children are going to be miserable adults with a nine-to-five desk job. So really I guess I want to say thank you. I support your message and wish you all the luck in the world in getting it across to others. Life's too short not to enjoy it.

You don't resign from these jobs; you escape from them.
—Dawn Steel

Well, take it easy. Best wishes.

Mat Moss

Pursuing a More Leisurely Lifestyle Is a Win/Win Situation No Matter What Happens

There is definitely risk involved in moving to a new career. There is, however, just as much risk involved in staying in a job you don't like. William T. David of Nashville, Tennessee, wrote to me in January 1999. Six months earlier, David had quit a high-paying job to pursue a more leisurely lifestyle. As he points out, the ability to take risks—even if it leads to failure—can have its rewards.

Dear Ernie,

I just finished reading *The Joy of Thinking Big* and *The Joy of Not Working*. What a wonderful way to start the new year!

In July of 1998, I walked out of a high-paid, high-stress factory job and never looked back. I spent four wonderful months relaxing and working on my condo. My current job pays much less, but I am happier now. My future plans include selling my condo and moving back to Wisconsin to be closer to my family.

Love of bustle is not industry.
—Seneca

It has taken some time, but I now know what I want to do in life. I am a very creative person and I have a ton of good ideas. I will pursue the things I've only dreamed about: writing songs, poetry, and a fictional novel; obtain patents on inventions; do more artwork; resume ballroom dance lessons; and learn to play the piano.

The wonderful news is that even if I fail, I never really fail as long as I am happy with what I want to do in life. It becomes a win/win situation no matter what happens.

Take care,

Bill David

On a Spiritual Path to More Leisure

James Paul Bauman of Oliver, B.C., wrote to me in August 2000. As Bauman indicates, living a more leisurely lifestyle can sometimes bring on guilt feelings. He gives us hints on how to overcome these feelings.

Dear Ernie,

I recently read your book *The Joy of Not Working*. I am very grateful for its message. Spirit sent it my way when I needed to learn its lesson. It gave me timely spiritual release. Thank you for writing it.

I'd long been laboring under some residual guilt feelings regarding my chosen lifestyle. I moved to a very simple life after I got separated several years ago. I wanted to have time to do all the things I'd rather do with my life, such as writing. As a result, I have been very fulfilled writing several books on economic freedom.

While I passionately love and believe in the simple, quiet life I lead, and have thrown off much of the guilt that came attendant with living radically differently from everyone else around me, and having so much free time to enjoy, I nevertheless retained an uneasy guilty feeling that I must work long hours, for no better reason than to *excuse* this lifestyle. I even avoided going into my local town during normal working hours, lest I appear as a "welfare bum." Silly, yes, but it's not always easy to go against years of social ingrainment.

On my spiritual path I am learning to accept myself wholly. The need for freedom in all aspects of my life has led to a natural way of being that has often met with disapproval from others and sometimes niggling residual fears and guilt of my own. But I've been overcoming these. The self-validation I've been receiving, including that which I've found in your book, has been overwhelming. Thank you!

Gratefully yours,

Jim

> Few people do business well who do nothing else.
> —Lord Chesterfield

A Loyal Leisure Convert

Mike Hood of London, Ontario, emphasized in his letter how he had refocused his life:

> Dear Ernie,
>
> Just a note to express how much I truly enjoyed your book *The Joy of Not Working*. Prior to reading it, my primary focus in life was work. (I still have the odd lapse.) However, now I am pleased to say that I have rediscovered the JOY OF FAMILY, FRIENDS, AND MOST DEFINITELY LEISURE. I bike regularly, take frequent trips to parks/beaches, see movies, and read novels.
>
> In closing, thanks a million. Your book has and continues to serve me well.
>
> Sincerely,
>
> Mike Hood (a loyal leisure convert)

A good rest is half the work.
—Yugoslav proverb

A Synchronistic Letter, Indeed

There was a bit of synchronicity involved in receiving the following letter. Allow me to lead into it. In December 2000, I received a phone call from Ronald Henares in California. Ronald told me that he and his friend Mark Craig, both in their late twenties, were employed in Silicon Valley and had become burned out from the hectic pace of working in the high-tech industry. Both Ronald and Mark had purchased a copy of *The Joy of Not Working;* the book had become, in Ronald's words, "their Bible for leisure."

Moreover, Ronald told me the book had influenced him and Mark to quit their jobs and move to Folsom, California, where they planned to open a smoothie shop. They wanted to sell *The Joy of Not Working* in the shop and were seeking my permission to do so. I suggested that Ronald contact Ten Speed Press to purchase the books directly from the publisher. During our conversation, I requested that Ronald and Mark both post a review of *The Joy of Not Working* on www.amazon.com, which they did within a week. (Only through these reviews was I able to get their full names.)

Approximately a year later, I was wondering how Ronald and Mark had made out with their smoothie shop and whether they were, in fact, selling *The Joy of Not Working* there. Because I did not have

Ronald's phone number or address, there was no easy way for me to find out. Much to my pleasant surprise, about a week later, in January 2002, I received a letter from Justin Matthew Onstot of Mather, California.

Dear Ernie,

Thank you for being true to your mission by publishing JONW. This book has, quite literally, changed my life.

It all began last summer when I walked into a smoothie store here in Folsom, CA. I was employed by a large high-tech company. This company is known as a meat grinder—and its reputation is well-deserved. I was having a bad day, and the proprietors of the smoothie shop picked up on it.

We got to talking, and it turned out that the two young men had both been corporate wage slaves. So they understood how I was feeling. One day they got hold of your book, and they became convinced to leave corporate America and follow their dream of owning their own business together.

Inspired by their story, I bought a copy of your book, which they were selling there in the store. I took it home that evening and savored the words of wisdom. There were some bitter pills to swallow, such as the idea that money could buy neither happiness nor security. But your ideas struck a chord in my soul.

It took me about six months to decide on my course of action. This last December I gave my notice. My employer was shocked, as apparently I was considered a "rising star." I worked my last day on December 31 and haven't looked back.

I love life again! I am able to start each day with coffee at my local caffeine dispenser. I sit and journal. And I am continuing to work on my first novel. The fact is, for the first time since graduate school, I can take full breaths of air again. The headaches, heartburn, and insomnia are gone. My goal now is to be faithful to the pursuit of my mission.

> A day's work is a day's work, neither more nor less, and the man who does it needs a day's sustenance, a night's repose, and due leisure, whether he be painter or ploughman.
>
> —George Bernard Shaw

I have you and your book to thank. Your book did more for me than anything else could ever do. God bless, and good luck in your endeavors.

Regards,

Justin Onstot

Pretty Ambitious for a Leisurely Person

After reading *The Joy of Not Working*, some people decide to slow down and take it easy; others are motivated to new heights. Kimberly Menard of Tinley Park, Illinois, was one of the latter. Kimberly wrote to me in April 2001.

Dear Ernie;

I just finished reading your book *The Joy of Not Working* and thoroughly enjoyed the entire book. I am forty-two years old and have been working in the purchasing profession for over sixteen years. Over the years I have set many work-related goals such as certifications and pursuing my degree to move ahead in my career. I have always loved learning in college and now will appreciate the classes more because they will provide me not only with career advancement (which was the only reason I was in college until reading your book). After reading your book I now see the opportunity for personal accomplishment and gaining knowledge not only for career advancement but also for self-improvement.

> The best career advice given to the young is "find out what you like doing best and get someone to pay you for doing it."
> —Katharine Whitehorn

Reading your book motivated me to now begin setting personal leisure goals which I have never previously done.

Goal number one: in high school I wanted to be a writer and somehow got sidetracked and ended up in purchasing. I will now pursue writing a book during my leisure time if only fifteen minutes a day (per your book)! I have always wanted to write a book but like your books says always came up with many excuses to not do it.

Goal number two: throughout my life I've always come up with a thousand excuses to not exercise. We have a golden retriever, and I have set a goal to walk her for one mile every day. Not only will this benefit me but also my dog. I am an insulin-dependent diabetic, so I must be careful when managing my insulin and exercise.

Goal number three: (can be tied to goal number two): I am involved in an islet cell transplant research program and UIC. This research program is a possible cure for diabetes. Eight people in Canada have previously been cured long-term through an identical islet cell transplantation protocol. My goal is to help find a cure for diabetes. If the islet transplantation does not cure me, at least I helped find a cure for future generations. The book I will write will be focused on coping with diabetes and will be basically my life's story. I want this book to be published to help all individuals who must cope with diabetes.

Thank you again for writing *The Joy of Not Working*. I'm certain that I will reflect back on the book throughout my lifetime.

Sincerely,

Kimberly Menard

People Think That She and Her Husband Are Odd to Be Leisurely

In April 2000, Melanie Martin of Medicine Hat, Alberta, wrote to me about how others don't agree with how she and her husband manage their lives.

Dear Ernie,

Thank you for writing your wonderful book *The Joy of Not Working*. It was amazing for me to read a book that reflected exactly how I think and feel about things. I didn't know people like you existed (aside from my husband and I, and we both always felt that we were odd). We've received nothing but criticism and negativity from people our entire six years of marriage, and now I understand why—because we are so happy, and people can't handle it.

In 1994, we married at twenty-one, and the life that followed was: a lay-off, then a move from Victoria, B.C., to Campbell River, B.C., for a job that fell through two months into it, another major move to Calgary, Alberta, where we were unemployed for another six months and homeless. Then I became very ill (but undiagnosed), husband got a great job for $45,000 a year, almost had a nervous breakdown as had no life outside of work and was treated horribly, he quit that job, came out to Medicine Hat, homeless for another month, jobless for almost a year, then I became severely ill and finally after long months of suffering was diagnosed with celiac disease (what a relief!).

> I haven't worked in twenty years;
> Guess I ain't so dumb.
> I may be a hobo;
> But, I ain't no bum.
> —*Unknown wise person*

My husband found a great job at $50,000 a year. And after all this, that's the icing on the cake as we're happy to be healthy and still in love. We receive tons of criticism from our friends and families back in B.C. But while they're complaining about the cost of living, etc., they are oblivious to the paradise in which they live—Victoria, B.C.

Come on, people! We are here in Alberta, watching the flat land, and the grass grow, and loving every minute. Inner peace is what it's all about. I feel blessed we've learned so much, so fast, so young. Failure. Failure. Failure, Failure, Success! (How exciting!)

By the way, my favorite pastimes are being by myself, coffee shops with my husband, reading, writing letters, and attempting books. Did your book ever make me feel good about myself! Everyone else judges me harshly for not working and not following "the norm." I'm happy. They're not.

Sincerely,

Melanie Martin

P.S. I left out 50% of the crap we went through—figured you'd get the general idea, and the past is the past. So don't run away. No negativity here.

> I have made this letter a rather long one, only because I didn't have the leisure to make it shorter.
>
> —Blaise Pascal

Not Everyone Likes *The Joy of Not Working*

Out of several hundred letters I have received, there have been only two negative ones. One was from a schoolteacher who complained about all the spelling errors in the first edition of the book, which was self-published and not properly edited. The other negative letter came from a gentleman in Ottawa, Ontario, whose name I have changed to Tom Blake.

Sir:

I have just finished reading your book *The Joy of Not Working*. I disliked the book intensely. You are irresponsible to encourage people not to work and to live off the efforts of others.

Who do you think pays the taxes that build the roads you drive on, maintain the public libraries, defend your person and property? Not only are you telling people not to contribute their share, but in not saving for hard times, misfortune, and retirement these people will require additional financial support from hard-working, responsible members of society.

Your book is nothing more than a shallow, long-winded advertisement for your worthless speaking engagements. You are encouraging people to add to the national debt, and you are making a living at this. I'm not all that

> A lazy person gives the workaholic something worthwhile to do and someone to feel happily superior to.
>
> —Julia Swiggum

surprised that you could not find a publisher. You are a traitor. You should be in prison.

Sincerely,

Tom Blake

Obviously, Tom Blake missed the whole drift of the book. Therefore, I immediately drafted a letter in which I shot holes through every criticism he made. I decided not to send the letter, however. Near as I can tell, you would have to be a certified psychiatrist, as well as a magician, to persuade negative people such as Blake to not work so hard and to enjoy life instead.

A Retired Teacher Who Wants to Teach People How to Retire Properly

Tim Westhead, a retiree from Whitby, Ontario, wrote to me in September 2002. Although he was looking forward to retirement, it turned out somewhat different from what he had expected.

Dear Ernie,

Let me begin by telling you how much I enjoyed and appreciated *The Joy of Not Working*, a book suggested to me this past August by my twenty-four-year-old son.

I retired at the end of June 2002 after teaching high school for thirty years in Toronto. I thoroughly enjoyed my job, the students, my department and school, and the conference circuit I've been on for more than two decades. But the key reason I decided to leave was to escape the brutal commute of one hour or more (one way) that I'd been doing for twenty-six years in Toronto traffic from my home outside Metro. I was fortunate enough to be able to take advantage of the 85 factor (age plus years of experience) for Ontario teachers that came into existence in the spring of 1998.

So from that time until last June, I had four years to consider my retirement, plan for it, and investigate possibilities of part-time employment. Like many who have worked for a number of decades—some who plan and some who don't—by mid-summer I began to feel pretty strange about being retired and about being jobless. You know, the "survivor guilt," the elation, etc., of not having a job to go to—the emotions that most people probably experience during the transition period, I experienced too.

I decided at that point that I'd better research retirement, leisure pursuits, and being jobless, and that's when my son suggested I read your book. The long and short of it is that I've created a workshop called "Keep Your Chins Up in Retirement—Practical Ways to Preplan Retirement." It deals neither with planning financial matters nor with filling out the proper forms; rather it focuses almost exclusively on the emotional aspects of retirement and how to deal with and enjoy one's new lifestyle. I believe this is a sig-nificant facet that retirement seminars and workshops gloss over or ignore altogether. I'm going to start pitching it to teacher's organizations, etc., in the near future.

> Leisure time is that five or six hours when you sleep at night.
> —George Allen

Again, I thank you, Ernie, for the emotional boost you've given me (and countless others, I'd wager) about how to take delight in a new lifestyle after the full-time grind.

My very best,

Tim Westhead (Retiree!! and Semi-working Stiff)

A Retired Couple Who Plan to Compare Their Leisure (Get-a-Life) Trees

Elaine Hamos of Palo, Iowa, wrote to me in October 2002. After setting it aside for two years or so, Elaine had rediscovered *The Joy of Not Working.*

Dear Ernie,

A couple of years ago my husband and I received two retirement books for Christmas from his son. Brian was worried about his dad adjusting to this new life.

We read both books, and I don't know what happened to the other one, but *The Joy of Not Working* was just excellent.

After two years, I decided to read the book again. It is amazing to me how much more I have learned. This sec-ond time around, everything made even more sense, and I completed some of the exercises that I hadn't bothered to do before. The Leisure Tree is especially helpful.

Reading your book has revved me up to make my life even more fulfilling. If a person will let the mind wander, many wonderful and exciting ideas come to mind. My husband plans on rereading the book also. It will be fun to compare our Leisure Trees!

Thanks for writing the book, and please let others know that it is even a better "read" the second time around. I plan to read it a third time sometime in the future. Your book is a real motivator.

Sincerely,

Elaine Hamos

Letter from an Early Retiree in Florida

Steve Reichard of Dublin, Ohio, sent me this email in January 2003. He was spending the winter in Florida at the time, something that I would like to be able to do so that I could escape the cold winters in my hometown.

Hi, Ernie.

First of all, let me say that I loved your books, especially *The Joy of Not Working*. I have definitely learned a lot from reading your books. I am a thirty-four-year-old software engineer with a wife and little boy. About two years after graduating from college, I started my own software company and have been self-employed ever since.

A few years ago, I became financially independent, so I have been facing the prospect of what to do with the rest of my life, which can actually be pretty stressful. I lead a life that is pretty similar to yours: I write software on a notebook computer whenever I please, and I enjoy a lot of free time. Right now I'm in Florida for the winter, staying with my wife's parents. My office consists of a notebook computer on a card table.

I run into a lot of the same problems that you probably deal with: everybody works, so it's hard to find someone to "play" with.

I also wanted to recommend a book to you: *Toxic Success* by Paul Pearsall. The author's views are similar to yours, in that everyone is working nowadays and letting their personal relationships and nonwork life suffer.

Anyway, I wish you the best, and wouldn't mind if you dropped me a line or two if you have some free time.

Thanks,

Steve Reichard

A Reader Who Discovered the Author
Is Not a "Welfare Bum"

Peter Borchers—who lives in my hometown of Edmonton, Alberta—
wrote to me in the late 1990s. Although I used to see Peter in some of the
coffee bars that I frequented at that time, I didn't get to know him until
some time later. Peter wrote to me to express his surprise at the content of
The Joy of Not Working once he actually got around to reading the book.

> Dear Ernie,
>
> I've come to read your book *The Joy of Not Working* from
> the opposite angle. As an adult education student, your
> book was one of ten on a list to write a book report on.
>
> To be truthful, the title stirred my senses in a
> very negative way. All I could think of was
> "welfare bum."
>
> I picked up the book at the library and right
> there started reading the first chapter. I didn't
> take the book out, but went to the nearest
> bookstore, bought my own copy, and went home to read it.
> I read it not once, not twice, but three times. I couldn't
> wait to present, alone in front of my peers and professor,
> your book, like a priest the gospel. My peers gave me a
> standing ovation and the professor top marks. I thank you
> for that; you deserve the praise; I was just a humble mes-
> senger of your message.
>
> I can happily confess that I, although still working full-time,
> am living most of your text. I am a very happy person with
> high esteem and various hobbies that will take up most of
> my time when I do retire. I will be taking a sabbatical of
> one year as a preretirement exercise to prove that your
> book is a living entity to many seekers.
>
> You will be hearing from me again.
>
> Greetings,
>
> Peter Borchers

Do not mistake a crowd of big wage earners for the leisure class.
—Clive Bell

Retirement Means Not Going Back
to the Tunnel with No Cheese

Job-sharing allowed Shirley Campbell of North York, Ontario, to
become semiretired. She was looking forward to full-time retirement,
however, and wrote to inform me how she planned to spend her time.

Dear Ernie:

I enjoyed your book very much, and it came along at the right time. It belongs to a friend who is a workaholic. I am retiring in March—sorry, I mean I plan to spend more time in self-realization/actualization.

I will be sixty-five in March, and my boss doesn't want me to quit and, in fact, was being very successful in making me feel guilty about it to the point where I was having second thoughts—but not anymore.

There are so many things that I want/enjoy doing. At the present I am job-sharing so only work three days a week. But how much better (it will be) not to work at all. No way do I want to sit in front of a computer for the rest of my life typing pathology reports.

> If you have a difficult task, give it to a lazy man—he will find an easier way to do it.
>
> —Hlade's law

My friend—the workaholic—said, "What are you going to do all day—lay on the couch and watch movies?" And I said, "No, I'll get up every once in awhile for a snack."

Seriously, I am going skiing in Banff in March with my grandson. I like to cook, bake, entertain, travel, and sew, so I do not believe I'll have a problem with too much leisure time. No—I am not going to keep going back to tunnel where there is no cheese—good analogy since I love cheese. Anyway, thanks so much.

Sincerely,

Shirley Campbell

An Invitation to Dinner

Over the years several readers have invited me to dinner, including Lorna (last name is withheld due to the nature of the letter) of Washington, D.C. I received her letter in February 2003.

Dear Ernie:

With all due respect I am writing to let you know that your book is too long to derive the right dose of leisure for me this Sunday morning.

You had me at first sight of your book's title. That was months ago, and I left your book at my bedside untouched!

Today it caught my eye again, and I opened it to the page with your picture. I needed great assurance that you are somebody alive, still on this planet. Therefore, please respond upon receipt of this (letter) immediately. You have dinner waiting here in Washington, D.C.—yes, to find out what "interesting subjects" you have to talk about (see page 5)!

Of course, your book says it all! The table of contents to be exact! I, myself, am enjoying *The Joy of Not Working* for I am JOBLESS and thankfully have found a kindred spirit in YOU.

I believe each topic in the table of contents of your book may very well be a book title unto itself, and believe me 99.999999 percent of the world's population (work force) needs these affirmations as expressed in your chapter headings.

> The word career is a divisive word. It's a word that divides the normal life from business or professional life.
>
> —Grace Paley

Let us therefore UNITE our minds of leisure! I wish to give away your book to each yuppie and definitely to corporate fools succeeding to promote MODERN SLAVERY! So, now let me not get all WORKED up! I certainly don't need the WORK!

Can we agree to meet soonest here in D.C.? Here is my card.

I am wrapping up your book to give to my daughter a most exciting birthday present for her thirtieth birthday. She is a disciple of leisure like you and me—although still struggles a bit with "society's programming," which I hope your book can successfully debug!

My thanks and praise for your wit and wisdom!

Call me,

Lorna

Paring of Old Beliefs and Attitudes Is Not Necessarily Easy

Louann Sanchez of Ridgeland, Mississippi, wrote to me in November 2001. Like many of the people who have written to me, Louann made a drastic change in her life to search for what she truly wants and be the person she always felt she could be.

Dear Ernie,

I just finished *The Joy of Not Working* and find that I am wishing it could continue. Not that there is more to be said (you do that superbly), but I really enjoyed the actual reading.

For an assortment of reasons, I quit my job of twenty-six years just before the tragic terrorist attacks in New York and Washington, D.C., in September and moved from the Midwest with a friend to Mississippi. Interesting time to make changes in one's life, hmm? The transfer job I had thought would be waiting for me did not work out and several other options proved unpalatable, so there I was unemployed and though unnerved by the prospect, I wasn't particularly worried. Lots of people are out of work due to the economic downturn and the terrorism. Unlike many desperately looking for work, I am glad that due to a stable financial base (for now) and my friend's help, I am able to take this time to do a complete reorientation of myself and decide what the future holds . . . I feel almost unpatriotic that I am not out there actively seeking reemployment or out shopping or traveling just to help the American economy. (Sounds a bit peculiar to me, this "shopping" to help the country, doesn't it? Finding a way to make an economically feasible and fiscally profitable economy based on saving and perpetuating the planet Earth and its dwindling resources seems like a much better way to help the country and the world.)

The many job positions I had held in my one company never completely satisfied me, although I liked doing many parts of the different jobs. It was a way to make money, to survive and continue. But in the past year, I found just bringing home a paycheck wasn't right for me anymore. Needs weren't being met, and I felt I had gotten lost somewhere along the way. With some misgivings and apprehension and lots of thoughtful reflection, I decided that radical change was the only way to effectively find a new way of living.

Anyway, in the face of family disapproval and puzzlement of friends, I have been dealing with the feelings derived from not having a job while trying to assess how to do what I want and be the person I've always felt I could be. It's harder than I thought, this paring of old beliefs and attitudes to find the real me and the passions that make life sweet and to find a better way to live. Your book has helped a great deal with the job loss issue and not working issue, besides pointing out marvelous ideas and jogging the ol' work-subdued creativity and wonder bubbling back to the surface. It hadn't disappeared entirely; just took a vacation from being front and forward. I've been delighted to work the exercises in the book, and equally delighted to find that in answering those questions, a whole slew of more questions (and answers and puzzles and contradictions and arguments) have arisen to add to the mix.

It is too difficult to think nobly when one thinks only of earning a living.
—Jean-Jacques Rousseau

I have asked for your book as my sole Christmas present (the one I finished is borrowed from the library and they frown mightily on highlighting pertinent information and writing in margins). Defacing your book is not my goal here; I just need to be able to refer to helpful sections, quotes, exercises, etc., to continue adding to the personal and career assessment that forms part of the structure of my day. I think adding your book to my collection of excellent thought-provoking books, articles, and personal journal entries is the best present I can give to myself this year and for years to come. Thank you once again, and here's to you. May health and happiness be your companions on the path.

Sincerely,

Louann Sanchez

Work Is That Thing That Interferes with Life— Don't Let It!

There is an old saying, "When the student is ready, the master will appear." Obviously, Jennifer Reinson of Calgary, Alberta, was ready for some guidance when she took a hiking trip on the West Coast Trail on Vancouver Island in British Columbia. The trip taught her a few important things about life.

Dear Ernie,

This past May I ventured out on a trip, little knowing the influence it would have on the rest of my life. It turned out to be the best thing I have ever done for myself. After graduating from university at Christmas, I decided to treat myself to a vacation and go on the West Coast Trail. Nothing could have opened my eyes to the wonders of the world more. This trip took me back to the basics of life, living in the now and mastering the moment for what it is. I realized on the second day of this nine-day trip that I worked far too much. At that time I had three jobs and numerous other side/part-time positions. One individual in this group that I traveled with pointed out that it was pretty sad to hear a twenty-two-year-old say that she worked too much. That is a comment that has stuck with me. I decided right then and there that life was not all about work, but about living now and enjoying the simple things in life. By the end of the trip, I had come up with the saying: WORK IS THAT THING THAT INTERFERES WITH LIFE—DON'T LET IT!

I promised myself that I would remember the feelings I experienced on the West Coast Trail when I returned to my hectic life at home. I decided on the trail to keep a journal of all the things I wanted to do with my life and how I planned to get there. I promised myself that I would never again hear myself say, "I work too much!" So, as the trip wound down, I began to think of what I had to go home to, three jobs and a summer full of work. Something had to be done!

Before returning to Calgary, our group stayed over in Victoria, and that's where I found your book. While strolling down a street, a few of us popped into Munro's bookstore. When I first saw the title *The Joy of Not Working*, I thought it would be a comedy about goofing off at work and ways of calling in sick, but all it took was for me to read up to the third paragraph of the Preface, when you talked about the zest for life and waking up every morning excited about the day, that I realized you and I were on the same wavelength. I couldn't believe that another person was thinking the way that I was! I had such a complete revelation about life on the West Coast Trail that I was sure when I returned home, reality would set in and I would be confronted by challenges and be forced to return to a lifestyle I had decided I no longer wanted.

Well, I returned home and quit two of my jobs, what a feeling! I was surprised to see that it really wasn't that hard! Simply put, I placed more pressure on myself because I didn't want to disappoint others that I almost stopped myself from doing it. Since then I have put some serious thought into what I want out of life. I thank the lucky gods every day for helping me to open my eyes and realize at a young age that I was headed in the wrong direction. I believe in your saying of "a little short-term pain for long-term gain" and have decided that I want to be my own boss and be able to take sabbaticals when I see fit and live the Life of Riley.

My summer plans have changed dramatically. I now will only be working one job until July 31, after which time I will be taking the entire month of August off. During this time I have plans to visit with family, travel and get a little R 'n' R. In September I have decided to return to school and take a two-year master's of kinesiology program. I already have my own company called ESSENTIAL FITNESS LTD. but instead of in the past doing that on the side and working for someone else at a job that brought me half the satisfaction, I have decided to be my own boss full-time.

> Idleness is an appendix to nobility.
>
> —Robert Burton

I've been back now from the West Coast Trail for just over a month, and I'm proud to say that every day I am thankful for allowing myself to enjoy the gifts of love, laughter, and life. I feel so fortunate to have discovered now at twenty-two that life is what you make it.

Thank you for your inspiration.

Sincerely,

Jennifer Reinson

A Woman Who No Longer Has to Feel Guilty about Not Working

Being retired gives you the freedom to do what you want, when you want, and with whom you want. Part of the equation for handling all this freedom is the ability to be creative and to become a highly independent person, if you aren't one already. Moreover, you must be able to overcome any feelings of guilt about not working while others less fortunate than you are working.

In March 2003, Susan Yates of Indianapolis, Indiana, wrote to inform me why she no longer has to feel guilty about not working.

Dear Mr. Zelinski,

I just finished your book *The Joy of Not Working* and wanted to let you know how much I enjoyed and appreciated it.

A few years ago, my husband and I took a look at our lives and decided to make some changes. At that time, I was working a nine-to-five office job, and he was flying for a commuter airline and working almost every weekend. When he was home, I was at work and vice versa. We realized his income was more than enough for our conservative tastes so I quit my highly unsatisfactory job with no regrets! Since then, we have had wonderful times together enjoying his many days off and I have had abundant time on my own to pursue my interests.

> We live in the age of the overworked, and the under-educated; the age in which people are so industrious that they become absolutely stupid.
>
> —Oscar Wilde

My problem has always been feeling guilty about not working. My family especially seemed to have a hard time with it, and some people have been downright hostile. But now, thanks to your wonderful book, I will no longer feel I need to apologize for my beautifully work-free existence, and I will know just what to say in response to those who attack it.

Thank you again for a wonderful book—I know I will read it again and again (it's already so highlighted now it looks like a coloring book!).

Sincerely,

Susan Yates

About the Author

Ernie Zelinski has negotiated eighty-seven book deals with publishers in twenty-four countries for his fifteen books. His latest irresistible smash hits include *How to Retire Happy, Wild, and Free* (over 40,000 copies sold) and *Real Success Without a Real Job: There Is No Life Like It!*

Photograph by Greg Gazin

Feature articles about Ernie and his books have appeared in major newspapers including *USA TODAY, Oakland Tribune, Boston Herald, The Washington Post, Toronto Star,* and *Vancouver Sun.* He has been interviewed by over one hundred radio stations and has appeared on CNN TV's Financial News and CBC TV's National News.

Ernie has an Engineering degree and an MBA from the University of Alberta. Because he is truly organizationally averse, he has not had a real job for over twenty-five years. Ernie speaks professionally on the subjects of real success, retirement, and applying creativity to business and leisure. You can e-mail Ernie at vip-books@telus.net or write to him at Visions International Publishing, P.O. Box 4072, Edmonton, AB, Canada, T6E 4S8.

Irresistible Websites by Ernie Zelinski

Ernie's two websites (listed on the bottom of this page) will further challenge and/or inspire you with cool stuff such as:

- The free e-book *1001 Best Things Ever Said about Work (and the Workplace)*
- Other free e-books including a fine slice of *The Joy of Not Working,* seven volumes in the *Graffiti for the Soul* Series, and over half of *How to Retire Happy, Wild, and Free*
- Resources to help you escape corporate life
- Real life success stories from readers
- What's new to help you attain real success without a real job
- News about Ernie's latest projects

www.Real-Success.ca

www.thejoyofnotworking.com

Irresistible Books by Ernie Zelinski

REAL SUCCESS WITHOUT A REAL JOB: There Is No Life Like It!

Career success is much more than having a real job and earning a decent income. Real career success is truly enjoying what you do for a living and having the personal freedom to perform your work virtually any time you want. This revolutionary book is for those millions of organizationally averse people who would like to break free of corporate life so that they have complete control over their lives. Ernie Zelinski uses experiences from his 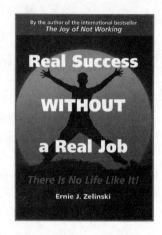 own life to show how the powerful success principles in this book can help you joyfully avoid the shackles of the corporate world for the rest of your life. Positive, lively, and captivating, *Real Success Without a Real Job* is designed to help you live an extraordinary lifestyle that is the envy of the corporate world – there is no life like it!

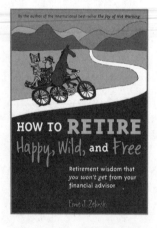

HOW TO RETIRE HAPPY, WILD, AND FREE: Retirement Wisdom That You Won't Get from Your Financial Advisor

With its friendly format, positive tone, and lively cartoons, this classic is for those individuals who absolutely, positively want to read The World's Best Retirement Book. Above all, retirees are granted the knowledge, freedom, and opportunity to live life like never before. Nancy Conroy of the Association of Pre-Retirement Planners raves: "*How to Retire Happy, Wild, and Free* is optimistic, practical, humorous, and provocative AND comprehensively addresses the many issues impacting individuals as they think about their retirement." The World's Best Retirement Book has already sold over 40,000 copies through word of mouth alone.